UNDERSTANDING
MEDICAL LAW

Cavendish
Publishing
Limited

UNDERSTANDING
MEDICAL LAW

Brendan Greene, LLB, MA

Cavendish
Publishing
Limited

London • Sydney • Portland, Oregon

First published in Great Britain 2005 by
Cavendish Publishing Limited, The Glass House,
Wharton Street, London WC1X 9PX, United Kingdom
Telephone: + 44 (0)20 7278 8000   Facsimile: + 44 (0)20 7278 8080
Email: info@cavendishpublishing.com
Website: www.cavendishpublishing.com

Published in the United States by Cavendish Publishing
c/o International Specialized Book Services,
5824 NE Hassalo Street, Portland,
Oregon 97213-3644, USA

Published in Australia by Cavendish Publishing (Australia) Pty Ltd
45 Beach Street, Coogee, NSW 2034, Australia
Telephone: + 61 (2)9664 0909   Facsimile: + 61 (2)9664 5420
Email: info@cavendishpublishing.com.au
Website: www.cavendishpublishing.com.au

British Library Cataloguing in Publication Data

Greene, Brendan
Understanding medical law
1 Medical laws and legislation – Great Britain
I Title
344.4'1'041

Library of Congress Cataloguing in Publication Data
Data available

ISBN 1-85941-888-0
ISBN 978-1-859-41888-8

1 3 5 7 9 10 8 6 4 2

Printed and bound in Great Britain by Antony Rowe Ltd.

CONTENTS

TABLE OF CASES

TABLE OF STATUTES

Table of Statutes

TABLE OF OTHER LEGISLATION

INTRODUCTION

Medical law is a challenging area of study not only because of the many difficult legal and ethical issues which it raises but also because it will have an impact on our individual lives. Some of these issues appear in the media on an almost daily basis and this is illustrated even as this book goes to print. On 8 February 2005, the Human Fertilisation and Embryology Authority granted a licence to create stem cells from embryos in order to facilitate study of motor neuron disease. *The Times* of 18 February 2005 carried three interesting articles: first, about three patients in Germany who contracted rabies after receiving organ transplants from a dead woman; secondly, the discovery in the United States of a new technique to use stem cells from a patient's fat which could be used to grow breast implants; and thirdly, research in Europe which showed that government advice to pregnant woman to take folic acid supplements in order to prevent birth defects in their babies was wrong, as the supplements had little effect.

This book is an introductory textbook on medical law and it also has some consideration of medical ethics, as the two are closely linked. It is aimed at law students who choose a medical law option, medical and nursing students who increasingly need some knowledge of the law, and others working in the health care professions and management, both within the National Health Service and in the private sector.

The aim of the book is to explain the basic principles of medical law and to raise important questions about both the law and about some of the ethical issues arising in medical practice. The book may also prove useful as a revision guide to students preparing for examinations. The main legal topics covered include consent to treatment, medical negligence, confidentiality, infertility, surrogacy, abortion, medical research, transplants and death. The impact of the Human Rights Act 1998 is also considered. Throughout the text, reference is made to leading cases, important statutes, reports, academic articles, other textbooks and there is a list of useful websites in Appendix B. It is hoped that the reader's interest will be stimulated to explore the subject further, by following up these sources! There is now a great wealth of material and resources on medical law and I hope that I have struck the right balance in explaining the main principles and issues but without drowning them in too much detail.

I would like to thank the staff at Cavendish Publishing for their support and encouragement while I was writing this book and their understanding as deadlines have approached and passed! Finally, I would like to thank my wife Michele and my boys Danny and Timmy for the patience they have shown. I can now look forward to playing football with the latter two (if only I could play football!).

I have endeavoured to state the law as it stood on 1 January 2005, although it has been possible to add a few later developments.

Brendan Greene
January 2005

CHAPTER 1

INTRODUCTION TO MEDICAL LAW

INTRODUCTION

Medical law touches the lives of everyone and raises fundamental questions about life, death and many of the things which happen in between those two events in people's lives. The law attempts to deal with a wide range of problems, such as what to do with patients who refuse treatment or patients who are unable to consent to treatment; how to respond to the increasing number of claims for medical negligence; and what rights children have in respect of treatment. There are many contemporary issues with which the law has to grapple. Should women have an automatic right to abortion? Should the 24 week limit on social abortions be reviewed, as foetuses of this age can now be kept alive? When may organs be removed from dead patients? Should the practice of euthanasia be made legal in the light of developments in Holland? The ethical and legal dilemmas confront us on an almost daily basis. Examples include: the discovery of the practice of removing organs from dead children at Alder Hey Children's Hospital in Liverpool and at Bristol Royal Infirmary; in 2000 the case of the conjoined twins, Jodie and Mary; in 2002 the struggle and ultimate failure of Diane Pretty, paralysed by motor neuron disease, to obtain permission for her husband to help her to die; Natalie Evans who, in June 2004, lost her appeal to use her frozen embryos to have a baby; and in January 2005 when Brian Blackburn, who made a suicide pact with his wife who was dying of cancer and killed her, pleaded guilty to manslaughter, he was given a suspended sentence of nine months' imprisonment.

ETHICAL THEORIES AND PRINCIPLES

Medical law is not simply a set of rules which can be applied to solve legal problems, because it frequently involves questions of morals – whether particular actions are the right thing to do – for example, the issue of abortion. Ethical rules are important because ethical principles sometimes underpin legal rules; for example, the law on consent to treatment is based on the principle of autonomy. Sometimes, there are no legal rules, or the rules are unclear and decisions have to be made on the basis of ethical principles; for example, if tissue is taken from a dead body. The Human Tissue Act 2004 sets out the circumstances in which tissue may be taken, but the substantive parts of the Act are not in force at the time of writing. There is also the question of individual moral perspectives – clearly, the law cannot satisfy everyone, as people have conflicting moral views. What should the role of the law be in such conflicts? Should it be a matter for the individual to decide, or should the law impose limits on people's rights? Again, the example of abortion may be used. Should the law give women an absolute right to abortion or should it make abortion illegal and protect the foetus? A second example is the conflict between the parents of Jodie and Mary, who did not want the twins to be separated, and the doctors at St Mary's Hospital, Manchester, who did want to separate the twins. The law is sometimes unclear and sometimes unsatisfactory. It is then that resort to ethical principles may help to determine how such problems should be approached, and the value of such principles can only be judged by their application in practical situations.

There are two main ethical theories: deontological – which is based on what is the right thing to do in any particular circumstances; and utilitarianism – which aims broadly to maximise happiness and evaluates an action on the consequences of that action:

- Deontological theory: 'deon' means duty and this approach determines whether an action is right by asking if there is a duty to do it or not to do it, for example, a duty not to kill. The focus is on the act and not the consequences. Immanuel Kant (1724–1804) was a proponent of this theory and believed that it could be used to judge whether any particular act was morally right or wrong. Kant believed that morality was based on reason and that human beings had rational powers. Kant argued that we should be moral for its own sake. Morality was an 'absolute' and people should not act on the basis that there was something in it for them or that it made the world a better place. To give an act moral worth we must act on the basis of duty or obligation and not for some other reason, such as self-interest. Kant's test for an act was the categorical imperative, 'I ought never to act except in such a way that I can also will that my maxim become a universal law'. Here 'maxim' means any principle which governs an individual's act. Kant means that if someone decides on a particular principle it must apply to everyone. Kant also believed that one should act in a way which treated every person as an end and never as a means. Each person had an absolute moral value which meant that they were ends in themselves. To treat a person as a means to an end was not respecting their autonomy. The duty approach frames actions in terms of various duties to do or not to do certain actions, normally as negative duties. It also tends to look for principles which can be followed, for example, the principle of autonomy. Autonomy means 'self-rule' and its wider meaning is the capacity to think and act freely. In a medical context, the doctor would be under a duty to respect the patient's autonomy, for example, by giving the patient enough information to make a decision whether to accept treatment or not. There are a number of problems with this theory. First, it provides no help regarding what action to take if there are two conflicting duties. Secondly, it ignores the consequences of an act.

- Utilitarian theory: this judges an action by what its consequences are, with the aim of maximising happiness. Jeremy Bentham (1748–1832) and John Stuart Mill (1806–73) were exponents of this theory. Bentham believed that an act could be judged by whether it produced more pleasure than pain. The right act was the one which produced more pleasure than pain. This can be seen as a 'goal-based' approach, the goal being to maximise the benefit, welfare or happiness to society. An action is right if it has good consequences and the nature of the action does not matter. The utilitarian approach does not take a stand on principle, but simply looks at the consequences of an action. For example, it would not consider abortion wrong in itself because it offends the principle of the 'sanctity of life', but would judge it on its overall effect on society, and whether it produces more pleasure than pain. A utilitarian approach would not distinguish between an act and an omission, so would not distinguish between killing someone and letting them die. A utilitarian approach will breach duties and violate rights if this maximises the good. In short, the end justifies the means. There are, however, some problems with this theory. It assumes that everyone knows what happiness is, there are difficulties with calculating the consequences of an action and it pays little regard to the individual in any particular case.

Apart from ethical theories, there are a variety of moral principles which play an important part in medical law and ethics. Four important principles relevant to medical ethics have been identified by Beauchamp and Childress in *Principles of Biomedical Ethics* (5th edn, 2001, Oxford: OUP). They include respect for autonomy, beneficence, non-maleficence and justice:

(a) Respect for autonomy: the word autonomy comes from the Greek, and literally means 'self-rule'. Autonomy is the capacity of an individual to think freely and to act on the basis of that thought. A doctor treating a patient can respect the patient's autonomy by keeping information about the patient secret – the duty of confidentiality. Another way would be to take note of whether the patient wishes to have treatment or not.

(b) Beneficence: this means to do good. It is a positive duty to help others. In a medical context, the doctor must act in the best interests of the patient. This will also involve respecting their autonomy.

(c) Non-maleficence: this means to do no harm and is a general moral duty not to harm others. A doctor must not harm his patient. However, as Gillon has pointed out, in the context of medical care the two principles of beneficence and non-maleficence must be considered together ('Medical ethics: four principles plus attention to scope', BMJ, Vol 309, 16 July 1994). A doctor treating a patient has a duty to produce a net benefit over harm. Many types of medical treatment involve harm, for example, surgical procedures or if a patient with cancer is given chemotherapy, but the net benefit in both cases may be to prolong their life for a number of years.

(d) Justice: this is the moral obligation to act fairly between competing claims. It is important in healthcare because resources are limited. A doctor treating a patient should not waste resources, for example, by prescribing an expensive drug if a cheaper one will have the same effect.

The traditional approach in medicine was based on the principle of beneficence, in that doctors saw their role as helping patients. All too often this became 'doctor knows best' and many doctors took a paternalistic approach to their patients. Over the last 30 years, patients' rights have grown more important and the principle of autonomy now has an important place in medical care.

THE WIDER CONTEXT OF MEDICAL LAW

Civil and criminal law

Although medical law is now recognised as a separate branch of law, it must be remembered that it operates in the wider context of the legal system. The distinction between civil and criminal law must be borne in mind. A civil matter is a dispute between individuals or between an individual and an authority, for example, an NHS hospital trust. The main aim of a civil claim is to obtain compensation or redress for an injury suffered. A criminal matter is a wrong committed by an individual against society in general and the State will take action. The aim with criminal law is mainly to punish the person committing the act. Most matters in medical law will be civil ones, for example, a patient suing a hospital trust for negligence. However, the criminal law will sometimes be relevant: for example, Harold Shipman, a general practitioner, was convicted of the murder of a number of his patients. This distinction between civil and criminal is reflected in the court structure and medical staff may need to attend both civil and criminal courts. One act may involve both civil and criminal liability; for example, if a member of staff hit a patient (or, increasingly more likely, a patient hit a member of staff!), this would be both a battery in civil law and a criminal assault under the Offences Against the Person Act 1861. Minor criminal matters such as assault will go to the magistrates' courts and more serious offences, such as manslaughter, will be dealt with at the Crown Court. A violent, unnatural or sudden death must be reported to the coroner, who may order a postmortem or hold an inquest. An inquest will take place in a coroner's court.

In civil law, negligence claims may be brought on the basis of a conditional fee agreement ('no win, no fee'). The client does not pay a fee unless they win the case. The lawyers for the winning side may claim a success fee of up to 100% for the case and this applies to all civil claims, including clinical negligence (formerly medical negligence), with the exception of family matters. Although the losing party did not have to pay their own lawyer, they did have to pay the other side's lawyer. To cover this cost, the claimant can take out an insurance policy.

Following Lord Woolf's reforms, the 'Clinical Negligence Protocol' was introduced to try to settle claims before they reach court. The claimant sends a 'preliminary notice' to the other side, setting out brief details and the value of the claim, and the other party must acknowledge this within 21 days. The parties may then decide to go through an alternative dispute resolution (ADR) procedure, under which they try to settle the claim. The next stage is a more detailed letter of claim, which must be acknowledged within 21 days. The parties should then conclude negotiations within six months. If the case should continue to court, then the procedure is set out in the Civil Procedure Rules 1998. These provide a common set of rules for both the county court and the High Court. The court now takes an active part in the management of cases and also allocates each case to one of three 'tracks':

(a) the small claims track, which deals with claims under £5,000. Claims for personal injury must be no more than £1,000 to be allocated to this track. Parties cannot claim their legal costs from the other side;

(b) the fast track, which is for claims up to £15,000 where the trial is not expected to last for more than one day. Only one oral expert is allowed for each party;

(c) the multi-track, for claims over £15,000 and for complex cases. Most medical negligence claims will be multi-track claims and, if they are for over £50,000, will be heard in the High Court.

Claims in contract

Patients who suffer harm as a result of NHS treatment can sue in tort for negligence. But can they sue for breach of contract? A contract is a legally binding *agreement* between two people or between a person and an organisation. A patient receiving treatment from the NHS does not have a contract with the NHS and therefore cannot sue for breach of contract if they suffer harm as a result of the treatment. Arguments have been put forward that a contract does exist with the NHS. In *Pfizer v Ministry of Health* (1965), the House of Lords considered whether a patient paying for a prescription under the NHS was a contract. It appeared to be a contract because the patient was paying for the prescription. The House of Lords said that there was no contract between a patient and the NHS, even though a payment was made. A contract was marked out by the fact that it was a voluntary agreement, but pharmacists were under a statutory duty to provide the drugs required, so they did not do so voluntarily.

In *Reynolds v Health First Medical Group* (2000), the claimant consulted her GP (the defendants) in 1996 and was told that she was not pregnant, even though she was. When she realised that she was pregnant, it was too late to have an abortion. After having a baby, she claimed damages for pain and suffering, loss of earnings and the cost of bringing up the child. Although the original claim was made in negligence, the decision of *McFarlane v Tayside Health Board* (2000) prevented claims for bringing up the child in such circumstances and the claimant therefore claimed for breach of contract. This was based on the argument that a GP received a fee (capitation fee) for each patient on his or her list and, hence, consideration was provided. It was held by the county court that the fact that a GP received payment for each patient was not consideration. Even if it was consideration, there was still no contract because the relationship was controlled by statute (the National Health Service Act 1977) and there was no room for bargaining between the doctor and patient. Also, either the doctor or the patient could end the relationship unilaterally, which could not be done in a contract.

If a patient paid for treatment at a private hospital and suffered harm as a result, they would have a claim for breach of contract. A patient suing in contract would have to show that the doctor did not reach the required standard of skill. At common law, the courts have said that the standard required is the same as that in negligence. In *Thake v Maurice* (1986), the Thakes had five children and did not want to have any more. Mr Thake paid a surgeon privately to carry out a vasectomy. The surgeon told Mr Thake that the operation was 'irreversible'. Later, Mrs Thake became pregnant but, not suspecting that she was, because of her husband's operation, she left it too late to have an abortion. The operation had been properly carried out but the effect had been reversed naturally. The Court of Appeal said that it was an implied term that the operation would be carried out with care and skill. Mr Thake argued that the surgeon had guaranteed that he would be sterile. The court held that the word 'irreversible' had to be interpreted in the context of medical science, where nothing could be guaranteed. It did not, therefore, mean irreversible, although it left open the possibility of a surgeon expressly guaranteeing a particular result. 'Of all sciences medicine is one of the least exact. In my view a doctor cannot be objectively regarded as guaranteeing the success of any operation or treatment unless he says as much in clear and unequivocal terms. The defendant did not do that in the present case' (Nourse LJ). But the failure of the surgeon to give his usual warning about the risk of reversal was a breach of the duty of care in negligence, and the claimants were entitled to damages for the distress suffered by both of them and for the pain of birth. It would be possible to claim in contract if the doctor guaranteed a particular result but such a claim would be unusual. In the Canadian case of *La Fleur v Cornelis* (1979), the claimant made a contract with the defendant cosmetic surgeon to reduce the size of her nose. The defendant told her: 'There will be no problem. You will be very happy.' He did not tell her of a 10% risk of scarring and the claimant was in fact scarred as a result of the operation. It was held that this was a breach of contract. The court said that a cosmetic surgeon was in a different position to a normal surgeon because he is carrying out a special service. He had agreed to do a particular thing and failed. Patricia Thompson made a contract with Sheffield Fertility Clinic to provide IVF treatment and implant two embryos. The clinic implanted three and Patricia had triplets. She sued the clinic for breach of contract and won the case in the High Court, obtaining £20,000 damages (BMJ 2001, vol 322, p 508).

It is now common practice for surgeons to warn of the risk of failure and this warning is contained in the consent form, which the patient will sign (see Appendix A, p 221).

The Supply of Goods and Services Act (SGSA) 1982 is also important where a contract exists. If the contract simply consists of providing a service (for example, carrying out an operation to repair a hernia), then ss 13–15 of the SGSA 1982 apply. Section 13 provides that where a service is provided in the course of a business, there is an implied term in the contract that it will be carried out with reasonable care and skill. Section 14 provides that where a service is provided in the course of a business and the timescale cannot be determined from the contract, there is an implied term that it will be carried out within a reasonable time. Under s 15, where the price is not fixed by the contract in a manner agreed in the contract or by a course of dealings, there is an implied term that a reasonable charge will be made.

If both goods and services are provided (for example, the fitting of a heart pacemaker), then, in addition to ss 13–15, ss 2–5 apply to the goods provided. Section 2 provides that there is an implied condition that the transferor has the right to transfer the property in the goods. If the sale is a sale by description, there is an implied condition that the goods will match the description (s 3). If the contract is made in the course of a business, there are implied conditions that the goods are of satisfactory quality unless any matter is brought to the buyer's attention, or an examination ought to have revealed the defect. Also, there is an implied condition that the goods must be fit for their purpose (s 4). If the contract is made by sample, there is an implied condition that the goods will match the sample (s 5).

The SGSA 1982 has been amended by the Sale and Supply of Goods to Consumers Regulations 2002. If the buyer deals as a consumer, any public statement on the characteristics of the goods made by the producer is taken into account in deciding if the goods are of satisfactory quality, etc. The Regulations also provide under reg 5 that goods which do not conform within six months of delivery must be taken not to have conformed at the time of delivery. Additionally, the Regulations provide new remedies of repair, replacement, rescission and reduction in price.

A patient suing for breach of contract will also have a possible claim in negligence.

Judicial review

The decisions of government and public bodies, which includes the NHS, are subject to judicial review. This means that the courts may examine the case to see whether the decision was made within the existing rules and in accordance with correct procedure. In considering the case, the courts will not look at the merits of a particular decision; for example, whether a particular patient should have been given a hip replacement. The application is made to a Divisional Court of the Queen's Bench Division. The court may quash a decision, stop a body from exceeding its powers or order it to carry out a particular duty. The courts have refused to become involved in decisions about whether a particular patient should receive treatment.

Section 3(1) of the National Health Service Act (NHSA) 1977 provides that it is the Secretary of State's duty to provide:

(a) hospital accommodation;

...

(e) such facilities for the prevention of illness, the care of persons suffering from illness and the aftercare of persons who have suffered from illness as he considers are appropriate as part of the health service;

(f) such other services as are required for the diagnosis and treatment of illness.

In *R v Secretary of State for Social Services ex p Hincks* (1979), patients complained that they had waited an unreasonable time for treatment because the hospital had postponed the building of a new block. They sought a declaration that the hospital was in breach of its duty under s 3(1) of the NHSA 1977. In rejecting the claim, it was held by the Court of Appeal that it was not the courts' function to say what funds should be given to the NHS and how to allocate them. Lord Denning said:

... it cannot be supposed that the Secretary of State has to provide all the kidney machines which are asked for, or for all the new developments such as heart transplants in every case where people would benefit from them.

The court would only intervene if the Secretary of State acted in a way that no reasonable minister would have acted (*Wednesbury* unreasonableness), and that was not the case here.

Other attempts to bring similar claims have all ended in failure. In *R v Central Birmingham HA ex p Walker* (1987), heart surgery on a premature baby was postponed five times because of a shortage of nurses. His mother applied for judicial review of the decision to postpone the operation. The Court of Appeal refused the application for judicial review. This was a matter about staffing and finance and the court said that the health authority would have to make a decision that no reasonable body could have reached, that is, '*Wednesbury* unreasonableness'. This does not completely rule out a claim, but it would have to be an extreme decision by the health authority. In *R v Cambridge HA ex p B* (1995), the defendants refused to provide expensive treatment for a 10 year old girl with acute myeloid leukaemia, as it would cost £75,000 and they believed that it had less than a 10% chance of success. The Court of Appeal held that it was not part of the job of the courts to rule on the merits of medical decisions – they could only rule on the lawfulness of such decisions; here, the authority had acted lawfully. Sir Thomas Bingham MR stated:

... the courts are not, contrary to what is sometimes believed, arbiters as to the merits of cases of this kind. Were we to express opinions as to the likelihood of the effectiveness of medical treatment, or as to the merits of medical judgment, then we should be straying far from the sphere which under our constitution is accorded to us. We have one function only, which is to rule upon the lawfulness of decisions.

In *R v Secretary of State for Health ex p Pfizer Ltd* (1999), the Secretary of State had issued a circular advising GPs not to prescribe Viagra for erectile dysfunction unless there were 'exceptional circumstances'. Pfizer sought judicial review, claiming that the circular prevented doctors from carrying out their statutory obligations. It was held that the advice overrode the professional judgment of doctors and therefore the circular was unlawful. Another recent claim for judicial review involved a refusal of treatment. In *R v North West Lancashire HA ex p A, D and G* (1999), the applicants were transsexuals. They had been living as women and all wished to have gender reassignment surgery. Their health authority refused to refer them to a specialist clinic and refused to pay for the surgery. The policy of the health authority was that, although it considered transsexualism to be an illness, it only provided counselling in cases of 'overriding clinical need'. The court quashed the authority's decision to refuse treatment and the authority appealed. The Court of Appeal said that determining priorities was a matter of judgment for each authority and transsexualism would normally be lower down the scale than, say, kidney failure. However, as the authority accepted that transsexualism was an illness, its policies ought to reflect that. The only exception it considered was if transsexualism led to mental illness, so that anyone seeking treatment had to establish another illness. Effectively, the exception of 'overriding clinical need' was meaningless. The health authority had acted in a way which was *Wednesbury* unreasonable and its appeal was dismissed. The court also said that general recourse to the European Convention on Human Rights was unhelpful and cluttered the development of domestic legal principles. Claims for breach of Art 8 (respect for private and family life) for failure to protect sexual identity and breach of Art 3 (freedom from inhuman treatment) for failure to provide treatment were rejected.

In the next case, the claim was for judicial review and breach of the EC Treaty. In *R (on the Application of Watts) v Bedford PCT* (2004), the claimant needed a hip replacement and the waiting list was for one year. The claimant asked the defendant to authorise treatment abroad but this was refused. The defendant reassessed her case and the claimant was told that she would only have to wait for 3–4 months. The claimant then went to France for the operation and claimed reimbursement from the defendant. She made a claim for judicial review and also argued that there was a breach of Art 49 of the EC Treaty, which prohibited restrictions on the freedom to provide services, and EC Council Regulation 1408/71 Art 22, which gave a right to be treated in another Member State if treatment could not be given in the normal time period for that treatment. The court said that in assessing undue delay, factors such as the patient's medical condition and degree of pain were relevant. Although delay for a year was undue delay, a period of 3–4 months was not and the claim was dismissed. The judge also held that provision of healthcare was within Art 49 and that a system which required prior authorisation to claim reimbursement restricted freedom to provide services. On appeal to the Court of Appeal, the court said that the question whether the NHS was under a duty to authorise medical treatment for patients in other Member States must be referred to the European Court of Justice.

The courts have made it clear that they cannot make judgments about the allocation of NHS resources, either in the case of individual patients or as regards types of treatment available. However, the mechanism of judicial review can bring wider benefits in focusing attention on treatments which are short of funds, and may sometimes help the individual patient. In *R v Cambridge HA ex p B* (1995), the girl with leukaemia received treatment which was paid for privately by a benefactor, and this extended the girl's life for a short time.

THE HUMAN RIGHTS ACT 1998

The Human Rights Act (HRA) 1998 took effect from 2 October 2000. The Act effectively incorporates most of the European Convention on Human Rights into English law. All English courts have the right to deal with claims under the Convention. Schedule 1 to the HRA 1998 sets out the Articles from the Convention incorporated into the Act:

- Art 2 Everyone's right to life shall be protected by law.
- Art 3 No one shall be subjected to torture or to inhuman or degrading treatment or punishment.
- Art 5 Everyone has the right to liberty. Some exceptions are made including lawful detention to prevent the spread of infectious diseases and to detain persons of unsound mind.
- Art 6 In the determination of his civil rights and any criminal charge, everyone is entitled to a fair and public hearing within a reasonable time.
- Art 8 (1) Everyone has the right to respect for his private and family life, his home and his correspondence.

  (2) There shall be no interference by a public authority with the exercise of this right except such as is in accordance with the law and is necessary in a democratic society in the interests of national security, public safety or the economic well-being of the country, for the prevention of disorder or crime, for the protection of health or morals, or for the protection of the rights and freedoms of others.
- Art 9 Everyone has the right to freedom of thought, conscience and religion.
- Art 10 Everyone has the right to freedom of expression.
- Art 12 Men and women of marriageable age have the right to marry and to found a family.
- Art 14 The enjoyment of the rights and freedoms in this Convention shall be secured without discrimination.

Some rights are absolute and cannot be interfered with by the State in any circumstances – these are Arts 2, 3, 4 and 14. Other rights are subject to derogations (Arts 5 and 6). This means that the government can apply restrictions to them; for example, Art 5, the right to liberty, is affected by legislation allowing suspected terrorists to be detained for seven days without appearing before a court. Other rights are qualified, for example, Arts 8 and 9, and these may be restricted in accordance with the law or if necessary for public safety or the protection of health and morals.

Under s 2 of the HRA 1998, courts dealing with Convention matters must take into account decisions of the European Court of Human Rights. The decisions are not binding but enable the law to move with changes in society. Under s 3, so far as it is possible to do so, primary and subordinate legislation must be read in such a way as to be compatible with the Convention. This means that, when interpreting legislation and statutory instruments, if the court is faced with a choice of interpretations, it must follow the one in keeping with the Convention. However, this is subject to the qualification, 'so far as it is possible to do so'. Under s 4, if a court determines that legislation is incompatible with the Convention, the High Court (and above) may make a 'declaration of incompatibility'. This does not make the legislation illegal, but it is then open to Parliament to change the law. Under s 6, it is unlawful for a 'public authority' to act in a way which is incompatible with the Convention. A public authority is any body carrying out public functions and includes courts and tribunals. This would also include the Department of Health, health authorities, NHS Trusts and doctors acting in their NHS role. Presumably, it would also include a private hospital carrying out work for the NHS. Under s 7, anyone who suffers, or is likely to suffer, through a breach of the Convention may sue. Claims must be brought before the end of one year from the act complained of or such period as the court thinks equitable.

Some courts took the HRA 1998 into consideration before it came into force on 2 October 2000. In *C v North Devon HA ex p Coughlan* (1999), a disabled woman moved from a hospital into a purpose built NHS home after being told that it would be her home for life. Five years later, it was decided to close the home. The woman applied for judicial review of that decision. The Court of Appeal said that, first, moving the woman was unfair because it frustrated her legitimate expectation of a 'home for life' and there was no overriding public interest to justify the move; therefore, it was an abuse of power. Secondly, this was a breach of Art 8 of the European Convention on Human Rights (the right to respect for private and family life) because it interfered with her right to a home and could not be justified unless a suitable alternative was provided. In *R v Brent, Kensington and Chelsea and Westminster Mental Health NHS Trust* (2002), the claimants were all long-term mental patients and had lived in hospital for many years. Under the 'care in the community scheme' the hospital was closed and in February 1998 they were moved to Harefield Lodge. In July 2002, it was decided to close Harefield Lodge. The claimants sought judicial review and claimed a breach of Art 8 (right to respect for private life). The court said that, even accepting that accommodation for long-term patients would be seen as a home, this had to be put in the context of the authority's wider obligations. These included the care needs of others and the resources available. Harefield Lodge was intended only as a temporary home. There was no breach of Art 8.

The courts considered Arts 2, 3 and 8 in *R (on the Application of Hegarty) v St Helens BC* (2003). The claimants lived in a private nursing home. The home was owned by a company which contracted with the defendant local authority. The defendant refused to renew the contract when the company substantially increased the fees. The company then decided to close the home. The claimants applied for judicial review and claimed a breach of Arts 2, 3 and 8. The court said that the risk to life was not severe enough to be within Art 2. Closure would not cause sufficient suffering to be within Art 3. There would not be great disruption to their home life under Art 8 and the interference by the defendant was justified on financial grounds. The claimants' case was dismissed.

Probably the most important Articles for medical law will be Arts 2, 3, 5 and 8 (see Gordon, R and Ward, T, 'Human Rights Act: health law' (2000) 144(17) SJ 1). The courts have made a number of significant judgments on these Articles and these are dealt with in the appropriate sections later in this book. Under Art 2 (the right to life), there is a duty on the State to preserve life, although this is not an absolute duty and it does not give a correlating right to die (*R (on the Application of Pretty) v UK* (2002)). Article 3 (freedom from torture and degrading treatment) could be used for failure to provide treatment. Article 5 (the right to liberty) allows detention of people of unsound mind and those with infectious diseases, but this must be according to law and must not be arbitrary. Article 8 (the right to private life) is important in relation to confidentiality (*H (A Healthcare Worker) v Associated Newspapers* (2002)). A breach of Art 12 was declared in *I v UK* (2002), in the case of a person who had had gender reassignment surgery.

SUMMARY – INTRODUCTION

1   *Ethical theories and principles*
   - Importance of ethical principles in medical law: rules based on them; useful if there is no law on a particular matter.
   - Deontological theory: duty to act; is the act right or wrong in itself? Kant – treat people as an end and never as a means.
   - Utilitarian theory: act is judged by the consequences; aim to maximise happiness. No regard to principle, just the results.
   - Principles of medical ethics: autonomy – self rule; beneficence – do good; non-maleficence – do no harm; justice – act fairly.

2   *Civil and criminal law*
- Civil: dispute between individuals, for example, negligence claim.
- Criminal: an act which society will punish, for example, an assault.
- Procedure for bringing claims in civil law: most medical claims on multi-track.

3   *Contract*
- No contract between patient and NHS: *Pfizer v Ministry of Health* (1965).
- Contract between patient and private hospital: breach of contract if doctor does not reach the standard required (same as negligence in tort) (*Thake v Maurice* (1986)).
- Doctors do not generally give a guarantee in contract.
- Supply of Goods and Services Act 1982: medical services must be carried out with skill and care.

4   *Judicial review*
- Public bodies must follow the correct procedures in making decisions and if they do not the decision may be quashed by judicial review.
- Courts reluctant to become involved in decisions about allocation of resources unless action is *Wednesbury* unreasonable: *R v Central Birmingham HA ex p Walker* (1987).

5   *Human Rights Act 1998*
- Main rights: Art 2, right to life; Art 3, no degrading treatment; Art 6, right to a fair trial; Art 8, right to respect for private and family life; Art 12, right to marry and have a family.
- *R v Brent, Kensington and Chelsea and Westminster Mental Health Trust* (2002): moving residents from local authority home not a breach of Art 8.

CHAPTER 2

CONSENT TO TREATMENT

INTRODUCTION

The requirement that, generally, a patient must consent to treatment is of fundamental importance in medical law. Before a doctor or nurse touches a patient they must obtain the patient's consent. In civil law, the tort of trespass to the person protects a person from being touched without giving their consent. It is a civil battery to do so. The tort of negligence is also relevant if a patient has not been given sufficient information before agreeing to treatment, for example, information about the risks of a particular treatment. In addition, an act which amounts to a battery in civil law may, at the same time, also be the criminal offence of battery. The person committing such an act may be prosecuted. The law dealing with competent adult patients is relatively clear but there are many difficulties with incompetent patients, largely stemming from the fact that no one can consent on behalf of an incompetent adult.

The ethical principle of autonomy, that people should have their autonomy respected, is reflected in the law of consent, in that by obtaining the patient's consent the doctor can then treat the patient in the way the patient wants. A patient undergoing surgery will usually be required to sign a 'consent form' and the legal significance of doing so needs to be examined.

CAPACITY TO CONSENT

To be able to give a legally valid consent, the patient must have the capacity (or competence) to do so. Some people will clearly not have this capacity; for example, they may be unconscious, mentally handicapped, too young or unable to communicate. Others who do not fall into any of these categories may still be seen as lacking capacity, but the problem for the law is to distinguish between those with and those without capacity. English law does not provide a universal test of capacity for all purposes. It depends on what a person is doing; for example, capacity to marry, or to enter a contract, or to manage one's property and affairs, will be different to capacity to agree to medical treatment. How does the law determine whether a person has the capacity to consent to treatment? As a general rule, the patient must be able to understand the nature and purpose of the treatment to be able to consent to it. Medical staff have to make the decision in individual cases whether that particular patient has the capacity to consent to that particular treatment. A number of factors will be relevant, including whether the patient can understand the nature of the treatment, whether the patient has been taking medication which may affect their understanding, the consequences of not having the treatment, etc. The Law Commission has recommended that capacity to make decisions should be assessed on the 'balance of probabilities' (*Mental Incapacity*, Law Com 231, 1995). The criteria to assess the capacity to consent to treatment (or to refuse treatment) were set out in *Re C (Adult: Refusal of Treatment)* (1994) as the ability (a) to understand and retain treatment information; (b) to believe the information; and (c) to weigh the information in the balance in making a decision.

A number of cases have given guidance on determining a patient's capacity. In *Re T (Adult: Refusal of Treatment)* (1992), T, a pregnant woman, was involved in a car accident. If she was not given a blood transfusion, she would die. T was not a Jehovah's Witness, although her mother was. After the mother spoke to T, T refused a transfusion. The Court of Appeal held that the hospital could ignore T's refusal, as T did not have the capacity to consent as her medication and the effect of her injuries affected that capacity. Also, the undue influence of her mother meant that T's decision was not given voluntarily.

However, in the following case, the courts accepted the importance of the patient's beliefs. In *Re C (Adult: Refusal of Treatment)* (1994), C, who suffered from paranoid schizophrenia and had delusions that he was a doctor, was detained in Broadmoor Hospital. He developed gangrene in his foot and the doctor said that amputation at the knee was necessary to save his life, but C refused this as he did not believe that he would die from gangrene. He was given other treatment which was successful, but C wanted a declaration from the court that no amputation should be done without his consent. The court had to consider whether C had capacity and used the test of whether he understood the nature, purpose and effect of medical treatment. The court said that he did understand the information he had been given and that he had made a clear choice. 'Although his general capacity is impaired by schizophrenia, it has not been established that he does not sufficiently understand the nature, purpose and effects of the treatment he refuses' (Thorpe J).

In *Re MB (Medical Treatment)* (1997), the Court of Appeal approved *Re C* in a case where a woman who was 40 weeks pregnant was admitted to hospital with the foetus in the breach position. Normal delivery would put both the woman's life and that of the baby in danger. She agreed to a Caesarean operation but refused at the last minute because of a fear of needles. The court held that a patient lacked capacity if: (a) the patient is unable to understand and retain information needed to make a decision; and (b) the patient cannot use information and weigh it in the balance, for example, if they suffer from a phobia. The court said that the patient temporarily lacked capacity because of her phobia, and it authorised the operation.

In *St George's Healthcare NHS Trust v S* (1998), the Court of Appeal laid down guidelines for dealing with patients who were believed to lack capacity. These are as follows:

- The guidelines do not apply if the patient is competent.
- If a competent patient refuses consent, application to the High Court is pointless. The hospital should make a written record of the patient's decision.
- If the patient is incapable of giving or refusing consent, the authority can act in the best interests of the patient. If there is an advance directive, that should normally be followed.
- The authority should identify as soon as possible if there is concern over competence.
- The patient's family doctor may be qualified to make the assessment but, in difficult cases about future health or the life of the patient, an independent psychiatrist should assess the patient. If there is still serious doubt about competence, the court should be involved.
- If the patient is unable or incapable of instructing solicitors, the Official Solicitor should be notified.

The guidelines then deal with the hearing of the matter, saying that both parties should be involved.

In response to the Law Commission's Report on *Mental Incapacity*, the government, in *Making Decisions* (Cm 4465, 1999), proposed a new test of capacity, based on the Law Commission's functional approach. This would focus on whether the individual is able to understand the nature and effect of the decision at the time that a particular decision is made (para 1.4).

The Mental Capacity Bill 2004 sets out a definition of those who lack capacity in cl 2 and the test for capacity in cl 3.

Clause 2 provides that a person lacks capacity in relation to a matter if at the material time he is unable to make a decision in relation to the matter because of an impairment or disturbance in the mind or brain. The impairment or disturbance may be permanent or temporary. The question of whether someone lacks capacity must be decided on a balance of probabilities:

3   Inability to make decisions

(1) For the purposes of section 2, a person is unable to make a decision if he is unable –

(a) to understand the information relevant to the decision,

(b) to retain that information,

(c) to use or weigh that information as part of the process of making the decision, or

(d) to communicate his decision (whether by talking, using sign language or any other means).

(2) The fact that a person is able to retain the information relevant to a decision for a short period only does not prevent him from being regarded as able to make the decision.

(3) The information relevant to a decision includes information about the reasonably foreseeable consequences of –

    (a) deciding one way or another, or

    (b) failing to make the decision.

REFUSING TREATMENT

What is the legal position on refusing treatment? A competent adult patient may consent to treatment or refuse treatment (*Re T (Adult: Refusal of Treatment* (1992)). But what if the effect of refusing treatment would lead to the death of the patient? In *Re AK* (2000), the patient suffered from motor neuron disease and had indicated that he wanted his ventilator switched off when he reached a point where he could no longer communicate. The court said that a refusal of treatment by a competent adult patient must be respected. This question was also addressed in *Re B (Adult: Refusal of Medical Treatment)* (2002). Ms B suffered damage to her spinal column and as a result became tetraplegic, which meant that she was paralysed from the neck down. She had to be put on a ventilator. She sought a declaration from the court that the ventilator should be switched off. The court had to consider the question of whether she had the mental capacity to accept treatment or to refuse treatment where such a refusal would lead to her death. The High Court said that there was a presumption of mental capacity. Unless the seriousness of the illness affected the patient's mental capacity, a patient with a serious physical disability had the same rights as any other person with capacity. The court said that in assessing the competence of a patient, doctors should not allow questions of mental capacity to become confused with the consequences of the decision, however serious. The patient's decision might reflect a difference in values rather than the fact that she lacked competence. Ms B had sufficient capacity to make decisions about her treatment, including the withdrawal of treatment, and the declaration was granted. She was entitled to damages for trespass. 'The right of the competent patient to request the cessation of treatment had to prevail over the natural desire of the medical and nursing profession to try to keep her alive' (Butler-Sloss P).

In *R (on the Application of L) v Newcastle Primary Care Trust* (2004), L, a haemophiliac, refused treatment with plasma derived Factor VIII and asked for another type. The hospital refused to give him another type. The court said that a person of full age and capacity could refuse treatment even though this meant that they would die. The hospital had no duty to provide a particular treatment.

CIVIL LAW

The tort of trespass to the person consists of assault, battery and false imprisonment. False imprisonment involves restricting a person's freedom of movement and it is much less likely to occur in medical treatment than assault and battery. However, in the *St George's* case, the patient was detained against her will and given a Caesarean section, so a claim could have been made for false imprisonment.

An assault is an act which causes someone to apprehend unlawful force against them. A battery is the infliction of unlawful force on another. 'An assault is an act which causes another person to apprehend the infliction of immediate, unlawful force on his person; a battery is the actual infliction of unlawful force on another person' (*Collins v Wilcock* (1984)). An example of assault would be a doctor holding a needle who approaches a patient, intending to give the patient an injection without their consent. An example of a battery would be an actual injection given without consent. Normally, assault and battery will go together because even in the medical context, using the needle example, the patient will see the doctor approaching and hence fear a battery. However, if the doctor approached the patient from behind and simply jabbed the needle into the patient, without the patient seeing the doctor approach, this would only be battery. Similarly, if the patient was unconscious and was given an injection, this would not be assault.

It has long been accepted that touching someone without consent is a battery. In *Scholendorff v Society of New York Hospital* (1914), Cardozo J stated:

> Every human being of adult years and sound mind has a right to determine what shall be done with his own body; and a surgeon who performs an operation without the patient's consent commits an assault.

Trespass to the person is an intentional tort, which means that the particular act, rather than the injury, is intended. This type of tort is in contrast to an unintentional tort, such as negligence, where the act is not intended. With intentional torts, legal action may be taken without proving actual damage: it is enough to prove that the act took place (this is sometimes referred to as being actionable *per se*, which just means without proof of damage). Consequently, a patient may sue for battery even though they have not suffered any injury. For example, if a nurse put a dressing on a wound without the patient's consent, that would be battery. With unintentional torts, actual damage must be proved; for example, a patient claiming negligence by a doctor must show that the doctor's negligent act caused the patient harm.

It was stated by the Court of Appeal in *Wilson v Pringle* (1986) that for a battery the touching must be 'hostile'. However, if this were the case it would mean that no one could sue doctors on the basis of battery because the doctor in giving treatment would not be acting in a hostile manner. However, in the later House of Lords case of *Re F (Mental Patient:*

Sterilisation) (1990), Lord Goff questioned this requirement: 'I respectfully doubt whether this is correct. A prank that gets out of hand, an over friendly slap on the back, surgical treatment by a surgeon who mistakenly thinks that the patient has consented to it, all these things may transcend the bounds of lawfulness, without being characterised as hostile.'

Consent by the patient may be expressly given or may be implied. An example of express consent is where the patient agrees to a proposed operation. This agreement could be given orally or it may be done in writing by asking the patient to sign a consent form. Consent may also be implied from the circumstances. In *O'Brien v Cunard SS Co* (1891) (US), the claimant immigrant arrived in New York and rolled up his sleeve for vaccination, thus giving an implied consent. It is standard practice to ask a patient to sign a consent form before an operation. However, it is important to realise that merely signing such a form would not in itself be a valid consent. It is important that medical staff have explained the nature of the procedure to the patient and the patient agrees to it. Clearly, if the patient agrees to a particular operation and the doctor carries out a different one by mistake, that is trespass. An example of a consent form appears in Appendix A, on p 221.

In order for a patient to give a valid consent to treatment, the patient must know what the proposed treatment is. However, the question arises of how much information the patient must be given. In the US, the concept of 'informed' consent requires that the patient must be given sufficient facts about the proposed treatment to give a proper consent. However, the exact scope of what is needed for 'informed consent' is unclear. It is sometimes explained on the basis of the 'prudent patient' test: what a reasonable person in the patient's position would want to know about the treatment. This concept has not been followed by the English courts. In *Sidaway v Bethlem Royal Hospital Governors and Others* (1984) in the Court of Appeal, Dunn LJ stated that 'The concept of informed consent forms no part of English law'. What information must be disclosed to the patient to obtain a valid consent in English law? In *Chatterton v Gerson* (1981), C suffered pain from a scar following a hernia operation. G, a surgeon, proposed an injection near the spinal cord to relieve the pain. Following this procedure, C lost all sensation in her right leg. The operation had been carried out carefully and without negligence by G. C argued that as she had not been given sufficient information about the risks of numbness, she could not give a valid consent and G was liable in battery. The court held that where the patient is told in 'broad terms' about the nature of the procedure that is sufficient. C's claim for battery failed, as she knew the general nature of the treatment. The court also said that if the nature of the operation has been explained but the risks have not, then any claim should be in negligence rather than trespass.

The application of the test from *Chatterton v Gerson* is not always straightforward. If a patient consents to a blood test but is not told that the test includes testing for HIV, has the patient consented? Because of the special nature of HIV, in that there is no cure, and the very fact that someone has been tested for HIV has insurance implications for the patient, it means that it can be argued that the patient should be told that the doctor is testing for HIV in order for the consent to be valid. John Keown has pointed out that a doctor who tells a patient he is taking blood for 'tests', but does not say that one of them is for HIV, has told the patient the nature of the procedure. '... *Chatterton* merely requires the patient to be informed in broad terms of the nature of the procedure. The doctor who tells the patient that the blood is to be removed for testing, even though he does not say that it is to be tested for HIV, has surely satisfied this requirement' (Keown, J, 'The ashes of AIDS and the phoenix of informed consent' (1989) 52 MLR 790). In practice, a doctor taking blood for routine tests will not inform the patient exactly what tests are to be done on the blood.

Consent and negligence

To establish negligence in a medical context, it has to be shown that the doctor owes the patient a duty of care, that the doctor has broken this duty and that the patient has suffered damage as a result, that is, that the breach caused the loss (*Donoghue v Stevenson* (1932)). Normally, this duty of care in negligence is about the actions of the doctor, who must not act in a careless manner and as a result cause harm to the patient (see Chapter 4, Medical Negligence). However, the doctor's duty of care in negligence has been interpreted by the courts to include omissions, and consequently includes a duty to give sufficient advice to enable the patient to make a rational decision about treatment and give a valid consent. A patient who brings a claim for negligence on the basis of lack of information has to show that this breach (that is, failing to tell the patient about the risks) caused the loss. To establish that the breach led to the loss, before *Chester v Afshar* (2004), the patient had to prove that if they had been given the extra information, they would not have consented to the procedure. The issue of causation arose in *Chester v Afshar*. The claimant was suffering severe back pain and she agreed to an operation to remove three spinal discs. The defendant surgeon did not tell her of a 1–2% risk of damage to the nerve root. As a result of the operation she suffered nerve damage and was paralysed. She claimed: (a) that the operation had been carried out negligently; and (b) that if she had been warned of the serious risks she would have postponed the operation to seek a further medical opinion. At first instance, the court found that there was no negligence in the performance of the operation, but that there was negligence in not warning the claimant of the risk of paralysis. The defendant argued on appeal that to establish that the failure to warn caused the harm, the claimant had to show that she would never have consented to the operation if she had been told the risks. The Court of Appeal held that the defendant's failure to warn the claimant of the risks caused her to have the operation, which she would not otherwise have had at that time. The claimant did not have to show that she would never have had the operation.

The House of Lords confirmed that the defendant surgeon was liable in negligence for failing to warn the claimant of the risk. The claimant did not have to prove that she would never have had the operation if told the risks; otherwise, claimants who were unsure about what they would decide would be left without a remedy. The injury to the claimant could therefore be regarded as caused by the failure to warn. This was a 3:2 majority decision (see Chapter 4, Medical Negligence, p 67).

Whether a doctor has acted negligently is not judged by the normal negligence standard of the 'reasonable man', but by the *Bolam* test. This provides that, if a doctor (or other health worker) reaches the standard of 'a responsible body of medical opinion' (*Bolam v Friern HMC* (1957), *per* McNair J), they are not negligent. If a patient is claiming that they have not been given sufficient information about the risks, their claim should be in negligence and not battery. In *Chatterton v Gerson* (1981), Bristow J stated:

> In my judgment, once the patient is informed in broad terms of the nature of the procedure which is intended and gives her consent, that consent is real and the cause of the action on which to base a claim for failure to go into risks and implications is negligence, not trespass.

In the US, the courts have adopted the 'prudent patient' test. This test uses the standard of a reasonable person in the patient's position – would they see the risks as an important factor in deciding whether or not to have treatment? This test was set out in the case of *Canterbury v Spence* (1972) (US), where the court considered how much information the doctor must tell the patient. The court dismissed full disclosure and good medical practice as the tests. The patient's right of autonomy required that the patient be told of risks which would be material to the decision on whether to consent to treatment. This would be the case when a reasonable person in the patient's position 'would be likely to attach significance to the risks' (Robinson J).

In Canada, the courts have said that a patient has the right to know about the risks (*Reibl v Hughes* (1980)). This has been qualified to the extent that a patient may waive this 'right to know' by giving the doctor the right to make the decision; this is known as 'therapeutic privilege'.

The English courts have followed the test of professional medical practice. The question of whether the *Bolam* test applied to giving information about risks as well as to diagnosis and medical treatment was determined in *Sidaway v Governors of Bethlem Royal Hospital* (1985). After an accident at work, S had pain in her shoulder. Dr F diagnosed pressure on a nerve root and recommended an operation on her spine. S consented to an operation which was carried out without negligence but as a result of which she became paralysed. S claimed that she had not been told about a 2% risk to a nerve root and a 1% risk of damage to her spinal cord. S claimed that failure to warn of the damage to the spinal cord meant that her consent was invalid and the doctor was liable in battery. S also claimed that not telling her of the risk was a breach of the doctor's duty of care in negligence to warn her of the risks, and she had not given an 'informed consent'. It was found by the trial judge that she had been told of the risk of damage to the nerve root. It was held by the House of Lords that, if S understood the general nature of the operation, not being told of the risks did not mean that it was battery. The majority in the House of Lords said that as regards her negligence claim, in warning of risks, if the doctor conformed to 'a responsible body of medical opinion' (*Bolam*) as to what to tell the patient, the doctor had fulfilled this duty. It was found that the doctor in this case had done so because not telling S of the risk of damage to her spinal cord was in line with the practice of a responsible body of neurosurgeons. Also, as the patient understood the nature of the operation, the claim in battery failed. In the House of Lords, Lord Scarman, in a dissenting judgment, argued in favour of the prudent patient test, rather than the *Bolam* test:

> ... I think that English law must recognise a duty of the doctor to warn his patient of risk inherent in the treatment he is proposing; and especially so if the treatment be surgery. The critical limitation is that the duty is confined to material risk. The test of materiality is whether in the circumstances of the particular case the court is satisfied that a reasonable person in the patient's position would be likely to attach significance to the risk.

The House of Lords also confirmed that a doctor could withhold information from a patient on the ground of 'therapeutic privilege' if the doctor considered that the information would be detrimental to the health of that patient. So, for example, telling the patient of certain risks would make the patient's condition worse.

If a patient asks the doctor questions about the risks, does the doctor have to answer? In the Australian case of *Rogers v Whitaker* (1992), R, who was blind in her right eye, was advised to have an operation on that eye to restore sight to it. She asked many questions about the operation but was not told of a one in 14,000 chance of going blind in her left eye as a result of the operation. The operation was carried out without negligence but she went blind in her left eye. It was held by the High Court, which refused to follow *Bolam*, that, as a matter of general principle, the doctor had been negligent in not telling R of this risk. It did not matter that the patient had not asked about that particular risk. The court applied a subjective test – what this particular patient needed to know. In the UK, however, the courts follow the *Bolam* test of whether a responsible body of medical opinion would answer such questions. In *Blyth v Bloomsbury AHA* (1985), the claimant, a nurse, had a baby. She was then given an injection of a contraceptive drug, Depo-Provera, to which she had consented. She had asked some questions about the drug but had not been told about the side effects. As a result of the injection she suffered bleeding. She sued for negligence, claiming that had she been told of the side effects, she would not have had the injection. The Court of Appeal allowed the appeal by the AHA and said that in answering general questions, medical staff would be judged by the *Bolam* test:

> The question of what a plaintiff should be told in answer to a general inquiry cannot be divorced from the *Bolam* test, any more than when no such inquiry is made. In both cases the answer must depend upon the circumstances, the

nature of the inquiry, the nature of the information which is available, its reliability, relevance, the condition of the patient, and so forth. [Kerr LJ]

If a duty to answer specific questions was imposed by the law, this would give a knowledgeable and articulate patient an advantage over others.

Non-therapeutic treatment

Non-therapeutic treatment is not given to make the patient better but for some other reason. Examples would include cosmetic surgery and treatment for contraceptive purposes. This is in contrast to therapeutic treatment, which is needed because the patient is suffering from an illness. Are the rules on consent different for non-therapeutic treatment? In *Gold v Haringay HA* (1987), Mrs G had three children and agreed with her husband that they would not have any more. She consented to be sterilised but was not told of the risk of natural reversal. She became pregnant and sued for negligence, claiming that she had not been told of the risks or alternatives such as vasectomy for her husband. It was held in the High Court that, in non-therapeutic cases, the *Bolam* test did not apply and the duty of care demanded that the patient should be given all the information that a reasonable patient would want to know (the prudent patient test). The Court of Appeal overruled this decision and said that giving treatment or advice involved professional skill and the *Bolam* test applied:

> The fact (if it be the fact) that giving contraceptive advice involves a different sort of skill and competence from carrying out a surgical operation does not mean that the *Bolam* test ceases to be applicable. It is clear from Lord Diplock's speech in *Sidaway* that a doctor's duty of care in relation to diagnoses, treatment and advice, whether the doctor be a specialist or a general practitioner, is not to be dissected into its component parts. [Lloyd LJ]

The court also said that the distinction between therapeutic and non-therapeutic treatment was often difficult to make and should not be made the basis for different standards of care. Some doctors did warn of the risk of reversal and others did not; therefore, Mrs G's claim failed.

CRIMINAL LAW

It is possible for medical staff to be charged with criminal offences arising out of their work. These offences range from minor criminal assaults to grievous bodily harm and, finally, manslaughter or murder. In all criminal offences the prosecution has to prove both that the defendant had *mens rea* (the intention to commit the act) and that he had committed the *actus reus* (the actual act).

As in civil law, a criminal assault at common law is a threat of violence and battery involves some physical contact. Statute, in the form of the Offences Against the Person Act (OAPA) 1861, also provides a number of offences. Under s 47 of the OAPA 1861, an 'assault occasioning actual bodily harm' is an offence. If a patient is given treatment without their consent or is given treatment in spite of their refusing to give consent, then medical staff could face prosecution. Treatment such as cauterising a blood vessel would fall within this section.

Section 18 of the OAPA 1861 provides that it is an offence to unlawfully and maliciously wound or cause any grievous bodily harm (GBH) with intent to do GBH. This is the most serious offence involving assault and includes both wounding, where the skin is broken (*C v Eisenhower* (1983)), and serious harm (GBH). The distinguishing factor from s 20 (see below) is that there must be a specific intent. If medical staff carry out a surgical procedure without consent, they could be charged under this section. A failure to treat, leading to serious harm, might also be regarded as 'causing' that harm, and could lead to prosecution.

Under s 20 of the OAPA 1861, it is an offence to 'unlawfully and maliciously wound or inflict any grievous bodily harm upon any person, either with or without any weapon or instrument'. Under this section, the damage must be inflicted, rather than caused, as under s 18. If medical staff fail to treat a patient, resulting in serious harm, they cannot be convicted under s 20, as they have not inflicted harm on the patient. In *R v Dica* (2004), the defendant was charged under s 20 with GBH after infecting two women with HIV. The question arose of whether the women had consented to the risk of infection with HIV even though the defendant had concealed his infection from them. The Court of Appeal held that because these were long-term relationships and the defendant had concealed his condition, they did not consent. The defendant would not have a defence under s 20. The court said that it was unlikely a person would consent to the risk of such a serious illness if they did not know about it. A retrial was ordered. The court refused to follow *R v Clarence* (1888), where the defendant had gonorrhoea but did not tell his wife. He had sex with her and she became infected. He was prosecuted under s 20. The appeal court said that his wife had consented to sex and he was not guilty. This is an important change in the law.

In all of the above offences, if the patient consents to the treatment this will provide a valid defence. However, this must be qualified, to the extent that there are certain things which a person cannot consent to at common law. For example, could a patient give a valid consent to having their arm amputated if there was nothing wrong with it? In *R v Brown* (1992), the court said that consent was not a defence to acts which caused actual bodily harm or wounding. Consequently, a patient could not give a valid consent to a medical procedure which was not medically necessary and which caused harm to the patient. A valid consent could be given to a procedure which involved harm but was medically needed, for example, amputation of a limb to stop the spread of gangrene.

Circumcision of men or women is generally non-therapeutic and performed for religious or cultural reasons. Female genital mutilation is painful and may have serious health consequences later in life. The Female

Genital Mutilation Act 2003 makes it a criminal offence to mutilate a girl's genitals (s 1). An exception is made in the case of a registered medical practitioner who carries out a surgical operation which is necessary for the physical or mental health of the girl. It is also an offence to carry out an act of female circumcision abroad on a UK national.

It would be rare for medical staff to face a prosecution for murder or manslaughter, although this is not unknown, as shown by the cases of the nurse, Beverly Allitt, and the prosecution in 1999 of the GP, Dr Harold Shipman. Murder is a common law offence, which requires the prosecution to prove the intention to kill or cause serious harm and the relevant act causing death. In *R v Cox* (1992), Dr Cox was charged with murder after he gave an elderly patient, who was in great pain, an injection of potassium chloride (which has no therapeutic value). The patient died within minutes, but the doctor was only convicted of attempted murder because it could not be proved that he gave the injection with the intention of killing the patient, rather than simply to ease her pain.

Manslaughter is divided into voluntary manslaughter, which falls under the Homicide Act 1957, and involuntary manslaughter. The latter is divided into unlawful act manslaughter and gross negligence manslaughter. Gross negligence manslaughter involves carrying out a lawful act but in a reckless way. In *R v Adomako* (1995), the defendant anaesthetist failed to notice that, during an operation, an oxygen tube had been disconnected for several minutes, as a result of which the patient died. It was held that the defendant owed a duty of care to the patient, that he had been grossly negligent and that the patient died as a result. The defendant was convicted of manslaughter. In this case, the negligence consisted of an omission to act.

TREATING WITHOUT CONSENT

To be able to give a legally valid consent to treatment, the patient must be recognised as competent to do so by the law. An adult patient is regarded as being able to consent to treatment unless there is evidence to show otherwise. However, in some circumstances a person may not be competent to give consent; for example, those suffering from mental impairment or from a physical injury which prevents them from giving consent. Children under 16 are not generally treated by the law as having competence to consent unless they are 'Gillick' competent (see Chapter 3, Children and Consent, p 40).

The law regards anyone who reaches the age of 18, and who is mentally competent, as an adult (s 1 of the Family Law Reform Act 1969). In the case of medical treatment, a child of 16 years who is mentally competent can consent to treatment (s 8(1) of the Family Law Reform Act 1969).

When someone reaches the age of 18, no one else may consent for them but, if the patient is over 18 and is mentally incompetent, this creates a problem. This situation has been described as a 'legal limbo' by Margaret

Brazier (*Medicine, Patients and the Law*, 3rd edn, 2003, London: Penguin), because the patient cannot consent and no one may consent on their behalf.

In some circumstances, treatment may be given without consent. At common law, treatment may be given on the basis of the doctrine of necessity, or on the basis of acting in the patient's 'best interests'. Children can be made wards of court and this enables the court to make decisions about their treatment, but the same cannot be done with adults. A number of statutes also provide that treatment may be given without the consent of the patient. If a patient is compulsorily detained under the Mental Health Act 1983, they may be given treatment for their mental condition without their consent if the treatment is given under the direction of the responsible medical officer (s 63). The Public Health (Control of Disease) Act 1984 provides that those suffering from certain notifiable diseases, such as cholera, typhoid, polio and meningitis, may be given a compulsory examination without their consent and may be detained in hospital. The Act is concerned more with protecting the public rather than treating the patient.

If a patient suffers from mental incapacity but has not been compulsorily detained, the problem of consent remains. In *F v West Berkshire HA* (1989) (also known as *Re F* (1990)), F was 36 years old but had a mental age of five. She was a voluntary patient in a mental hospital. She began a sexual relationship with another patient and, as she would be unable to look after any child which might be born, the question arose as to whether F could be sterilised. Clearly, F was unable to give a valid consent to such a procedure. A declaration was sought as to the legality of sterilisation. The House of Lords confirmed that if an adult patient could not give consent because they were unconscious or suffered from mental disability, a doctor could provide treatment on the basis of the principle of necessity only if it would save their life, improve their health or prevent a deterioration in their health. A declaration was granted that F could lawfully be sterilised. The court said that if the proposed treatment was radical or irreversible, the doctor should apply to the court for a declaration.

It may often be difficult for doctors to judge whether an adult has the capacity to consent. In *St George's Healthcare NHS Trust v S* (1998), S was a 36 year old pregnant woman who was diagnosed with pre-eclampsia and advised that she should go to hospital for an induced birth. S wanted a natural birth and refused to go into hospital. S was then seen by a social worker and two doctors and was compulsorily admitted under the Mental Health Act 1983. The hospital obtained a declaration from the court, which enabled them to act without S's consent and they carried out a Caesarean operation. S then appealed to the Court of Appeal, which said that a competent pregnant woman has the right to refuse treatment, even if refusing put her life in danger, and the hospital had committed trespass. The court criticised the use of the Mental Health Act 1983 to detain a patient who simply had different views from the majority.

Guidance has been given on obtaining declarations for adults who lack capacity (*Practice Note (Official Solicitor: Declaratory Proceedings: Medical and*

Welfare Decisions for Adults Who Lack Capacity) [2001] 2 FLR 158). There are two categories which require the sanction of a High Court judge: (a) sterilisation of a person who cannot consent; and (b) discontinuing artificial nutrition and hydration of a patient in a persistent vegetative state. In other cases, applications should be made where there are disputes about the patient's capacity or the patient's best interests. Applications should be made to the Family Division of the High Court.

The principle of necessity

In *Re F (Mental Patient: Sterilisation)* (1990), Lord Goff stated:

> Upon what principle can medical treatment be justified when given without consent? We are searching for a principle upon which, in limited circumstances, recognition may be given to a need, in the interests of the patient, that treatment should be given to him in circumstances where he is (temporarily or permanently) disabled from consenting to it. It is this criterion of a need which points to the principle of necessity as providing justification ...

In order for the principle of necessity to operate, two requirements must be met: (a) there must be a necessity to act in a situation where medical staff cannot communicate with the patient; and (b) the action taken must be what a reasonable person would do in the best interests of the patient (*Re F (Mental Patient: Sterilisation)* (1990), *per* Lord Goff); for example, if an injured patient is brought to a hospital unconscious after a road accident. Guidance on how this principle works can be found in two Canadian cases. In *Marshall v Curry* (1933), during an operation to repair a hernia, the patient was found to have a diseased and gangrenous testicle. The doctor believed that the testicle was a danger to the patient's life and removed it. When the patient found out, he sued for battery. The court held that, in an emergency, a doctor may act without the patient's consent to save their life or preserve their health. In the circumstances, this was not a battery because it was removed both in order to repair the hernia and to protect the patient's health and possibly save his life. It was unreasonable to postpone the procedure. In *Murray v McMurchy* (1949), during a Caesarean operation, it was found that tumours in the patient's uterus would have made it dangerous for her if she became pregnant again. The doctor tied her fallopian tubes to prevent her becoming pregnant in the future. The court held that there was no evidence that the tumours were an immediate danger to her life or health. The doctor could quite easily have waited and obtained the consent of the patient. The doctor was liable for battery.

These cases illustrate that a distinction can be made between doing an act which is a necessity and doing something which is simply convenient. In the English case of *Devi v West Midlands RHA* (1981), the patient had consented to the repair of her uterus and the surgeon also performed a sterilisation operation, which he believed was in her best interests. It was held that the surgeon was liable in battery.

When a doctor acts on the basis of the principle of necessity, the doctor is limited to the extent that he should do 'no more than is reasonably required'.

The best interests of the patient

Another basis on which a doctor may treat a patient without their consent is if the doctor acts in the 'best interests' of the patient. This raises the question of who decides what is in the best interests of the patient. The answer to this is that the *Bolam* test applies – what a responsible body of medical opinion would say was in the best interests of the patient. In *F v West Berkshire HA* (1989), the House of Lords confirmed that the *Bolam* test applied when determining the best interests of a patient who could not consent. Neill LJ had argued in the Court of Appeal that the test should be that it was 'unreasonable, in the opinion of most experts in the field', not to carry out the operation. This test is stricter than *Bolam*, which merely requires a group of doctors who would agree to carry out such an operation.

Although *F v West Berkshire HA* effectively decided that doctors make the decision of what is in the best interests of the patient, it still left open the question of what exactly is in the patient's 'best interests'. What is in the patient's best interests is not simply a matter of clinical judgment by doctors, but may include the patient's beliefs and way of life. The Court of Appeal has recently qualified the approach to be taken in two cases. In *R-B (A Patient) v Official Solicitor* (2000), the Court of Appeal considered the case of A, a 28 year old man with Down's syndrome, who lived with his mother and attended a day centre. The mother was not in good health and was concerned that if A went into local authority care, he may have sexual relations with another patient and make them pregnant. A could not understand the link between sex and pregnancy and, although he had said that he did not want to be sterilised, he could not validly consent or refuse. His mother applied to the High Court to exercise its inherent jurisdiction to allow A to be sterilised in his best interests, but the court refused the application, saying that a vasectomy was not essential for A's well-being.

On appeal, the Court of Appeal applied *Re F (Mental Patient: Sterilisation)* (1990) and said that, as regards the sterilisation of an adult who was unable to consent, it had to be shown that the procedure was in their best interests. The court said that 'best interests' included medical, emotional and other welfare issues. Doctors making decisions about best interests had a duty to act in accordance with a responsible body of medical opinion. But there was also a second duty – to act in the best interests of the mentally incapacitated patient. In such applications, it was the judge, not the doctor, who decided whether the operation was in the best interests of the patient. In applying these principles, the court said that sterilisation would not give A more freedom, save him from exploitation or help him to deal with the emotional implications of a close relationship; the operation was not in his best interests. The court emphasised that the interests of the patient were paramount but left open the question of whether third party interests should be considered.

In *Re S* (2000), S was a 29 year old woman who had severe learning difficulties and lived with her mother. She was moving into a local authority home and her mother was worried that S may become pregnant. The choice was either to have a hysterectomy or to have a coil fitted and both procedures would effectively sterilise S. The judge at first instance said that it was for the mother to decide. The Court of Appeal said that once a court decided that the proposed treatment was within the range covered by the *Bolam* test, that test then became irrelevant to the decision of what was in the 'best interests' of the patient. It was for the court to decide this, taking into account broader ethical, social and moral considerations than those in *Bolam*. The court said that a disabled patient had the right not to have drastic surgery imposed unless this was in their best interests; here, the less invasive treatment was best. *Re S* was applied in the later case of *The Queen (on the Application of N) v Doctor 'M' and Others* (2003), concerning a patient detained under the Mental Health Act 1983. As required under the Act, two doctors had diagnosed N as being psychotic and in need of medication. However, N refused to consent and obtained an independent report from another doctor that she was not psychotic and did not need medication. The Court of Appeal had to consider the question whether, even though there was a responsible body of medical opinion that medication was not needed, it was still in N's best interests that medication should be given. The High Court had said that it was in N's best interests to have medication. The Court of Appeal said that it had to be 'convincingly shown' that medication was necessary. A number of factors were relevant, including whether the disorder was treatable; how serious it was; the risk to others; how likely it was that the treatment would cure the disorder; and the likelihood of adverse consequences to the patient. The treatment must satisfy the *Bolam* test but the fact that it does will not necessarily mean that it is in the patient's best interests. Conversely, even if there was a responsible body of medical opinion to show that treatment was not in the best interests, this did not mean that it cannot be shown that the treatment was in the best interests of the patient.

The question of whether an incompetent patient should be given experimental treatment arose in the next case. In *JS v An NHS Trust; JA v An NHS Trust* (2002), a boy of 18, JS, and a girl of 16, JA, suffered from variant Creutzfeldt-Jakob disease (vCJD). The two patients had sustained brain damage and were confined to bed but could recognise people. Both were bound to die from the disease and a new treatment was proposed, which had not been tested on human beings and which had to be given under anaesthetic. There was a slight chance that the treatment would be beneficial and prolong their lives. The parents sought a declaration that the patients lacked capacity to consent and that it was lawful for them to have the treatment. It was held by the High Court that a responsible body of medical opinion supported using the new treatment. The court said that the *Bolam* test should not be allowed to inhibit medical progress. A 5% risk of haemorrhage from the treatment was not outside the bounds of responsible medical treatment and an unacceptable risk. It was accepted by the court that both JS and JA lacked mental capacity to make decisions about treatment, but a patient who could not consent to a new treatment ought not to be deprived of the chance. It was in the best interests of the patients that the treatment be given, even though there was only a slight chance of improvement. Where an application is made to a court, it is the court not the doctor who makes the decision of what is in the best interests of the patient:

> In my judgment, I have to assess the best interests in the widest possible way to include the medical and non-medical benefits and disadvantages, the broader welfare issues of the two patients, their abilities, their future with or without treatment, the views of the families, and the impact of refusal of the applications. All of these matters have to be weighed up and balanced in order for the court to come to a decision in the exercise of its discretion. [Butler-Sloss P]

Should relatives be consulted about the best interests of the patient? Although relatives are often asked in practice, they have no legal right to consent to treatment for adult patients. However, see the proposals for reform, below, under 'Reform of the Law on Mental Incapacity'.

If there is disagreement between parents and doctors, then it is up to the courts to decide what is in the best interests of the patient. In *A Hospital NHS Trust v S* (2003), S, aged 18, had learning difficulties, was epileptic, autistic and had a mental age of between five and six years. He was admitted to hospital with kidney failure and was on haemodialysis. The staff found him difficult to control and he sometimes needed sedation before treatment. Two questions arose: (a) because of problems with the dialysis, whether a different method of dialysis could be used which required the use of two large needles; and (b) whether a transplant was suitable for S. S's family wanted these two things to be considered but the trust did not. It was held by the High Court that S did not have the capacity to make decisions about his treatment. As there was disagreement between S's family and the doctors, it was the duty of the court to decide by considering medical, emotional and other welfare issues to determine what was in S's best interests. It was important that someone who lacked capacity should not receive lesser treatment than someone with full capacity who was able to understand the risks. It was in S's best interests to be given dialysis and if there were problems to change to a different method, but a kidney transplant should not be carried out as he would have the same life span with dialysis. However, if in the future medical reasons favoured a transplant, then it should not be rejected on the grounds that S could not understand the purpose and consequences, nor because of worries over how his behavioural difficulties would be managed.

REFORM OF THE LAW ON MENTAL INCAPACITY

The Law Commission examined the law in this area in *Mental Incapacity* (Law Com 231, 1995) and made a number of proposals:

- There should be a presumption against lack of capacity.
- Any decisions made on behalf of someone without capacity should be made in their best interests (as there is no other viable alternative). Clause 4 of the Mental Capacity Bill sets out the test for best interests:

4 Best interests

(1) In determining for the purposes of this Act what is in a person's best interests, the person making the determination must consider all the circumstances appearing to him to be relevant.

(2) In particular, he must take the following steps.

(3) He must consider –

  (a) whether it is likely that the person will at some time have capacity in relation to the matter in question, and

  (b) if it appears likely that he will, when that is likely to be.

(4) He must, so far as reasonably practicable, permit and encourage the person to participate, or to improve his ability to participate, as fully as possible in any act done for him and any decision affecting him.

(5) He must consider, so far as is reasonably ascertainable –

  (a) the person's past and present wishes and feelings,

  (b) the beliefs and values that would be likely to influence his decision if he had capacity, and

  (c) the other factors that he would be likely to consider if he were able to do so.

(6) He must take into account, if it is practicable and appropriate to consult them, the views of –

  (a) anyone named by the person as someone to be consulted on the matter in question or on matters of that kind,

  (b) anyone engaged in caring for the person or interested in his welfare,

  (c) any donee of a lasting power of attorney granted by the person, and

  (d) any deputy appointed for the person by the court,

  as to what would be in the person's best interests and, in particular, as to the matters mentioned in subsection (5).

...

(8) In the case of an act done, or a decision made, by a person other than the court, there is sufficient compliance with this section if (having complied with the requirements of subsections (1) to (6)) he reasonably believes that what he does or decides is in the best interests of the person concerned.

- There should be a general authority to act reasonably for the personal welfare or healthcare of a person without capacity. The Mental Capacity Bill deals with this in cl 9:

  9 Lasting powers of attorney

  (1) A lasting power of attorney is a power of attorney under which the donor ('P') confers on the donee (or donees) authority to make decisions about all or any of the following –

    (a) P's personal welfare or specified matters concerning P's personal welfare, and

    (b) P's property and affairs or specified matters concerning P's property and affairs,

    And which includes authority to make such decisions in circumstances where P no longer has capacity.

The Report made a number of other proposals, including the following: 'advance refusals of treatment' (advance directives) should be respected when the patient later lacks capacity; certain treatments, such as sterilisation and organ donation, would need the permission of the court; and there should be a new power – a 'continuing power of attorney' – which would give the donee of that power the right to make decisions for a donor who lacks capacity. This power should cover the donor's personal welfare, healthcare, property and affairs. The Mental Capacity Bill calls it a 'lasting power of attorney'.

The government's response included a Consultation Paper (*Who Decides? Making Decisions on Behalf of Mentally Incapacitated Adults*, 1997) and a Report, *Making Decisions* (Cm 4465, 1999). The government proposals in *Making Decisions* would apply to those people aged 16 or over who lack capacity. The government accepted most of the proposals, including the three main points listed above. However, it did not accept the proposals for advance directives. The Report stated:

> The government believes that a clear statement of the present legal position concerning advance statements would be helpful to lawyers, doctors and patients. [Chapter 1, para 16]

But it added:

> Given the division of opinion which exists on this complex subject, and given the flexibility inherent in developing case law, the government believes that it would not be appropriate to legislate at the present time and thus fix the statutory position once and for all. [Chapter 1, para 20]

Some of the main proposals are set out below:

- Capacity: there will be a presumption against lack of capacity. This means that it is presumed that someone can make decisions, unless it is proven otherwise. There will be a 'functional approach' to determining capacity; that is, can the person make that particular decision at the time? A new statutory definition of incapacity is based on the fact that someone is 'unable to make a decision for himself in relation to the matter because of an impairment of, or a disturbance in the functioning of, the mind or brain' (cl 2(1)). Also, all practical steps must be taken to enable someone without capacity to communicate their decisions.

- Best interests: decisions made on behalf of people without capacity must be made in their best interests. The factors suggested in the Law Commission's draft Bill were accepted.

- General authority to act reasonably: there should be a general authority to act reasonably for the personal welfare or healthcare of someone lacking capacity. This was proposed by the Law Commission. Such a general authority would help those making day to day decisions for people who lack capacity. The present law protects neither the person without capacity nor the carer. The general authority will not cover some decisions which no one may make on behalf of someone lacking capacity. These decisions include consent to marriage, consent to sexual relations, consent to divorce, consent to adoption, discharging parental responsibilities and consent under the Human Fertilisation and Embryology Act 1990 (cl 27); and voting at elections or referendums (cl 29).

- Lasting power of attorney: proposals to introduce this new power were accepted. It will replace the existing system of enduring power of attorney, which only covers financial matters. The new power would cover financial, personal welfare and healthcare matters.

- Court of Protection: there should be a new court known as the Court of Protection, which will have the same powers as the High Court to replace the existing Court of Protection. The new court would be able to make decisions on behalf of those lacking capacity. The new court should have regional centres and not simply be based in London like the existing Court of Protection.

The law on incapacity has been in need of reform for several years and these proposals should eliminate many of the existing problems. A draft Mental Incapacity Bill was published in 2003 and a revised Mental Capacity Bill was introduced in Parliament in June 2004. The Bill was carried over after the end of the Parliamentary session and was reintroduced on 23 November 2004 with a number of amendments. It incorporates many of the above recommendations and a person will be able to give someone power to make health decisions for them when they become incapable. The Mental Capacity Bill has been criticised by a number of people because they believe it fails to protect the rights of those who lack capacity. For example, by giving powers to another person to consent to or refuse treatment for a patient, this effectively gives them the right to decide whether a patient lives or dies (Laing, J, 'Mental Capacity Bill – threat to the vulnerable', NLJ, Vol 154, No 7139, p 1165).

CODES OF PRACTICE

In 1999, the General Medical Council issued guidance for doctors in *Seeking Patients' Consent: The Ethical Considerations*. This sets out in detail how doctors should approach obtaining consent and, amongst other things, covers the following matters: providing sufficient information for patients; obtaining consent with adults; the mentally incompetent; children; dealing with questions; advance statements; and when to apply to the court.

THE HUMAN RIGHTS ACT 1998

Article 3 (the right not to be subjected to degrading treatment) could be used in situations like *S v St George's NHS Trust* (1998), where S was forced to have a Caesarean section against her will. It may also be used by an anorexic patient who is fed against his or her wishes or if a patient is refused treatment and suffers as a result. Article 8(1) provides that everyone has the right to respect for private and family life. This covers physical integrity and could be used if a patient is given treatment without consent. However, Art 8(2) allows interference with that right in the interests of public safety, the protection of health and the protection of the rights of others. This would allow compulsory vaccination in some circumstances. Article 9 (freedom of religion) may be relied upon if someone's religious beliefs are ignored and they are given treatment, for example, Jehovah's Witnesses who are given a blood transfusion.

SUMMARY – CONSENT

1   *Requirement for consent*
   - Doctor must obtain patient's consent before treatment – otherwise a battery.
   - Not giving enough information about risks could be negligence.
2   *Capacity to consent*
   - For a valid consent, patient must have capacity: test of capacity is that patient understands nature and purpose of treatment. *Re T (Adult: Refusal of Treatment)* (1992) – patient refused transfusion; *Re C (Adult: Refusal of Treatment)* (1994) – gangrene in foot.
   - Guidelines: if competent patient refuses treatment, that refusal is valid; if patient incapable, medical staff can act in best interests; if staff have serious doubt about capacity, go to court.
   - Mental Capacity Bill 2004 has definition of capacity.
   - Valid refusal must be respected – otherwise it is trespass: *Re B (Adult: Refusal of Medical Treatment)* (2002).

3 *Civil law*

- Tort of trespass: assault – fear of unlawful force; battery – actual touching of another.

- Trespass is an intentional tort – no need to prove damage with assault and battery.

- No need for touching to be hostile: *Re F (Mental Patient: Sterilisation)* (1990).

- Doctor must obtain patient's consent to avoid claim for battery; for a valid consent, patient must know nature of treatment in broad terms: *Chatterton v Gerson* (1981).

- Tort of negligence: need to prove duty of care, breach and that the breach caused the damage.

- Negligence includes giving sufficient advice for patient to give consent; originally patient had to prove that if they had been given more information, they would not have had the operation, but note the effect of *Chester v Afshar* (2004).

- Test applied to decide if a doctor has given enough information is the *Bolam* test – responsible body of medical opinion: *Sidaway v Governors of Bethlem Royal Hospital* (1985).

- No duty to answer questions, but note the Australian case of *Rogers v Whitaker* (1992).

- Courts are against making a distinction between therapeutic and non-therapeutic treatment.

4 *Criminal law*

- Various types of assault under ss 18, 20 and 47 of the OAPA 1861.

- *R v Dica* (2004): infecting with HIV through sex – victims did not consent.

- Patient cannot consent to serious harm with no benefit: *R v Brown* (1992).

- Manslaughter by gross negligence; murder.

5 *Treating without consent*

- When patient reaches 18 years, even if they are incompetent, no one can consent for them.

- Treatment can be given on the basis of necessity: must be a necessity and patient cannot communicate and medical staff act in best interests of patient; Canadian cases of *Marshall v Curry* (1933) and *Murray v McMurchy* (1949).

- Treatment can be given in 'best interests' of patient: test for best interests is *Bolam*, but note qualification in *The Queen (on the Application of Dr N) v Doctor 'M' and Others* (2003) that *Bolam* was not necessarily sufficient.

6   *Reform of law*
   - Law Commission proposals 1995: presumption of capacity; if someone lacks capacity, decisions should be made in best interests.
   - Mental Capacity Bill 2004.

7   *Human Rights Act 1998*
   - Main Articles: Art 3, no degrading treatment; Art 8, private and family life if given treatment without consent.

CHAPTER 3

CHILDREN AND CONSENT

INTRODUCTION

This chapter will examine the circumstances where children are competent to consent to treatment and where parents may consent on behalf of children, and the problems which arise when there is a conflict between the views of parents and children or between parents and medical staff. The area of refusal of treatment causes difficulties for the law, particularly in determining the extent to which children may refuse treatment where that refusal may result in serious harm or death. Applications may be made to the court under s 8 of the Children Act 1989 for a specific issue order; or the child (if under 18) may be made a ward of court; or the court may use its inherent power under its *parens patriae* jurisdiction to make decisions for a child.

Consent not needed

Treatment may be given without consent under the principle of necessity, for example, in an emergency. Also, if a child has been abandoned by his or her parents, treatment may be given without consent.

CAPACITY TO CONSENT

A child, or minor, is someone under the age of 18. It is important for medical staff to obtain consent before treating a child for the same reasons as for adult patients: it would otherwise be trespass to the person. The question arises of when a child is competent to consent to medical treatment. Section 8(1) of the Family Law Reform Act 1969 provides:

> The consent of a minor who has attained the age of 16 years to any surgical, medical or dental treatment which, in the absence of consent, would constitute a trespass to the person ... shall be effective as it would be if he were of full age.

Section 8(2) provides:

> In this section 'surgical, medical or dental treatment' includes any procedure undertaken for the purposes of diagnosis, and this section applies to any procedure (including, in particular, the administration of an anaesthetic) which is ancillary to any treatment as it applies to that treatment.

A child aged 16 can, therefore, consent to treatment. A parent cannot override consent by the child. But s 8 does not cover the child donating blood or an organ as these are not 'treatment' or within 'diagnosis'.

What about children under 16?

The common law has developed rules for such children. The leading case is *Gillick v West Norfolk and Wisbech AHA* (1985). The Department of Health and Social Security (DHSS) issued guidance to doctors, stating that they could give contraceptive advice and treatment to girls under 16. They could do this without the consent of the parents if the child did not want the parents to be involved. Mrs Gillick, who had several daughters under 16, sought a declaration that it was unlawful to treat children under 16 without their parents' consent. The House of Lords held by a majority of 3:2 that this advice by the DHSS was not unlawful. The majority were Lords Fraser, Scarman and Bridge and dissenting judgments were given by Lords Brandon and Templeman. The majority said that a child under 16 could give a valid consent to medical treatment in certain circumstances without their parents' consent. Lord Scarman said that the parents' right to consent for their child who is under 16 yields to the child's right when he reaches 'a sufficient understanding and intelligence' to be able to make up his own mind. However, in applying this test to contraceptive advice and treatment he said:

> It is not enough that she should understand the nature of the advice which is being given; she must also have a sufficient maturity to understand what is involved. There are moral and family questions, especially her relationship with her parents; long term problems associated with the emotional impact of pregnancy and its termination; and there are risks to health of sexual intercourse at her age, risks which contraception may diminish but cannot eliminate. It follows that a doctor will have to satisfy himself that she is able to appraise these factors before he can safely proceed on the basis that she has the capacity at law to consent to contraceptive advice and treatment.

Lord Fraser said that the doctor could give contraceptive advice and treatment but must be satisfied about five matters:

(a) the girl will understand the advice;

(b) the doctor cannot persuade her to tell her parents;

(c) she is likely to begin having sex, or continue to have sex, without contraception;

(d) unless she receives advice/treatment, her health will suffer;

(e) it is in her best interests to receive advice/treatment.

Lord Templeman agreed that consent depended on age and understanding but saw contraception as a special case:

> The effect of the consent of an infant depends on the nature of the treatment and the age and understanding of the infant. For example, a doctor with the consent of an intelligent boy or girl of 15 could, in my opinion, safely remove tonsils or a troublesome appendix. But any decision on the part of a girl to practise sex and contraception requires not only knowledge of the facts of life and of the dangers of pregnancy and disease but also an understanding of the emotional and other consequences to her family, her male partner and to herself.

He considered that a girl under 16 was not capable of making such a decision.

In July 2004, the Department of Health published revised guidelines on the provision of contraceptive services for the under 16s. The doctor or health professional should establish a rapport with the young person. This can be done by discussing: the emotional and physical implications of sex; the risks of pregnancy and sexually transmitted disease; whether the relationship is mutual or whether there is coercion or abuse; and the importance of informing the GP and a parent, but a refusal to do this should be respected. In the case of abortion, if the young woman does not wish to tell her parents, efforts should be made to find another adult to provide support.

The *Gillick* case laid down the test for determining whether a child under 16 could consent to medical treatment, and it became known as the *'Gillick* test', or the test of *'Gillick* competence'. Although the test can work for many treatments, the boundaries of the test are not clear. For example, a 15 year old may consent to having their tonsils removed, a 10 year old may consent to treatment for minor cuts and bruises, and a *'Gillick* competent' child can consent to giving blood. But could a child under 18 consent to donating a kidney? Although this latter example seems unlikely, there are cases in between the above examples in which the legal position is not clear.

As regards young children who are not *Gillick* competent, their parents may give a legally valid consent for them. Margaret Brazier, in *Medicine, Patients and the Law* (3rd edn, 2003, London: Penguin), considers that children under 12 virtually never have the maturity to consent to treatment. The parents' right to consent is limited, in that it must be exercised in the 'best interests' of the child. A parent can therefore consent to everyday treatments and procedures, but problems may arise if a child needs complex surgery.

If a parent refuses to allow a child to have any medical treatment when they need it, this would amount to wilful neglect causing injury to health under s 1 of the Children and Young Persons Act 1933, which is a criminal offence. The Act only applies to those with parental responsibility and does not therefore apply to doctors.

REFUSAL OF CONSENT

(a) By a minor

If a child refuses to consent to treatment, can anyone consent for the child? Although the Family Law Reform Act 1969 gave children aged 16 the right to consent to treatment, it did not deal with the power to refuse treatment. What is the position of the *Gillick* competent child – can they refuse treatment? The matter was dealt with in *R (A Minor) (Wardship: Medical Treatment)* (1991). R was a 15 year old girl who was placed in a children's home after a fight with her father. Her mental state deteriorated and she attacked her father with a hammer. She was then placed in a psychiatric unit, where doctors wanted to give her anti-psychotic drugs, which she refused. The local authority made her a ward of court so as to obtain the court's permission to give her the drugs without her consent. The court considered Lord Scarman's speech in *Gillick* and said that the parents' right to consent does not end when the child becomes *Gillick* competent. Lord Donaldson drew an analogy between having the power to give consent and having the key to a door. The child can obtain this 'key' by reaching 16 years or by becoming *Gillick* competent, but the parents also have keys and they can give consent even if a competent child refuses. On the facts, even though R had periods of lucidity, she was incompetent and the court authorised the doctors to give her medication. Lord Donaldson said: 'However, consent by itself creates no obligation to treat. It is merely a key which unlocks the door ... No doctor can be required to treat a child, whether by the court in the exercise of its wardship jurisdiction, by the parents, by the child or anyone else.'

A doctor who is faced with a child who refuses treatment may obtain consent to treatment from a parent. The Court of Appeal again considered the matter in *Re W (A Minor) (Medical Treatment)* (1992). W, a 16 year old girl who had anorexia, was taken into a residential home but her condition worsened and doctors wished to move her to a special hospital. W refused to consent to the move. The local authority applied to the court under the Children Act 1989 for a declaration that it would be lawful to move her. The Court of Appeal held that, although W was over 16 years and could therefore consent to treatment, the court had an inherent power to override a refusal of treatment if this would lead to severe injury to the child or death. The nature of the illness was such that patients did not wish to be cured. Lord Donaldson said that his 'keyholder' analogy was wrong, because keys could lock doors but a child could not refuse treatment. Instead, he drew an analogy with a 'flak jacket'. A valid consent acted like a flak jacket for a doctor and provided a defence to a claim in trespass. The flak jacket could be provided by a competent child or a parent. The right of a 16 year old to consent cannot be overridden by a parent but this can be done by the court; and the right of a *Gillick* competent child to consent cannot be overridden by a parent but can be overridden by the court. However, if any child under 18 refuses treatment, consent may be given by a parent or the court. Lord Donaldson said:

> No minor, of whatever age, has power, by refusing consent to treatment, to override a consent to treatment by someone who has parental responsibility for the minor and, *a fortiori*, a consent by the court.

Both Lord Donaldson MR and Balcombe LJ pointed out that one of the effects of anorexia nervosa was to take away a person's ability to make an informed choice, although on the facts W was considered competent.

A number of commentators have argued that the power to refuse treatment is the corollary of the power to consent to treatment and, logically, someone who can consent should be able to refuse:

> It seems obvious that a right to give consent must also mean the right to refuse consent. Otherwise the right to consent would seem to be no more than the right to agree with the medical practitioner. Many medical ethicists have commented wryly on the catch 22 by which patients whose competence is in doubt will be found rational if they accept the doctor's proposal but incompetent if they reject professional advice. [Devereux, J, Jones, D and Dickenson, D, 'Can children withhold consent to treatment?' BMJ, Vol 306, p 1459]

But Mason, McCall-Smith and Laurie (*Law and Medical Ethics*, 6th edn, 2002, London: Butterworths) point out that a distinction can be made between consent and refusal. Consent is an acceptance of the view of an experienced doctor, while refusal is rejecting this experience. The consequences of the latter may be far more serious.

The court did accept in *Re W* that, in making a decision, the fact that the minor refused treatment would be taken into account.

The power of the court to overrule a minor's refusal of treatment stems from its *parens patriae* jurisdiction. This means 'parent of the country' and formed part of the prerogative powers of the Crown to look after those citizens who needed protection. The court will look to see whether the minor has the capacity to refuse treatment and, if this is not established, it will authorise treatment, as in *Re R* (1991) and *Re W (A Minor)* (1992), above. In exercising its powers, the court will act in the best interests of the child. As to the circumstances in which the courts will override a refusal by a child, in *Re W*, the Court of Appeal said that it would intervene if the refusal would lead to death or permanent injury. Kennedy and Grubb (*Medical Law*, 3rd edn, 2000, London: Butterworths) have pointed out that the decisions in *Re R* and *Re W* threaten to undermine *Gillick* because they detract from children's rights and they should be reconsidered by the House of Lords when the opportunity arises.

A parent can also overrule a refusal by a minor, because the parent can consent to treatment for the minor.

(b) By a parent

What if the parents refuse to consent to medical treatment for their child? If the child is over 16 or is *Gillick* competent, then the child may consent to treatment. But if the child is too young or too immature and cannot give a valid consent, what is the legal position of the doctor as regards giving treatment?

The classic example is a critically ill baby whose parents refuse to consent to treatment because of their own religious beliefs. In *Re R (A Minor) (Blood Transfusion)* (1993), R was a 10 month old girl with leukaemia who needed blood transfusions. Her parents, who were Jehovah's Witnesses, refused to consent. The local authority applied, under s 8 of the Children Act 1989, for a specific issue order to allow the transfusions to be given. The court said that the main consideration was the welfare of the child. The child was too young to express her wishes and, without treatment, she would suffer harm. The court could override the parents, as it was in the child's best interests.

However, this type of decision is not an easy one for the court to make, because it must consider the effect on the child if the court goes against the wishes of the parents. The child could, for example, be rejected by the religious community. The circumstances of the case are also important, whether it is an emergency or whether there is time to refer it to court for a considered decision. The court must balance the various factors, including the religious beliefs of the parents. In *Re S (A Minor)* (1993), S was a four year old boy with leukaemia who needed treatment, including a blood transfusion. His parents were Jehovah's Witnesses and refused to allow him to undergo a transfusion. The local authority asked the court for an order under the court's inherent jurisdiction. The court took into account the fact that the treatment would give the boy a 50% chance of living and granted the order allowing treatment. As regards the argument that the child would suffer rejection, the court said that it had made the decision and, thus, the parents were absolved of blame. 'The reality seems to me to be that family reaction will recognise that the responsibility for consent was taken from them and, as a judicial act, absolved their conscience from liability' (Thorpe J).

In *Re C (A Child) (HIV Testing)* (1999), the parents refused to have their child tested for HIV, although her mother was HIV positive. Both parents opposed the traditional method of treating the disease and believed that it would not be to C's benefit because such treatment would cause harm. When the baby was five months old, the doctors believed that it would be in the child's best interests to be tested, as knowledge of her HIV status was important in determining future treatment. If the child was found to be free of the disease, doctors would then recommend that breast feeding should stop, which would further improve the child's chances of avoiding the disease. An application was made by the local authority for a specific issue order under the Children Act 1989 that C be tested, and the Official Solicitor acted as the child's guardian *ad litem*. At first instance, an order was granted because it was deemed to be in the child's best interests that her HIV status should be known. An application for leave to appeal was made by the parents. The Court of Appeal said that a court could overrule the decision of a reasonable parent and, on the scientific evidence, the case for testing was overwhelming: '... the parents' views, which are not the views of the majority, cannot stand against the right of the child to be properly cared for in every sense' (Butler-Sloss LJ). Leave to appeal was refused.

The High Court issued a *Practice Direction* [2003] 1 FLR 1299 on 15 May 2003 concerning the appropriate court for applications with regard to the HIV testing of a child. If this is necessary, application should be made to the County Court unless proceedings are pending in the High Court. If a child of sufficient understanding opposes the testing, application should be made under the inherent jurisdiction of the High Court. Where all those with parental authority agree to the testing, no reference to the court is necessary.

In *Re A (Children)* (2000), the Court of Appeal had to consider the very difficult case of the conjoined Siamese twins, Jodie and Mary. Jodie had the potential to lead a separate, independent existence but Mary's heart and lungs did not function properly and she was dependent on Jodie for oxygenated blood. If an operation to separate them was not carried out, they would die within three to six months because Jodie's heart would fail. The parents were Roman Catholics and they refused to consent to the operation, as they believed that both twins had a right to life. The doctors wanted to carry out an operation to separate the twins because they believed that Jodie could have a worthwhile life, although Mary would inevitably die. An application was made by the NHS Trust under the inherent jurisdiction of the court. The leading judgment was given by Ward LJ. Such an operation could not be in Mary's best interests because it took away her right to life, but it was in Jodie's best interests. In resolving this conflict, the court had to choose the lesser of two evils. It also had to consider the wishes of the parents, which should be given great respect; however, their wishes were not in the children's best interests. The best interests of the twins was to give the chance of life to the one who could benefit from it, even if to do that was to end the life of the other twin. The other important question to decide was whether the proposed operation was lawful, as it would involve the killing of an innocent person. It had been accepted by the court that the twins were two persons in law. The doctors were under a duty to Mary not to carry out the operation because it would kill Mary, but they were under a duty to Jodie to operate because not to operate would kill her.

In this seemingly irreconcilable conflict, the doctors, like the court, had to balance the welfare of each child against the other child and make a decision based on the lesser of two evils. Carrying out the operation could be justified as the lesser of two evils and would not be unlawful. The operation would not offend the sanctity of life principle because Mary was, in effect, slowly killing Jodie and doctors could come to Jodie's defence by carrying out the operation. A majority of the court said that the defence of necessity could be used to justify the murder of Mary. The decision is based on a utilitarian approach rather than a duty to respect human life. The operation to separate the twins was later carried out and, as a result, Mary died.

The case has raised many important issues, not least of which is the fact that although the court took the views of the parents into account, it overrode those views. 'The best interests of the twins is to give the chance of life to the child whose actual bodily condition is capable of accepting the chance to her advantage even if that has to be at the cost of the sacrifice of the life which is so unnaturally supported' (Ward LJ).

The Court of Appeal decided against treatment in the following case and followed the wishes of the parents in refusing medical treatment. In *Re T (A Minor) (Wardship: Medical Treatment)* (1997), T was born with a liver defect and without a transplant would only live for two years. Doctors said that the operation would be successful and believed that it was in the baby's best interests. The parents, who both worked in the health service, refused to consent to the transplant and moved abroad. The local authority applied to the court under the Children Act 1989 for the court to exercise its inherent jurisdiction. The High Court held that the mother had acted unreasonably and overruled the parents' refusal of treatment. The Court of Appeal said that the most important consideration was the welfare of the child. It was important not to base the decision simply on the medical assessment of the situation, namely, that the operation would succeed. The mother knew that the baby only had a short time to live without a transplant and wanted the baby to continue his peaceful and painless life. The fact that the mother had refused treatment for the baby also had to be considered, as the mother would have to look after the baby after an operation. Further, the disruption to the whole family in moving back to England for the operation had to be taken into account. The court concluded that it was in the best interests of the baby to leave his treatment in the hands of his parents. The Court of Appeal stressed that it was not determining whether the decision of the parents was reasonable but was deciding on the basis of the best interests of the child.

The decisions in *Re T* (1997), where the court followed the wishes of the mother not to carry out a transplant on the child, and in *Re S* (1993), where the court overruled the wishes of the parents to refuse a transplant, are clearly conflicting.

Parents requesting treatment against medical advice

Sometimes, parents disagree with medical staff and want their child to have treatment. In *Re C (A Minor) (Medical Treatment)* (1998), C suffered from a deteriorating condition and the doctors considered that any treatment would simply be delaying death. They wished to withdraw ventilation and, if C suffered further breathing difficulties, they did not wish to ventilate her. The parents agreed to the withdrawal of ventilation but wanted it to be given again if needed, because, as Orthodox Jews, they believed that life had to be preserved. The High Court had to consider what was in the best interests of the child. It took account of the medical evidence that further treatment would be futile and granted an order that ventilation could be withdrawn.

This case illustrates that the courts will not order treatment against the wishes of medical staff. In *R v Portsmouth Hospital NHS Trust* (1999), a child born with cerebral palsy was now 12 years old. After a tonsillectomy, he suffered from various infections; doctors considered that the child was dying and wanted to stop treatment and give him diamorphine to alleviate his pain. This was against the wishes of the parents, who then intervened to stop the administration of diamorphine and to resuscitate the child. Following this incident, the hospital wrote to the parents saying that the child should be treated elsewhere if further treatment was needed. His mother applied for judicial review of the lawfulness of the hospital's actions in withdrawing lifesaving treatment against the wishes of the parents. The application was dismissed at first instance and the mother applied to the Court of Appeal for leave to appeal. The Court of Appeal said that if the parents did not agree with medical staff, then, in serious cases, the matter had to go to court and the court could decide what was in the best interests of the child. Using judicial review should be a last resort, as more suitable remedies were available. These included a specific issue order under s 8 of the Children Act 1989 or a declaration about a proposed course of action; alternatively, the child could be made a ward of court. It would not be helpful to set out guidance, as the considerations with such children were infinite.

More recently, in *Re Wyatt (A Child) (Medical Treatment: Parents' Consent)* (2004), a baby had been born prematurely and had never left hospital. She suffered from brain damage, breathing difficulties and kidney damage. The baby was now one year old and was unlikely to survive for a further year. The parents had strong religious beliefs and wished treatment to continue but doctors wanted to discontinue treatment which was invasive and aggressive. The High Court granted a declaration allowing treatment to be discontinued. It was not in the baby's best interests to continue treatment (also see Chapter 9, Death, 'Neonaticide', p 178).

Limits on parents' powers to consent to treatment

The right of parents to consent to treatment for their child must be exercised in the 'best interests' of the child. Clearly, consenting to routine medical treatment which will benefit the child is within the parents' powers. But can parents consent to other treatment, such as major surgery, sterilisation, cosmetic surgery, circumcision, medical research or transplants?

The result of a sterilisation operation is that a woman cannot have children. The right to bear children is seen as a fundamental human right and Art 12 of the European Convention on Human Rights says men and women have a right to found a family. In *Re D (A Minor) (Wardship: Sterilisation)* (1976), D was an 11 year old girl who suffered from Sotos Syndrome, which meant that she developed physically at a young age. She also suffered from epilepsy, was mentally deficient and had behavioural problems. The child's mother was worried that D might become pregnant and that D would not be able to look after a child. D would not be able to manage contraception and the mother wished to have her sterilised. A doctor agreed to carry out the operation but an educational psychologist disagreed and applied to the court to make D a ward of court. The High Court said that a sterilisation operation was irrevocable. D could not understand the implications of having such an operation. However, in the future, it was likely that D would have a greater understanding of such an operation and would then be able to make her own choice. The operation was not medically necessary and sterilisation for non-therapeutic purposes was not in D's best interests.

This can be contrasted with *Re B (A Minor) (Wardship: Sterilisation)* (1988), which concerned a 17 year old patient, B, who lived in a residential home. She had a mental age of five or six and suffered from epilepsy, rendering her virtually unable to communicate. Although she was sexually mature, she had no understanding of the link between sex and pregnancy and her mother was worried that B might become pregnant, as she would not be able to manage contraceptives. If she became pregnant and needed a Caesarean operation, this would lead to problems, as she had a habit of picking at wounds. The mother and the local authority applied to the court for an order that the sterilisation would be lawful. The House of Lords said that B would never understand what was involved and would never be able to make a choice herself.

This case can be distinguished from *Re D* (1976). Here, B could not be seen as having a right to bear children, as she had no understanding of the concept. If B became pregnant, this would seriously affect her health. Sterilisation was allowed. Lord Templeman said that, in his opinion, a girl under 18 should not be sterilised without the permission of the court.

A distinction can be made between sterilisation which is needed as part of therapeutic medical treatment, and sterilisation for social purposes. In the latter case, the opinion of the court should be obtained. In *Re E (A Minor) (Medical Treatment)* (1991), a 17 year old mentally handicapped girl had menstrual problems, which could only be solved by a hysterectomy. The court said that:

... there is a clear distinction to be made between cases where an operation is required for genuine therapeutic reasons and those where the operation is designed to achieve sterilisation.

The consent of the court was not needed and the parents could consent.

A Practice Note on sterilisation was issued in 1996 (*Official Solicitor: Sterilisation* [1996] 2 FLR 111). Applications for minors should go to the Family Division of the High Court under its inherent jurisdiction, or under the Children Act 1989 for a specific issue order under s 8. The preferred course is under the inherent jurisdiction.

Can parents consent to cosmetic surgery for children? If the child has an obvious facial blemish or 'bat ears', then the parents can consent. A balance has to be struck between the child undergoing the treatment and the pain and suffering such treatment entails, and being left without the treatment, thus having to suffer unwanted attention and 'offensive' remarks.

Circumcision of both males and females is practised in some cultures. Under s 1(1) of the Female Genital Mutilation Act 2003, it is a criminal offence to mutilate a girl's genitals. An exception is made if a surgical operation is carried out by an approved person and it is necessary for her physical or mental health (s 1(2)). The Act also makes it an offence to aid, abet, counsel or procure a person who is not a UK national to carry out an act of female genital mutilation outside the UK (s 3). The Female Genital Mutilation Act 2003 repeals the Prohibition of Female Circumcision Act 1985. The 2003 Act aims to stop the practice of taking girls abroad for the operation. However, male circumcision remains legal.

What is the legal position if one parent agrees to treatment but the other does not? The same applies equally to those with parental responsibility who disagree over treatment. In *Re J (A Minor) (Specific Issue Orders: Muslim Upbringing and Circumcision)* (1999), the parents of a five year old boy were separated but lived in the UK. The father was Turkish and a Muslim, the mother was English and a Christian. The father wanted to have the boy circumcised in accordance with his beliefs and culture but his mother refused. The father applied for a specific issue order. The Court of Appeal said that this was an irreversible procedure and no one with parental responsibility could authorise it against the wishes of another. A court order was needed. On the facts of the case, this was an irreversible operation; the child would not be brought up in the Muslim culture and it was not in his best interests to have the operation.

The problem has been highlighted more recently by arguments over the MMR vaccine (Measles, Mumps, Rubella), as there is some evidence that it has been linked to autism and bowel disease. In *Re C (Welfare of Child: Immunisation)* (2003), two girls aged four and 10 years old were looked after by their mothers, who did not want the children to be given the MMR vaccine. The two fathers applied to the court under s 8 of the Children Act 1989 for specific issue orders for the MMR vaccine. The High Court granted the orders, saying that the benefits outweighed the risks and vaccination should be allowed. The mothers appealed, arguing that the judge had taken the wrong approach by using a two stage test: (a) asking whether on medical grounds immunisation was in the best interests of the children; and having answered 'yes'; (b) considering if there were good non-medical reasons to reject the application. The Court of Appeal said that the judge had made the decision putting the welfare of the children as the paramount consideration. The order in which factors were looked at was up to the judge. The appeals were dismissed. The court said that where those with parental responsibility for a child were in dispute about immunisation against an infectious disease, one person did not have the right to make the decision and it had to be done with the approval of the court.

Can parents consent to young children being involved in medical research? If the research is for therapeutic purposes, the parents can consent. Clearly, this will be for the benefit of the child. If the research is for non-therapeutic purposes, then the question is whether any particular procedure is in the child's best interests. This may be difficult to establish if there is no direct benefit to the child. An adult may consent to research on themselves for non-therapeutic reasons, as this may be seen as altruistic. The legal position is not clear as to whether an adult may consent for a child in the same circumstances.

Can parents consent to transplants to or from their child? Such a transplant may involve tissue or organs. A transplant to the child will depend on whether it is in the best interests of the child (see *Re T* (1997), where consent to a liver transplant was refused). Transplants *from* children are not covered by the Family Law Reform Act 1969 and the decision would have to be made under common law rules. But could a child be regarded as *Gillick* competent in respect of organ donation? This seems doubtful. Bone marrow transplants by children are not uncommon and parents can give permission for this.

Refusal of treatment by both children and parents

If both the child and the parents refuse treatment, can the doctor carry on with treatment? The doctor would have to explain the consequences of refusing the treatment. The most difficult situation is if the refusal would lead to the death of the patient. In *Re E (A Minor) (Wardship: Medical Treatment)* (1993), a boy aged 15 and three quarters with leukaemia needed treatment involving blood transfusions. Both he and his parents were Jehovah's Witnesses and they all refused to consent to the treatment. The treatment had an 80–90% chance of success. The boy was made a ward of court by the hospital and, when he was dying, the hospital applied for permission to treat him. The court accepted that the boy was intelligent and had made the decision of his own free will but said that it could override the boy's and his parents' decision. The court said that the boy did not fully understand the implications of dying and, although he had a strong belief, that could change in the future. The court allowed the hospital to treat the boy.

More usually, a court faced by this type of dilemma will find that the child is not competent. In *Re S (A Minor) (Medical Treatment)* (1994), S, a girl aged 15 and a half, had a condition which required daily injections and monthly blood transfusions. When S was 10 years old, her mother became a Jehovah's Witness and took S to meetings. S refused to consent to any further transfusions and the local authority applied to the High Court to use its inherent jurisdiction to override S's refusal. The court said that S was not *Gillick* competent and the doctors were authorised to give transfusions.

GUIDANCE ON WITHHOLDING LIFE-PROLONGING TREATMENT

In 1999, the British Medical Association issued guidance on withholding treatment: *Withholding and Withdrawing Life-Prolonging Medical Treatment*. This includes guidance on decisions made in the case of children and young people (see, for example, paras 14–19).

THE HUMAN RIGHTS ACT 1998

Article 2 (the right to life) could be invoked by a child who needs treatment to save their life, for example, in *Re C (A Child) (HIV Testing)* (1999). In *Re A (Children)* (2000), the court said that the death of Mary as a result of the operation would not be a breach of Art 2 because the court had to balance the death of both twins if nothing was done against the survival of Jodie. In *Simms v Simms and Another* (2003), where the two patients suffered from vCJD, the court said each patient had a right to life under Art 2 and the right to respect for family life under Art 8, and considered that prolonging their life was in their best interests. 'A reduced enjoyment of life even at quite a low level is to be respected and protected' (Butler-Sloss LJ). Article 3 (freedom from inhuman and degrading treatment) could be used if treatment is given against the wishes of the child. In *Re A* (2000), the court did not consider that the proposed operation could be regarded as inhuman and degrading to Mary under Art 3.

Article 9 (freedom of religion) could be used in cases where a child is given treatment against his religious beliefs, as in the case of Jehovah's Witnesses who are given blood transfusions. However, a conflict may arise in such cases between the right to life and freedom of religion. It would then be up to the court to decide which should prevail. A conflict may also arise between the views of the parents, as in *Re J* (1999), where the father was in favour of circumcision but the mother was against it. The father claimed a right to freedom of religion under Art 9, as he wanted the boy to be brought up a Muslim. The Court of Appeal said that, if there was a conflict between two parents or between the parents and the child, the court could impose limitations and act in the best interests of the child. In the High Court, the father argued on the basis of Art 9 that it included the right to have his son circumcised in accordance with the beliefs of his religion. The judge accepted this but said that it had to be balanced against the rights of the mother and had to be in the best interests of the child.

SUMMARY – CHILDREN AND CONSENT

1 *General rule*
  - Consent of competent child or parent needed for treatment – otherwise trespass; unless necessity or child is abandoned.

2 *Capacity to consent*
  - Child of 16 years can consent to medical treatment: the Family Law Reform Act 1969.
  - Child under 16 years can consent if *Gillick* competent.
  - If child not *Gillick* competent, a parent can give a valid consent.

3 *Refusal of consent by minor*
  - Family Law Reform Act 1969 did not give a child of 16 years the right to refuse consent; if child refuses treatment, a doctor can obtain consent from a parent: *Re W (A Minor) (Medical Treatment)* (1992).
  - The court can also override the minor and give consent under *parens patriae*.

4   *Refusal of consent by parent*
  - If child is too young or not *Gillick* competent – court can overrule parent and give consent: *Re R (A Minor) (Blood Transfusion)* (1993); *Re A (Children)* (2000) – conjoined twins.
  - But note *Re T (A Minor) (Wardship: Medical Treatment)* (1997): parents and court refused consent.

5   *Requests for treatment against doctors' wishes*
  - If there is conflict between doctors and parents, the matter should be referred to court under s 8 of the Children Act 1989, a declaration made or child made a ward of court: *R v Portsmouth Hospital NHS Trust* (1999).

6   *Limits on parents' power to consent*
  - Cannot give consent to some operations like sterilisation for non-therapeutic reasons.
  - Female Genital Mutilation Act 2003 – cannot consent.
  - Cosmetic surgery, medical research and transplants – can consent but with conditions.

7   *Refusal of consent by child and parent*
  - If this would lead to the death of the child, court usually rules child is incompetent: *Re E* (1993).

8   *Human Rights Act 1998*
  - The most important Articles are Art 2, right to life and Art 3, freedom from degrading treatment.

CHAPTER 4

MEDICAL NEGLIGENCE

INTRODUCTION

The cost of medical negligence claims has soared over the last 25 years. In 1980, the combined medical defence unions, which defend doctors in negligence claims, reported that the payment of damages in negligence claims had reached a total of £1 m in that year.

In 1999–2000, the NHS Litigation Authority (NHSLA) paid out £386 m (Fenn, P, 'Counting the cost of medical negligence', BMJ, Vol 325, 2002). Estimates of what the NHS owes in compensation to victims of medical negligence range up to £8 billion. There are many reasons for the growth in negligence claims, the main ones being the greater awareness that people have of their rights to claim, the desire to blame someone if something should go wrong, and the belief that doctors and hospitals should be able to 'cure' patients. The development of medical technology has meant that riskier and more invasive procedures can be carried out. As life expectancy increases, the diseases and problems of old age create more claims. New services, for example, NHS telephone advice lines, also create the potential for claims arising from negligent advice or misdiagnosis. Some lawyers specialise in medical claims and lawyers giving advice in such cases now have to be on a specialist panel approved by the Law Society. Cases may also be brought on a conditional fee basis, which means that the claimant does not have to worry about paying legal bills if they lose their case.

Nonetheless, there are still particular difficulties with bringing successful claims as a result of negligent medical treatment, and claimants who bring their claim on this basis are less likely to win than general negligence claimants. When things go wrong, many patients (or their relatives) simply want an explanation, rather than taking legal action, and, in providing explanations, hospitals can reduce the number of claims made.

In 1995, the NHSLA was set up to deal centrally with claims for negligence against NHS Trusts. This is a voluntary scheme and individual trusts pay a sum of money based on their size and estimates of risk to the NHSLA to cover claims. At the end of March 2003, there were 19,580 outstanding claims worth approximately £6 billion.

Medical negligence is not regarded as a particular type of civil wrong in its own right – it is simply the general rules of the tort of negligence applied to medical accidents. If someone suffers an injury in the course of treatment under the NHS, they can bring a claim in negligence. They cannot claim for breach of contract because a patient does not have a contract with the NHS (see Chapter 1, Introduction to Medical Law).

A report by the government's Chief Medical Officer in June 2003 made recommendations for reform of the current system of negligence claims in the NHS (*Making Amends*). The National Patient Safety Agency (NPSA) was set up in 2001 to deal with errors in the NHS. In February 2004, the NPSA started the first national reporting system for failures in the health system. Health workers will be able to report online any failures and this is done in an anonymous way. It is hoped that this will enable solutions to be developed to tackle recurring problems and hence reduce the number of claims.

ELEMENTS OF THE TORT OF NEGLIGENCE

The claimant who wishes to bring a claim in negligence has to meet the requirements set out by the House of Lords in *Donoghue v Stevenson* (1932). In this case, the claimant's friend bought her a bottle of ginger beer in a café. As the claimant was drinking the ginger beer, she saw the remains of a snail in her glass, was promptly sick and suffered shock. The House of Lords said that a manufacturer owed a duty of care to the ultimate consumer, because the manufacturer should reasonably have foreseen that if he was careless in making the ginger beer, someone drinking it would suffer harm. Lord Atkin set out the 'neighbour principle':

> You must take reasonable care to avoid acts and omissions which you can reasonably foresee would be likely to injure your neighbour.

The court set out the three requirements for a successful claim in negligence:

(a) the defendant owed the claimant a duty of care;

(b) the defendant broke that duty of care; and

(c) the defendant's breach of duty caused the damage to the claimant.

The duty in negligence applies to both acts and omissions.

(a) The duty of care

There is no general duty on doctors to provide treatment for people; for example, a doctor who is watching a film at the cinema does not have to help someone who faints. The claimant must establish that the defendant doctor owes the claimant a duty of care. The 'universal test' for establishing a duty was set out in *Marc Rich v Bishop Rock Marine* (1995), and the three factors of 'foreseeability', 'proximity' and 'just and reasonableness' have to be proved. Proving that a duty is owed does not usually cause any problem, as the duty of a doctor (or other health staff) to a patient is well established.

It may be more of a problem to pinpoint when that duty arises. Is this when the patient:

- telephones for an ambulance?;
- has their emergency call accepted?;

- arrives at the hospital in an ambulance?;
- arrives at the hospital entrance?;
- reports to reception?; or
- is given treatment?

A duty would certainly be owed to a patient arriving in an ambulance or reporting to reception. A patient who simply walks into the hospital may have difficulty showing that a duty is owed to them at that point. The courts have been reluctant to make the emergency services liable in negligence for policy reasons, as illustrated by *Capital Counties v Hampshire CC* (1997), where the court said that the fire service could only be liable if they made an error which no reasonable fire service would make and which made the position worse. In *Kent v Griffiths and The London Ambulance Service* (2000), the pregnant claimant suffered an asthma attack and called her doctor, who arrived at the house, examined the claimant and dialled 999 for an ambulance. The ambulance took nearly 40 minutes to arrive and, because of the delay, the claimant suffered respiratory arrest and a miscarriage. The claimant sued the doctor and the ambulance service for negligence, and the ambulance service argued that it was not legally bound to respond to an emergency call and could only be liable if it made the claimant's position worse by a negligent act. The Court of Appeal said that the ambulance service was part of the NHS and should be seen as providing services similar to hospitals, rather than the police or the fire brigade. Once an emergency call was accepted, a duty of care was owed and the defendant was liable. It was accepted that there was no question of an ambulance not being available in this case and a failure to attend within a reasonable time was negligent.

A general practitioner is also under a duty to treat anyone who is a victim of an accident or other emergency in his practice area (National Health Service (General Medical Services) Regulations 1992).

In determining whether a duty of care exists in a medical context, using the three factors from *Marc Rich*, it may sometimes be argued that as a matter of policy a duty should or should not be owed. In *Rees v Darlington Memorial Hospital NHS Trust* (2003), the claimant was severely visually handicapped and she had been sterilised but later had a child as the sterilisation had been performed negligently. The question arose whether she should be able to claim the cost of rearing the child. The House of Lords accepted the policy that the cost of bringing up the child could not be recovered. Nonetheless, it said that a conventional award of £15,000 should be given to acknowledge that a legal wrong had been committed and that some compensation should therefore be given.

The question arose as to the extent of the duty of care in *A v Ministry of Defence* (2003). The claimant was born in Germany to the wife of a serving soldier. During the birth in a German hospital the claimant suffered brain damage. The Ministry of Defence (MOD) had appointed an NHS Trust hospital to provide medical care for servicemen, and that hospital in turn had appointed the German hospital. It was accepted that the treatment provided was negligent. Could the claimant sue the MOD or the German hospital? The court said that there was a special relationship between the MOD and soldiers and their dependants, which created a duty to provide appropriate secondary healthcare. That duty involved exercising reasonable care in selecting the providers. The MOD had fulfilled that duty by making a contract with the NHS Trust hospital. The NHS Trust hospital in turn was under a duty to patients to exercise reasonable care in procuring the services of a German hospital. But there was no duty on the MOD or the NHS Trust to ensure that skill and care was used in the treatment in Germany. That meant that any proceedings had to be taken in Germany against the German hospital. The claimant appealed, first on the ground that the MOD's duty of care to provide medical treatment given with skill and care was a non-delegable duty. Secondly, as a matter of policy British soldiers and their dependants should be able to sue the MOD in the English courts for medical negligence in a foreign hospital. The Court of Appeal said that the first argument should fail, as it would extend the law of negligence too far. As regards the second argument, the claimant relied on guidance published by the Department of Health in November 2002 that the NHS authorised treatment abroad to reduce waiting lists. The guidance stated that patients should be able to sue the NHS in the English courts. The court said that was about claims for breach of an organisational duty rather than specific negligent treatment. Even if it was accepted that the NHS owed a non-delegable duty that patients receive careful medical treatment abroad, this did not mean that the same duty applied to the MOD. The MOD no longer provided medical treatment itself and its role was simply to arrange for others to provide treatment. The claimant's appeal was dismissed.

The normal doctor-patient relationship gives rise to a duty of care in tort, for example, a patient and a hospital doctor or a general practitioner (family doctor) and patients on their list. But what of a relationship which arises outside such contexts? If an employer asks a doctor to carry out a medical examination of a job applicant and the doctor does this negligently, the doctor owes a duty of care to the employer. If, as a result, the applicant does not obtain the job, they can sue the doctor for economic loss. What is the position if the doctor simply gives advice based on the applicant's medical record? In *Kapfunde v Abbey National plc* (1998), the defendants sent the claimant's completed application form to a doctor, who acted as their independent advisor. The claimant had stated that she had been off work with sickle cell anaemia and the doctor advised the defendants that she was unsuitable. The defendants refused to employ the claimant and she sued the doctor in negligence. The Court of Appeal said that, even if it was foreseeable that the claimant would suffer financial loss if the doctor was careless, there was no direct doctor-patient relationship and the doctor had not assumed a duty to the claimant. The doctor was not liable.

In *N v Agrawal* (1999), the defendant doctor examined the claimant, who was a suspected rape victim, but did not appear at the trial as a witness. The claimant argued that the doctor owed her a duty of care to attend and, because of breach of this duty, the trial collapsed and the claimant suffered psychiatric harm. The Court of Appeal held that, in carrying out such an examination, the doctor did not assume responsibility for the claimant's psychiatric welfare and the doctor-patient relationship did not arise. The duty was simply to take care during the examination in not making the claimant's position worse. There was not sufficient proximity to create a duty of care. The court used the analogy of a doctor who witnesses a road accident and gives assistance: there, no doctor-patient relationship arises.

(b) Breach of the duty of care

The second matter for the claimant to prove is that the doctor is in breach of his duty of care. The question that needs to be addressed is, what standard of conduct does the doctor have to reach to fulfil the duty? The usual standard used in the tort of negligence is the standard of the 'reasonable man', which is an objective standard, but this does not work if the defendant has a particular skill, because the reasonable man does not have that skill. Instead, the law applies the 'Bolam test'. In Bolam v Friern HMC (1957), the claimant was mentally ill and was advised to have electro-convulsive therapy. This involved passing an electric current through the brain and one of the effects of the treatment was to cause convulsions. He consented to this treatment but was not told of the risk of fractures. At that time, patients having this treatment were given relaxant drugs or were physically restrained, or neither of these. The claimant was given treatment without drugs or restraints although there was a nurse at each side of his bed. As a result of the treatment, he fractured his hips. He claimed that the defendants were liable for giving him the treatment without giving him drugs or restraining him. The court said that a doctor was not negligent if he acted in accordance with 'a responsible body of medical men skilled in that particular art'. Evidence was given of diverse practices: some doctors used relaxant drugs, some used manual control and some used neither. The doctor in this case was not negligent because he had used neither.

A doctor does not have to reach the standard of the 'best' doctor, but simply the average, competent doctor in that particular field. A general practitioner will be judged by the standard of a competent general practitioner and is not expected to reach the standard of a specialist surgeon.

The Bolam test was applied in Whitehouse v Jordan (1981). The claimant went to hospital to have a baby and had been identified as likely to have a difficult birth. The defendant surgeon first tried delivery by forceps but this was unsuccessful and he then carried out a Caesarean delivery. The baby suffered brain damage and the claimant argued that too much force had been used in trying the forceps delivery, and this caused asphyxia and brain damage. The House of Lords, in dismissing the claimant's appeal, said that the test whether a surgeon has been negligent is whether he has met the standard of the ordinary skilled surgeon.

The *Bolam* test has been criticised for a number of reasons. First, it allows the medical profession to determine what standard of care is acceptable. Secondly, there are problems in deciding what is meant by 'a responsible body' of medical opinion. For example, how many doctors are needed to constitute 'a responsible body'?

However, the courts have always retained the power to override the view of doctors in certain circumstances. In *Hucks v Cole* (1968), evidence was given that in order to treat the patient's skin complaint, some doctors would have used penicillin and some doctors would not have used it. The defendant did not use penicillin and as a result the patient developed septicaemia. The Court of Appeal said that the doctor's failure to use penicillin was negligent. Sachs LJ remarked about not changing to penicillin, 'failure to do this was not merely wrong but clearly unreasonable'. More recently, in *Bolitho v City and Hackney HA* (1992), the House of Lords ruled that before accepting medical opinion as 'responsible', a court had to be sure that the doctors had considered the risks and benefits and had reached a defensible conclusion. Effectively this gives the courts the ultimate right to make decisions (see '(c) Breach caused damage', below, p 64).

Factors relevant in determining the standard of care

The courts in determining the standard of care take all the circumstances into account.

The magnitude of the risk

The risks associated with a particular course of treatment are relevant in deciding if a doctor has reached the appropriate standard. If a patient is suffering from a relatively minor illness the doctor must not treat it with dangerous drugs.

The cost of avoiding the harm

Doctors are only under a duty in negligence to do what is reasonable. This includes taking the cost of a particular course of treatment into account. In *Hucks v Cole* (1968), the cost of prescribing penicillin, which would have cured the patient's infection, was relatively inexpensive. A doctor would not be under a duty to always give a patient the most expensive treatments whatever the circumstances.

National Health Service Acts

These set out various statutory duties. For example, under s 1 of the National Health Service Act 1977, the Secretary of State for Health is under a duty to provide 'a comprehensive health service'. Attempts have been made to enforce these statutory duties, but without success (see, for example, *R v Central Birmingham HA ex p Collier* (1988)). The question here is whether a failure to fulfil a statutory duty can also lead to breach of a duty in negligence. In *Re HIV Haemophiliac Litigation* (1990), haemophiliacs were given contaminated Factor VIII, which gave them the HIV virus. They argued that there was a breach of statutory duty and negligence. The court said that there was not a breach of statutory duty, but that in itself did not preclude a claim in negligence. A successful claim in negligence is not, therefore, ruled out, but it seems remote.

Professional codes

These are guidelines produced by various medical professional bodies, such as the General Medical Council. Breach of a code is not negligence in itself, but will be relevant in deciding whether someone has acted in breach of duty.

Keeping up to date

All medical staff must keep up with major developments in their particular specialism. For example, a cancer specialist must know about important new treatments. The courts accept, however, that medical staff cannot be expected to know about every new development. In *Crawford v Charing Cross Hospital* (1953), the claimant developed paralysis because his arm had been put at a right angle to his body during an operation. An article in *The Lancet* six months previously had pointed out this danger. The court held that it would be impossible to require doctors to read every article in the medical press. The anaesthetist had not read the article but was nonetheless found not to be negligent.

At the present time, the vast amount of medical literature and research and the advent of the internet make it impossible for any individual to keep up with all current developments in their field, but they do need to know about major changes. Mason, McCall-Smith and Laurie warn that 'It is no longer possible for a doctor to coast along on the basis of long experience' (*Law and Medical Ethics*, 6th edn, 2002, London: Butterworths).

Following a general practice

It will usually be a good defence that medical staff have followed the generally accepted practice. The first matter to establish is that there was an accepted practice. In *Roe v Minister of Health* (1954), Roe went into hospital in 1947 for an operation and was given a spinal anaesthetic (nupercaine). The anaesthetic, in ampoule form, was kept in a clear solution of phenol, but tiny cracks in the ampoules had let phenol in, which contaminated the anaesthetic. As a result of being given the anaesthetic, Roe was paralysed from the waist down. It was held by the Court of Appeal that the defendants had followed the normal practice and no one could have foreseen the risk, so they were not negligent. Denning LJ said: 'We must not look at the 1947 accident with 1954 spectacles.' Clearly, after this accident, hospitals had to change the practice and Denning LJ pointed out that, in 1951, after the accident, a leading medical textbook had warned that keeping the anaesthetic solution in a clear spirit so that cracks could not be seen could cause permanent paralysis. He added: 'Nowadays it would be negligence not to realise the danger, but it was not then.'

Different medical opinions

In medical matters, it is common for there to be different opinions. If a doctor follows a minority practice, is this negligent? In *Maynard v West Midlands RHA* (1985), doctors believed that the patient had tuberculosis, but symptoms showed that it might be Hodgkin's disease, which is fatal unless treated quickly. Instead of waiting for the test results for tuberculosis, the doctors carried out an exploratory operation to see whether the patient had Hodgkin's disease, which in fact showed that he had tuberculosis. The operation caused damage to a nerve, even though it was carried out without negligence. However, the patient claimed that the operation was not necessary and that it had been negligent to carry it out. The House of Lords said that this was not negligent, as a competent body of medical opinion would have agreed with this course of action. Lord Scarman quoted the words of Lord President Clyde in *Hunter v Hanley* (1955):

> In the realm of diagnosis and treatment, there is ample scope for genuine differences of opinion and one man clearly is not negligent merely because his conclusion differs from that of other professional men. The true test for establishing negligence in diagnosis or treatment on the part of a doctor is whether he has been proved to be guilty of such failure as no doctor of ordinary skill would be guilty of if acting with ordinary care ...

In *Bolitho v City and Hackney HA* (1992), Dillon LJ, in the Court of Appeal, said that a court could reject a body of medical opinion if the court considered that it was '*Wednesbury* unreasonable', that is, that it was a view which no reasonable body of doctors would have held. The test of *Wednesbury* unreasonableness derives from *Associated Provincial Picture House v Wednesbury Corp* (1948), in which the Court of Appeal said that a decision made by a public authority could be challenged if it was so unreasonable that no reasonable authority would have made it. This covers taking irrelevant matters into account or ignoring relevant matters and it applies to health authorities.

New treatments

The law has to allow medical staff to try new procedures and new drugs, otherwise developments would be stifled. In deciding whether a new treatment was negligent, the courts have to take account of whether existing treatments had failed; what would happen to the patient without trying the new treatment; and the risks to the patient of having the new treatment. In *Clark v MacLennan* (1983), the claimant suffered incontinence after the birth of a child and normal treatment failed to work. A gynaecologist then carried out a procedure which left the claimant with permanent incontinence. This procedure would not normally have been tried until three months after the birth. It was held that the doctor should have waited, and it was negligence to depart form the normal practice.

Misdiagnosis

A mistake in diagnosing a medical condition is not in itself negligent. Many conditions have similar symptoms – see, for example, *Maynard v West Midlands RHA*, above. A doctor is judged by the *'Bolam* test' of what a competent doctor would do in the circumstances. This will involve looking at medical notes, asking the patient questions, carrying out an examination of the patient and, if necessary, carrying out tests or X-rays. In *Wood v Thurston* (1951), the claimant was taken to hospital by his friends. He was in a drunken state and his friends told the doctor that the claimant had been seen under a moving lorry. He was examined, his facial cuts were dressed and he was sent home in a taxi. A few hours later he died and it was found that he had broken most of his ribs and his collarbone, and had a congested lung. The doctor argued that he was not liable because the claimant's drunken state had dulled his reaction to pain. It was held that this was negligence, as the claimant's condition could easily have been detected by using a stethoscope. In *Langley v Campbell* (1975), a GP who failed to diagnose malaria in a patient who had recently been to Africa was held to be negligent.

Particular knowledge of the claimant

If medical staff have particular knowledge about a patient, this may mean that a higher duty of care is owed to that patient, for example, if a patient is very young, very old, has particular allergies, is known to be violent, etc. In *Selfe v Ilford and District HMC* (1970), a 17 year old boy was admitted to hospital after taking an overdose. He was put in a ward on the ground floor with 27 patients and three nurses. One nurse went to the toilet, one went to make tea and one was called to a patient. The boy then climbed out of an open window and onto the roof, and jumped off. As a result, he was paralysed. It was held that the hospital was negligent, as it knew that he was a suicide risk and not enough supervision had been provided. However, the courts have accepted that supervision cannot be provided at every moment. In one case, a patient suffering from mental deficiency went to the toilet, ate a lavatory freshener and died. This was held not to be negligence.

Particular characteristics of the patient

If a patient has particular characteristics that make treatment more difficult, these are taken into account. In *Williams v North Liverpool HMC* (1959), the defendants gave the claimant an injection into the arm tissue instead of a vein and this caused an abscess. It was held that, because the patient was overweight and it was difficult to find a vein, the defendants were not liable.

Failure of communication between staff

The practice of medicine has always involved teamwork, and this in turn relies on communication of information between medical staff. Particular problems arise if patients are transferred to other hospitals. In *Coles v Reading HMC* (1963), the claimant's finger was crushed in an accident at work. He went to a small local hospital where his wound was cleaned and dressed, and was told to go to Reading Hospital for further treatment. Instead, he went home and, some time later, the wound became infected and he died of blood poisoning. It was held that the local hospital had been negligent, as the claimant should have been given a note by the local hospital referring him to Reading Hospital for further treatment and should have been told to go there immediately. This was a failure by the doctors to communicate with each other.

Newly qualified staff

It is not a defence to a claim for negligence that the doctor has recently qualified. The law applies an objective standard and, under the *Bolam* test, a doctor must reach the standard of a competent and experienced doctor. In *Wilsher v Essex AHA* (1987), Mustill LJ said that the standard of care is defined by the particular post that the doctor occupies, rather than the status of the doctor in the hospital hierarchy. A doctor in a specialist baby unit would need to reach the standard of an experienced doctor in such a unit. Although this seems harsh, the standard may be reached through supervision or by a young, inexperienced doctor asking a consultant for advice.

Alternative medical practitioners

What standard should be applied to someone practising a different type of medicine from the normal, orthodox type? Is it enough to judge them by the standard of the competent practitioner of that type of medicine? In *Shakoor (Deceased) v Situ* (2000), the deceased consulted the defendant about a skin condition which needed surgery using orthodox medicine. The defendant, who practised Chinese herbal medicine, prescribed a herbal remedy. After taking nine doses, the deceased suffered liver failure and died. His widow sued for negligence. The evidence showed that the remedy had produced a rare reaction which could not be predicted. The claimant argued that the defendant was negligent in prescribing the remedy or for not warning of the risk of liver damage. The court said that the defendant owed a duty of care to the deceased and the question was what criteria should be used to decide whether the defendant was in breach of his duty: the standard of the careful practitioner of Chinese herbal medicine or the standard of orthodox doctors? A practitioner of herbal medicine practised alongside orthodox medicine and this had to be taken into account. This was an internal remedy and the practitioner had to have regard to the following:

- he worked in a system of law and medicine which would review the standard of care;
- the practitioner had a duty to ensure that any remedy was not harmful;
- he must realise that someone suffering an adverse reaction would go to an orthodox hospital and such incidents might appear in medical journals.

It was up to the practitioner to check that there were no adverse reports, or to subscribe to a body that checked for him. The defendant had acted in accordance with the standard of care required to practise Chinese herbal medicine and was not liable.

Lack of resources

If a hospital is sued for negligence, could it claim that it was a lack of resources which led to a lower standard of care and that therefore they should not be liable? It is a feature of the NHS that funds are short and there is frequently a shortage of staff, beds or equipment (or all three!). It would not be acceptable for a hospital to rely on lack of resources as a defence to a claim for negligence because, if a particular service was provided, the hospital would have to reach the *Bolam* standard for that service. If they could not reach the *Bolam* standard, then they should not provide that particular service. For example, if a hospital could not provide an accident and emergency service to the *Bolam* standard, they should not provide one. The situation can be illustrated by *Bull v Devon AHA* (1993), where the claimant was pregnant with twins. A problem arose with the delivery of the second twin and there was a delay of over one hour in the attendance of a suitably qualified doctor because facilities were on two sites and, under the system operated by the defendants, doctors were not available quickly enough. As a result of the delay, the second twin was born with brain damage. The court said that a proper system needed to be in place if maternity services were provided. In practice, a hospital facing a shortage of resources or staff would withdraw certain facilities, for example, by closing a particular ward. It would have been better in the circumstances if the hospital had not provided facilities for childbirth.

Emergencies

If a doctor is acting in an emergency situation, the courts will take this into account in deciding if the doctor has acted negligently. If, for example, there has been a train accident and there are hundreds of casualties taken to one particular hospital, this will be taken into account. Similarly, if a doctor goes to help someone who has collapsed in the street, the doctor will not have the same resources available as in a modern hospital and this is taken into consideration in setting the standard.

Duty to third parties

In tort, as a general rule, a person is not liable for an injury caused to another by a third party. In *Smith v Littlewoods* (1987), a third party set fire to the defendant's disused cinema and the fire damaged the claimant's property next door. It was held by the House of Lords that the defendants were not liable as, even though the damage was foreseeable, the defendants did not know about the third party and an intolerable burden would be imposed on owners of property if a duty was found in these circumstances. There are exceptions to this rule where:

- there is a special relationship between the claimant and the defendant;
- there is a special relationship between the defendant and third party; or
- the defendant creates the danger.

In *Palmer v Tees HA* (1999), an inpatient at the defendant's mental hospital threatened to kill a child in June 1993. Shortly after this, he was released and became an outpatient. Over a year later, the patient abducted and murdered the claimant's daughter and, as a result, the claimant suffered nervous shock. The patient lived in the same street as the child he murdered. The Court of Appeal considered whether proximity could be established between the claimant and the defendant. The claimant victim had to be identified and, clearly, the defendant could not do this. What precautions could the defendant have taken? It was difficult to detain outpatients. The best precaution was to warn the victim, but the defendant did not know who to warn. In the circumstances, the defendant could not be liable.

Another possibility is that a doctor or hospital gives advice to a patient, which the patient acts on and which causes harm to a third party. Does a doctor owe a duty to the third party? In *Goodwill v British Pregnancy Advisory Service* (1996), the defendant carried out a vasectomy for M. Three years later, M, a married man, started a relationship with the claimant. He told her about his vasectomy. The claimant became pregnant and sued the defendants for the cost of bringing up the child. The Court of Appeal applied the principles from *Hedley Byrne v Heller* (1964), saying that, in a claim for financial loss, the claimant had to show that the defendant knew that the advice was likely to be acted on and had been acted on. It was held that the defendant could not reasonably foresee that the claimant would act on their advice, as they did not know about M's future sexual partners and there was no assumption of responsibility to the claimant. The claimant could obtain independent advice herself. The defendants were not liable.

(c) Breach caused damage

The claimant must prove that the defendant's breach caused the damage. Two matters must be proved:

(a) as a matter of fact, the defendant's breach caused the claimant's loss; and

(b) the damage was not too remote.

Point (a) is known as causation in fact. The courts use the 'but for' test to determine whether the defendant caused the loss; that is, would the claimant have suffered loss but for the defendant's negligence? If the answer is 'no', then the defendant must logically have caused the harm and is liable. The operation of this test can be seen in *Barnett v Chelsea Hospital* (1969). Three night watchmen called at the hospital's casualty department early one morning, complaining that they had been vomiting since drinking tea at 5 am. The nurse contacted the duty doctor, who advised that they should go home and see their own doctor. A few hours later, one of the men died. It was discovered that they had mistakenly put arsenic in their tea but, even if they had been admitted to the hospital, the deceased would have died, because it would have taken some time to diagnose the problem. The widow sued for negligence. It was held that the defendants owed a duty of care to the deceased and they had broken that duty by sending him away without an examination. If the test was applied – would the deceased have died 'but for' the negligence of the defendants? – the answer would be 'yes'. Therefore, the breach did not cause the death because he would have died anyway. The hospital was not liable.

There are often problems in proving causation in fact in medical cases because there may be a number of causes for illnesses and medical conditions. There is the added requirement that it is up to the claimant to prove his case on the balance of probabilities, which is often difficult in medical matters. In *Kay v Ayrshire and Arran Health Board* (1987), the claimant was a two year old boy who was admitted to hospital with suspected meningitis and was given an overdose of penicillin. The boy later became deaf and claimed that the overdose caused the deafness. It was held that the evidence showed that it was probably the meningitis, not the overdose, which caused the deafness. A similar result occurred in *Wilsher v Essex AHA* (1988), where the claimant was born prematurely. A junior doctor mistakenly put a catheter into a vein instead of an artery and the baby was given too much oxygen. The baby later went blind. One of the possible causes was too much oxygen and the claimant sued. The House of Lords said that, although too much oxygen caused blindness, there were four other possible causes and the baby had these four conditions. It was not possible for the claimant to show that the blindness was caused by too much oxygen.

In *Bolitho v City and Hackney HA* (1997), the claimant, a boy aged two who had breathing difficulties, was taken to the defendant's hospital. He suffered acute shortage of breath and the nurse summoned the doctor, but the doctor did not attend. Later, the boy had a similar shortage of breath and suffered cardiac arrest and brain damage. The claimant argued that failure to attend was negligent. The defendant accepted the failure to attend but said that it was not liable because, even if the doctor had attended, she would not have intubated him and he would still have suffered brain damage. Each side called experts to show that a responsible body of medical opinion would intubate and would not intubate. The House of Lords held that the defendant was not liable in negligence, as a responsible body of medical opinion would not have intubated the boy. Lord Browne-Wilkinson said:

> ... the judge, before accepting a body of opinion as being responsible, reasonable or respectable, will need to be satisfied that, in forming their views, the experts have directed their minds to the question of comparative risks and benefits and have reached a defensible conclusion on the matter.

Effectively, what the House of Lords is saying is that the courts have the ultimate decision as to whether an act is negligent or not. *Bolitho* was applied in *Marriott v West Midlands HA* (1999), where the claimant fell downstairs at home in 1984 and injured his head and was unconscious for 20–30 minutes. He was taken to hospital and X-rays of his skull were taken, but no abnormalities were noticed and he was discharged. A week later, his condition had not improved and he still had headaches, and so his GP (the third defendant) was called. The GP examined the claimant but tests showed no abnormality. A few days after this, the claimant's condition deteriorated and he was admitted to hospital. He was found to have a fractured skull and had sustained a haematoma; he was left disabled. The claimant argued that the GP was negligent in failing to realise the claimant's position and in failing to send him back to hospital. Experts were called for each side to give evidence of what a GP should do in such circumstances. The judge agreed with the claimant's expert – a doctor seeing such a patient who had shown no improvement and was suffering from headaches ought to send the patient to hospital. The defendant's body of professional opinion was not reasonably prudent. On appeal, the Court of Appeal said that the judge could subject medical opinion to analysis to see if it was reasonable, and was entitled to find that it was unreasonable. The appeal was dismissed.

The Court of Appeal reiterated that expert medical evidence of sound medical practice had to be capable of withstanding logical analysis in *Penney, Palmer and Cannon v East Kent HA* (2000). This case involved the negligent reading of cervical smears by the defendants, resulting in the claimants being wrongly told that they were free of cancer. In *D v South Tyneside Health Care NHS Trust* (2003), D was detained under the Mental Health Act 1983 because she suffered from a mental disorder. She had a history of absconding from hospital but usually returned herself. On this occasion, she left the hospital and took a drug overdose which caused brain damage. The hospital had been observing D every hour. The Court of Appeal said that the question was whether the practice of hourly observations could be supported by a reasonable body of professional opinion (*Bolitho*). The judge in the High court had said that the view of the defendants was logically defensible. Even if D had been observed every 15 minutes and the police told when she went missing, it was unlikely that the police would have found her before she took the overdose. Therefore, D's appeal was dismissed. However, the courts have declared medical practice illogical on some occasions. In *Reynolds v North Tyneside HA* (2002), the claimant was born in 1979 but lack of oxygen at birth due to umbilical cord prolapse caused her to develop cerebral palsy. When the mother was admitted to hospital she was not given a vaginal examination. Later, the cord prolapse was discovered and an emergency Caesarean section was performed. The claimant argued that a vaginal examination should have been carried out and that if it had been the claimant would not have suffered damage. The defendants argued that it was hospital practice not to carry out an immediate vaginal examination. The court said that even if there was a body of opinion not to perform a vaginal examination on admission, the only reason for that view was a risk of infection. That did not withstand scrutiny and was illogical and there was no proper basis for such an opinion. Failing to perform a vaginal examination was negligent.

If the damage was caused by more than one factor, the 'but for' test does not work. Instead, the law asks the question, did the defendant's act 'materially contribute' to the claimant's damage? If the answer is 'yes', the defendant is liable. This was illustrated in *McGhee v NCB* (1972), where the claimant worked in a brick works and because no showers were provided he cycled home covered in brick dust. He developed dermatitis and the question arose whether this was caused by the brick dust on him at work or the brick dust on him on the way home. He could not prove it was the dust on the way home, for which the defendants would have been negligent. The House of Lords held that by not providing showers the defendants had 'materially increased' the risk of dermatitis and were liable. In *Wilsher v Essex AHA* (1988), the claimant was unable to prove that giving the baby too much oxygen made a 'material contribution' to the blindness. A difficult case in this area is *Hotson v East Berkshire AHA* (1987), decided by the House of Lords. The claimant, a 13 year old boy, fell out of a tree and was taken to hospital, but he was sent home. Five days later, he returned to hospital and an X-ray showed that he had a fractured hip. He developed avascular necrosis, a deformity of the hip joint. The defendants admitted negligence in not diagnosing the injury but argued that the condition was not caused by the delay. It was held by the High Court that, if the claimant's condition had been diagnosed immediately, there was still a 75% chance that the condition would occur. The defendant's breach had caused the loss of a 25% chance of recovery and the claimant was entitled to 25% compensation. The House of Lords said that the claimant had to prove that the delay in treatment was a material cause of the condition. The evidence was that the fall damaged blood vessels and this caused the condition. The claimant was not entitled to any compensation, as he was not able to prove on a balance of probabilities that, but for the delay, his injury would have healed without developing the condition. He could not prove this on a balance of probabilities because, statistically, he only had a 25% chance of recovery. The claimant was trying to claim for the loss of the chance of recovering. But the claimant's argument was based on a hypothetical situation because, even if he had been treated immediately, he may have been in the group (the 75%) which would not have made a full recovery. However, the House of Lords did not say that a claim for loss of a chance could never succeed.

In *Chappell v Hart* (1999), H had a pharyngeal pouch, a condition affecting the pharynx, which connects the back of the nose to the back of the mouth. This condition would eventually need surgery. The operation had a risk of damage to the oesophagus, which is the part of the throat leading from the mouth to the stomach. This in turn would cause infection and consequent damage to the voice. C did not warn H of this risk and, although C carried out the operation carefully, H's voice was damaged. H claimed that if she had been warned, she would have waited and had the operation performed by the best specialist. H was awarded damages. C appealed, arguing that there was no causal connection between the failure to warn and the injury, because, as surgery was inevitable, H had lost nothing because she had not lost the chance of the risk being avoided. Also, the injury resulted from a random risk which H accepted. The High Court of Australia dismissed C's appeal. They said that the claim was for physical injury, not the loss of a chance. The injury was foreseeable, C had a duty to warn H of the risk and the injury would not have happened without C's breach of duty; therefore, C's breach caused the damage. The fact that H would have been exposed to the risk later did not mean that she would have suffered it, and *Hotson v East Berkshire HA* (1987) could be distinguished.

The House of Lords has recently considered causation in *Fairchild v Glenhaven Funeral Services Ltd* (2002), which involved claims by employees who developed mesothelioma (a form of lung cancer) caused by asbestos dust. It was accepted that the disease could be caused by a single fibre. The problem facing the claimants was that they had worked for a number of different employers and could not prove which employer was responsible. The House of Lords said that the employers were in breach of their duty in exposing employees to asbestos dust. Existing medical knowledge could not identify on which particular occasion the disease started. In the circumstances, a different approach to causation could be taken and the fact that each employer's actions had materially increased the risk of contracting the disease was enough to prove causation, and the defendants were liable. The court here is bringing policy into its decision and even though the 'but for' test would not help the claimants, the court believes that it would not be just and reasonable to deny the claims. The Court of Appeal, in *Gregg v Scott* (2002), applied *Hotson* and distinguished *Fairchild*. The claimant developed a lump under his arm in 1994 but the defendant GP wrongly diagnosed it as benign. In 1995 the lump was correctly diagnosed as a malignant tumour. In 1996 he was given treatment, but by 1998 was told he could not be cured. The claimant established that the failure to diagnose and refer for treatment delayed treatment for nine months and reduced his chance of survival to 25%, whereas he would otherwise have had a 42% chance of surviving five years. The claimant claimed damages for loss of life expectancy. The court held by a majority of 2:1 that, on the balance of probabilities, the claimant would not be in a better position than he was now if the first diagnosis had been correct. The evidence showed that he would probably have relapsed even if he had been diagnosed and treated earlier. Only 42% of patients in his position would be cured. His present condition was not caused by the delay but by the disease. The claimant in most situations had to show, using the 'but for' test, that his injury was caused by the defendant's negligence. This did not apply in exceptional cases like *Fairchild* where proof was impossible.

On appeal to the House of Lords, the appeal was dismissed by a majority of 3:2 and the leading judgment was given by Lord Hoffmann. The court said that as regards the argument that the delay in treatment deprived him of survival, the question was whether the spread of cancer caused this. It was likely that he would not have survived anyway, so that the delay had not deprived him of survival. As regards a second argument that the loss of a chance should give a right to damages, this was not allowed in cases of clinical negligence and the exception in *Fairchild* did not apply (*The Times*, 28 January 2005).

The House of Lords also had to deal with issues of causation in *Chester v Afshar* (2004). Chester suffered from back pain. Afshar, a surgeon, advised her to have an operation and C agreed. A carried out the operation without negligence but it resulted in nerve damage and C was left partially paralysed. There was a 1–2% risk of such damage and C argued that the failure to tell her of this risk was negligent. It was accepted that there was a duty to warn of such a risk under the *Bolam* principle. The court found that A had failed to warn C of that risk. The House of Lords asked the question, did C have to prove that if she was warned of the risk she would not have consented at that time or that she would never have consented? The law which required doctors to warn of risks was based on the right of the patient to make a choice whether to have the operation or not. Some patients would find this decision easy but others would find it difficult. The latter group would not be able to say that they would have refused the operation for all time, if they had been warned. This would mean that under the normal rule of causation they would not be entitled to damages. One of the functions of the law was to uphold rights. The injury to C could be regarded as caused by breach of the duty to warn. The House of Lords was effectively saying that as a matter of policy C should have a remedy and A was found negligent. But this was a majority decision of 3:2 with Lords Bingham and Hoffmann dissenting. Lord Hoffmann said that where the breach of duty is a failure to warn of a risk, the claimant must prove that he would have taken the opportunity to avoid that risk. Here, C would have to prove that she would not have had the operation. C argued that it was sufficient to show that she would not have had the operation at that time, even though the evidence was that the risk would have been the same at a later time. Lord Hoffmann said of this: '... this argument is about as logical as saying that if one had been told, on entering a casino, that the odds on number seven coming up at roulette were only one in 37, one would have gone away and come back next week or gone to a different casino.' The Court of Appeal considered *Chester v Afshar* in *White v Taylor* (2004). White was given wrong advice by his solicitors. The trial judge found that if he had been given the correct advice he would still have made the same decision and he could not therefore prove causation. In the Court of Appeal, he argued that it was impossible to say what he would have done if he had been given the correct advice and therefore, on the basis of *Chester v Afshar*, he was entitled to damages. The Court of Appeal agreed with the trial judge that White would have made the same decision even with the correct advice and therefore had failed to prove causation. Arden LJ made some observations on *Chester v Afshar*: 'In my judgment, this case does not establish a new general rule in causation. It is an application of the principle established in *Fairchild v Glenhaven Funeral Services Ltd* (2003) that, in exceptional circumstances, rules as to causation may be modified on policy grounds.' She went on to explain that consent to medical treatment has special importance in the law and patients had to be informed of risks, so that policy reasons existed in *Chester v Afshar* to change the normal rule. But no such policy reasons existed in *White v Taylor* and therefore *Chester v Afshar* did not apply. 'The basic rule remains that a tortfeasor is not liable for harm when his wrongful conduct did not cause that harm' (Arden LJ). (Also see Willis, M and Brown, W, 'A change in the rules?' NLJ, Vol 54, 1882.)

Even if the claimant establishes factual causation, it still has to be proved that the defendant's act is a legal cause of the harm (point (b) in the two stage causation test). This is also known as the principle of remoteness. The defendant cannot be made liable for everything that happens as a result of a negligent act. The law uses this principle to limit liability. Applying the rule from *The Wagon Mound (No 1)* (1961), the test for determining whether the damage is too remote is the test of reasonable foreseeability. The courts often use this requirement to deny liability on policy grounds.

THE THIN SKULL RULE

The thin skull rule can be explained by the principle of 'you must take your victim as you find him'. The effect of this is that if the claimant has a special sensitivity and suffers more serious harm than a normal person, the defendant is liable for all of that harm. Even though the extra harm is not foreseeable, the defendant is liable. The rule protects sensitive claimants. The classic example is *Smith v Leech Brain* (1961), where, due to the defendant's negligence, the husband of the claimant suffered a small burn on his lip. This caused a latent cancer to develop and the husband died. The defendants were held liable. Similarly, in *Robinson v Post Office* (1974), due to the defendant's negligence, the claimant slipped at work and cut his leg. He was given an anti-tetanus injection by a doctor but he was allergic to this and suffered brain damage. The court said that the defendants had to take the claimant as they found him and they were liable for the full extent of the injuries.

Examples of where the thin skull rule applies would include patients with allergies, weak hearts, brittle bones and haemophilia.

RES IPSA LOQUITUR

The normal rule is that it is up to the claimant to prove, on a balance of probabilities, that the defendant has been negligent. Sometimes, the claimant will be able to rely on the maxim of *res ipsa loquitur* (the thing speaks for itself). The circumstances when this will apply are when it is obvious that the defendant has been negligent. The requirements to establish it are:

(a) there is no explanation for the injury; and

(b) such an injury would not normally happen if care is taken; and

(c) the defendant had control of the 'instrument' causing the damage.

It has been argued that the effect of *res ipsa loquitur* is to reverse the burden of proof, so that once the claimant establishes *res ipsa loquitur* it is up to the defendant to show that he was not negligent. This view was disproved by Lord Bridge in *Wilsher v Essex AHA* (1988). More recently, in *Ratcliffe v Plymouth and Torbay HA* (1998), Hobhouse LJ said: '*res ipsa loquitur* is not a principle of law; it does not relate to or raise any presumption. It is merely a guide to help to identify when a *prima facie* case is being made out.'

Res ipsa loquitur does not reverse the burden of proof and it is still up to the claimant to produce evidence to show that the defendant is liable. In *Cassidy v Ministry of Health* (1951), Lord Denning said that the claimant could say, 'I went into hospital to be cured of two stiff fingers. I have come out with four stiff fingers and my hand is useless. That should not happen if due care had been used. Explain it if you can'. The principle was applied in *Roe v Ministry of Health* (1954). The two claimants went into hospital for minor operations and were given a spinal anaesthetic. The anaesthetic was in glass ampoules, which were kept in a solution of phenol. Phenol had seeped through invisible cracks in the glass ampoules and contaminated the anaesthetic with the result that both claimants were paralysed from the waist down. Lord Denning said that it was up to the hospital to explain how this had happened. The hospital were able to explain what had happened and, in fact, the practice of storing anaesthetic in such a way was not negligent at the time of the operations because it could not be foreseen that it would be contaminated.

The principle has not been used often in medical cases, but the typical example is *Mahon v Osborne* (1939). The claimant had an abdominal operation and, two months later, it was found that a swab had been left in his body. As a result of this, he died. It was held by the Court of Appeal that *res ipsa loquitur* applied and the surgeon was liable.

In *Leckie v Brent and Harrow AHA* (1982), the claimant suffered a 1.5 cm cut to her cheek while her mother was having a Caesarean section. It was held that *res ipsa loquitur* applied and, in the absence of an explanation, the surgeon was negligent.

CONTRIBUTORY NEGLIGENCE

Under s 1(1) of the Law Reform (Contributory Negligence) Act 1945, if the defendant can show that the claimant has been partly to blame for the injury, then the compensation payable may be reduced to the extent the court believes is just and equitable. Under s 1(2), the court should assess the total damages and then make the reduction.

Contributory negligence could arise in medical cases, for example, if a patient discharged him or herself from hospital against medical advice and suffered harm as a result. The courts have been reluctant to say that a claimant has been contributorily negligent. In *Coles v Reading HMC* (1963), even though the claimant had failed to go to the main hospital for further treatment when told to do so by his doctor, he was not considered to be contributorily negligent. Medical staff must be on the alert for patients who are reluctant to follow advice or co-operate with treatment. As patients now have more say about their treatment, it is possible that the courts may find them contributorily negligent in appropriate circumstances.

THE LIMITATION ACTS

The law limits the time period within which a claimant must bring his claim because of difficulties of proof many years after the event and because it is unfair that someone should have a potential claim outstanding for an indefinite period. The effect of the limitation period is that it provides a defence for a defendant against whom a claim is made. Under s 11 of the Limitation Act 1980, if the claim is for personal injuries, the claim must be brought (a) within three years from when the cause of action accrued; or (b) three years from the date of the claimant's knowledge of the right of action, whichever is later. Under s 14, the date of knowledge is when the claimant had, or should have had, knowledge that the injury was significant and that it was attributable, wholly or in part, to the act, and had knowledge of the identity of the defendant. The test used by the courts is what a reasonable man would have known, but this is given a subjective element, as the claimant's age, intelligence, etc, is taken into account. In *Spargo v North Essex DHA* (1997), the claimant was detained in a mental hospital for 22 years after being diagnosed as suffering brain damage as a result of dieting. Five years after leaving hospital, the claimant saw a solicitor, claiming that she had been misdiagnosed. She did not issue a writ (now a claim form) until 12 years after leaving hospital. The Court of Appeal held that she realised the connection between the hospital's negligence and her suffering when she saw her solicitor. She had three years from that time and therefore had left it too late.

Under s 33 of the Limitation Act 1980, the court has a discretion to extend the three year period if there are valid reasons for the delay and if it would be just in all the circumstances. In *Das v Ganju* (1999), the claimant's daughter was born severely disabled in 1978 because the claimant had had German measles during the pregnancy. In 1988, her lawyers wrongly told her that her claim was not for personal injury and that it was too late to sue. The claimant consulted new solicitors and, in 1996, 18 years after the birth, the claimant sued the defendant doctor for failing to warn her that a rash in pregnancy could have been German measles. The defendant argued that the claim was too late. The Court of Appeal, in exercising its discretion under s 33, took into account the fact that the claimant had been given the wrong legal advice and that she was not at fault. It allowed the claim to proceed.

For other tort claims, the limitation period is fixed at six years from when the right of action accrued, under s 2 of the Limitation Act 1980. One example would be a claim for economic loss (financial loss) for the cost of bringing up a child after a failed sterilisation. This fixed period also covers intentional torts, for example, assault. In *Stubbings v Webb* (1993), W was abused by her stepfather in 1971, but did not realise that this abuse caused her psychiatric problems until 1984, when she consulted a psychiatrist. In 1987, when she was 30 years old, she issued a writ. The House of Lords held that s 11 did not apply to intentional acts and s 2 gave a fixed period of six years, which could not be extended. W had to sue within six years of reaching 18 and was therefore outside the limitation period. This is clearly a disadvantage for someone suing under the six year period, as no extension may be given.

If someone is under a legal disability, for example, if they are under 18 years old or of unsound mind, the limitation period runs from when the disability ends or when they die, whichever occurs first. For example, in the case of a minor suing for personal injuries caused by medical negligence when they were 10, the limitation period is three years after their 18th birthday (as in *Stubbings v Webb*).

If the claimant dies before the three year limitation period expires, a new period of three years runs from the date of death or the date of the personal representative's knowledge of the right to sue, whichever is later.

It should be noted that the Limitation Act 1980 also fixes a six year period for claims in contract.

COMMON LAW CLAIMS IN NEGLIGENCE AND BREACH OF STATUTORY DUTY

Public authorities like the NHS are given powers by Parliament and the exercise of these powers is subject to judicial review (as seen in Chapter 1). However, there may also be some overlap with claims in negligence at common law. Such a claim was brought in the following case. In *Smith v Secretary of State for Health* (2002), the claimant was born in July 1979. In May 1986, when she was six years old, she caught chicken pox at school and her mother gave her aspirin. Her condition worsened and she was taken to hospital, where it was discovered that she had Reye's Syndrome. This affected her brain and she became totally dependent on others. The Committee on the Safety of Medicines (CSM) gave the government advice that aspirin could trigger Reye's Syndrome, and in June 1986 the government issued a warning to the public not to give aspirin to children under 12 years old. Under the Medicines Act 1968, the Secretary of State for Health was responsible for the grant, renewal and revocation of licences for medicine. If any alteration was made to a licence, the Licensing Authority was required to give licence holders 28 days to make representations. Alternatively, an agreement could be made between the Licensing Authority, the CSM and the licence holder. The CSM gave the government advice in March 1986 that there was overwhelming evidence that aspirin was a causative factor in Reye's Syndrome and recommended that a warning should be given immediately. In April 1986, a meeting was held between the Secretary of State and aspirin manufacturers about a voluntary withdrawal of children's aspirins. The Secretary of State agreed not to publish a warning but proceed by co-operation as it was believed that would be more effective. A public announcement was made on 10 June 1986. The claimant argued that the delay in publishing a warning was negligent. If the claimant's mother had been given a warning, she would not have given the claimant aspirin. The court said that the decision in April 1986 to postpone the warning was a policy decision, not an operational one. A policy decision was not subject to judicial review by the courts. On the facts, neither the Secretary of State nor the CSM owed the claimant a duty of care in negligence. This did not mean that they could never be liable to an individual member of the public for a failure to exercise a statutory power. In any event, the decision in April to postpone the warning could be justified. Delaying the warning created a grave risk to a few children but on the other hand there was a clear benefit to having a co-ordinated campaign to alert medical staff and the general public.

VICARIOUS LIABILITY

One problem faced by a patient bringing a claim in negligence will often be who to sue. A patient who is treated in a hospital may have been injured by a doctor, nurse, radiologist, physiotherapist, etc. Under the principle of 'vicarious liability', an employer is liable for the torts of employees which are committed 'in the course of employment'. An employer is not liable for the negligent acts of an independent contractor. Rather than suing the individual member of staff for negligence, the patient can sue the hospital using the principle of vicarious liability. To establish vicarious liability, it must be shown that *the tort was committed by an employee*. The law developed a number of tests to determine whether someone is an employee, including the control test, the organisation test and the multiple test. Most of the staff in a hospital will clearly be employees and will be full time, but what is the position of a consultant surgeon who works at the hospital for one day each week? In *Roe v Minister of Health* (1954), Denning LJ said:

> I think that the hospital authorities are responsible for the whole of their staff ...
> It does not matter whether they are permanent or temporary, resident or
> visiting, whole time or part time. The hospital authorities are responsible for all
> of them. The reason is because, even if they are not servants, they are the agents
> of the hospital to give the treatment.

The legal position of agency staff who are taken on by the hospital on an *ad
hoc* basis is unclear – for example, nurses hired from an agency. They may be
seen as employees because of the control exercised over them by the
hospital. Alternatively, the nurse may be seen as an agent of the hospital,
which would then be liable for her torts.

The tort must be *committed in the course of employment*. If a nurse carried
out an operation on a patient and the patient was harmed, then this would
not be in the course of the nurse's employment. The hospital may, however,
be made liable for negligence in allowing such a situation to arise.

In applying the above principles to a hospital situation, the patient can
sue the hospital (or the health authority) and does not need to identify the
individual responsible for the negligent act. In fact, the individual member of
staff is also liable in tort and it would be possible to sue that individual,
although it would be unusual to do so, as they would be unlikely to be able
to pay compensation.

It has been argued that a hospital owes a non-delegable, direct duty to
patients. In *Ellis v Wallsend District Hospital* (1989), the Australian courts held
that a direct duty was owed by the hospital where a patient went directly to
the hospital for treatment. This principle of direct liability may also apply in
English law, although the point has not been directly addressed. In *Wilsher v
Essex AHA* (1987), in the Court of Appeal, Lord Browne-Wilkinson said: 'I
can see no reason why, in principle, the health authority should not be
[directly] liable if its organisation is at fault.' It can be argued, therefore, that
a health authority is directly liable for providing medical care to patients and
will be liable for breach of that duty. The principle of direct liability is more
likely to apply if there is negligence in the organisation and management of
the hospital, rather than in the actual provision of treatment.

If the patient was injured by a GP (family doctor), then that individual
doctor is liable, rather than the health authority, as the GP is an independent
contractor. The GP is vicariously liable for the actions of the staff of the
practice. Hospital doctors are covered by the NHS indemnity scheme, but
GPs are not covered by the scheme and have to insure against claims
through their professional bodies.

NEGLIGENT MISSTATEMENTS

Most negligence claims involve the commission of a negligent act, but
negligence may also take the form of negligent advice. Negligent advice may
lead to physical injury or, more usually, economic (that is, financial) loss. In

Hedley Byrne v Heller (1963), the House of Lords said that if a 'special relationship' could be established between the claimant and the defendant, in that the defendant knew that the claimant would rely on the advice, and the defendant assumed responsibility, the defendant could be liable. A doctor giving advice to a patient would have a special relationship with that patient and would owe them a duty not to give negligent advice. It is likely that negligent advice would lead to physical injury, for example, if a doctor told a patient to put butter on a burn and this caused further harm. A doctor may also be liable to a third party in respect of that advice if the requirements of *Hedley Byrne v Heller* are met. Such a claim was made in *Goodwill v British Pregnancy Advisory Service* (1996) (see above, p 64).

NERVOUS SHOCK (PSYCHIATRIC INJURY)

Nervous shock, or psychiatric injury, means some medically recognised psychiatric illness, which results from being exposed to an accident caused by the defendant's negligence. It does not include normal grief or shock, for which no claim can be made. Following the Hillsborough football tragedy, many relatives of the victims suffered nervous shock, although they lost their claims in the courts (*Alcock v Chief Constable of South Yorkshire Police* (1991)). In *Page v Smith* (1995), the House of Lords set out two categories of claimants:

(a) Primary victims, who are at the scene of the event and within the range of foreseeable physical harm. The claimant must show that the defendant could foresee 'personal injury'.

(b) Secondary victims are those who are not directly involved but suffer shock as a result of what they see or hear.

In *Alcock v Chief Constable of South Yorkshire Police* (1991), the Hillsborough case, the Court of Appeal set out the requirements for a secondary victim to claim:

- there had to be a relationship of 'love and affection' between the claimant and the victim;

- the claimant had to be present at the accident or in the aftermath – in *Alcock*, relatives who suffered nervous shock after identifying bodies eight hours afterwards were not considered to be present in the aftermath;

- the claimant must see or hear the event or aftermath – being told by someone else is not sufficient;

- there must be a sudden shock – so seeing something on television would not be sufficient.

With secondary victims, the claimant must show that the defendant could foresee nervous shock. In addition, the claimant has to show that a person of 'reasonable fortitude' would have suffered nervous shock.

In a medical context, it is unlikely that someone would have a claim as a primary victim unless they were present at the time of the negligent act and within range of harm. Someone may claim as a secondary victim; for example, if a child dies as a result of negligent medical treatment and the parents suffer nervous shock, they may have a claim. In *Sion v Hampstead HA* (1994), the claimant's son was injured in a road accident and was taken to hospital. His father stayed by him in hospital every day for 14 days and watched his condition worsen before the son eventually died. The father suffered nervous shock as a result and claimed that the hospital was negligent in not diagnosing bleeding from his son's left kidney. The Court of Appeal said that the claimant did not suffer a sudden shock but suffered as a result of seeing his son deteriorate over a period of time. This was not sufficient and his claim failed. The Court of Appeal considered a claim by a mother of a patient in *North Glamorgan NHS Trust v Walters* (2002). The claimant's 10 month old son became ill and was taken to the local hospital. The hospital failed to diagnose that he had acute hepatitis. The claimant was sleeping in her son's room when she was woken by him choking. He had an epileptic fit. The mother was told that her son had not suffered any brain damage but that he needed a transplant. He was taken to a London hospital by ambulance and the claimant followed the ambulance. When the claimant arrived she was told that her son had suffered irreparable brain damage. The next day she was told it would be best to turn off his life support, to which she agreed. Her son died in her arms. The claimant then suffered pathological grief reaction. At first instance the court rejected her claim that she was a primary victim as she was not likely to suffer physical injury. It treated her as a secondary victim and she was awarded damages. The hospital appealed on the grounds that the period from the fit to her son dying 36 hours later could not be one event; neither could events over such a period be treated as a 'sudden' shock. The Court of Appeal said that the period from the fit to the death of the child could be regarded as one horrific 'event', even though it was over a period of 36 hours. Also, the claimant could be seen as suffering a sudden shock in waking to find her son in convulsions, later being told about the brain damage and the next day being asked to agree to terminate the life support, rather than it being a gradual unfolding of events. She satisfied the test of proximity as she was there as all this was happening. It was not a case of merely being informed of an incident and she was entitled to compensation for nervous shock as a secondary victim.

In *Creutzfeldt-Jakob Disease Litigation Group B, Plaintiffs v Medical Research Council and Secretary of State for Health* (2000), the claimants suffered from dwarfism (achondroplasia). This is a condition caused by damage to or destruction of the pituitary gland, which stops the development of growth hormone and the child never grows up. By 1 July 1977, the defendants knew that a drug, HGH, which was used to treat dwarfism, carried a risk of CJD. However, the defendants used HGH in clinical trials on the claimants after 1 July. The claimants later discovered, either from their doctors or from the media, that CJD could be fatal. They suffered nervous shock as a result of knowing that they might develop CJD. It was held that the defendants could have realised that injections of HGH could have led to CJD, and it was reasonably foreseeable that patients would be given this news over a wide time span. The risk of the claimants suffering psychiatric injury as a result of learning about CJD was reasonably foreseeable. Claimants who could prove nervous shock caused by knowledge of the risk of CJD were entitled to compensation.

Claims for nervous shock were made by parents of dead children whose organs had been removed at postmortem. In *A, B and Others v Leeds Teaching Hospital NHS Trust and Cardiff Vale NHS Trust* (2004), three claimants, H, M and S, suffered nervous shock caused by removal of organs from their dead children without their consent. The question for the court was whether the defendants owed a duty of care to the claimants. When consent was given for a postmortem, there was proximity between the doctor and the parents of a dead child. This created a duty to explain the nature of the postmortem and to tell the parents that organs might be retained. That duty was broken. The claims of H and M were dismissed, as the risk of them suffering nervous shock was not foreseeable, but S was awarded damages.

The Law Commission has issued a Report on *Liability for Psychiatric Illness* (No 249, 1998), in which it is argued that the law is too restrictive and claims for nervous shock should be made simply on the basis of the requirement of love and affection. The Law Commission proposes that liability should be based on 'a close tie of love and affection' between the claimant and the victim, and that there is no need for the claimant to prove that they were close to the accident or the aftermath in both time and space, as required by *Alcock v Chief Constable of South Yorkshire Police* (1991).

The Law Commission has set out a list of relationships where a close tie of love and affection is presumed. These are spouse, parent, child, brother or sister and a cohabitant of at least two years' standing. Claimants outside this list would have to establish a close tie of love and affection, for example, grandparents.

THE CONSUMER PROTECTION ACT 1987

Patients may be given a wide variety of medical products in the course of their treatment. These can include drugs, blood, artificial limbs, heart pacemakers, etc. In June 2000, patients who had been given breast implants filled with soya oil were warned that there was a risk they could cause cancer, and they were advised to have them removed. Patients who suffer harm as a result of being provided with a product may have possible claims in contract, in negligence and under the Consumer Protection Act (CPA) 1987. If the product is supplied under the NHS, then no claim can be made in contract. If the product is supplied in the course of private treatment, a claim in contract could be made. However, an NHS patient could bring a claim for negligence at common law and would have to prove duty, breach and damage (*Donoghue v Stevenson* (1932)). Another possibility is to bring a claim under the CPA 1987 for harm caused by a 'defective' product.

The CPA 1987 was passed to implement the European Community Product Liability Directive (85/374/EEC). There are some differences in wording between the Directive and the CPA, but s 1 of the latter provides that the Act must be interpreted so as to comply with the Directive.

The CPA makes the producer strictly liable for harm caused by defective products. Under s 2(1), 'where any damage is caused wholly or partly by a defect in a product, every person to whom sub-section (2) applies shall be liable for the damage'. A person claiming under the CPA must prove that: (a) the product was defective; (b) damage was suffered; and (c) the damage was caused by the defect. This last requirement still poses a problem for claimants in, for example, proving that a drug caused particular side effects.

Product

Under s 1(2) of the CPA 1987, 'product' is defined widely to include any goods, components and raw materials incorporated in other products. 'Goods' is further defined as including any substance or growing crops. *A v National Blood Authority* (2001) involved a claim by a large number of patients infected with hepatitis C from blood transfusions given between 1988 and 1991. They sued under the CPA 1987, claiming that they had been given a 'defective' product. It was accepted that blood was a product and therefore covered by the Act. In deciding if the product was defective, the court applied the wording of Art 6 that it does not provide the safety which 'a person is entitled to expect'. The court distinguished between 'standard' and 'non-standard' products. With standard products, the question was whether it was safe for its foreseeable use. With a non-standard product, the question was whether the public accepted that because of its nature some of the products would be defective. Blood was a non-standard product and the public did not know that it carried a risk of infection, so they did not accept the risk that there was something wrong with it and expected it to be 100% free from infection. The blood was therefore a defective product. The defendants also put forward the defence under s 4(1)(e), which is dealt with below.

Goods are defective if their safety is not such as persons generally are entitled to expect (s 3(1)). This imposes an objective standard, but the Directive (Art 6) provides that goods are defective if they do not reach the standard that 'a person is entitled to expect', which is a subjective standard and wider than that of the CPA 1987. In deciding whether goods are defective, the courts must take into account all the circumstances, including matters set out in s 3(2), which include:

(a) the way in which goods are sold and the purposes for which they are sold, for example, for adults or children;

(b) any instructions or warnings – with medicines, it is important to give clear instructions on use and information about side effects because, if this is not done and harm results, the medicine will be treated as a 'defective' product. If the medicines are for children, they may need to be in a childproof container, so that only adults may give the medicine;

(c) what might reasonably be expected to be done with the goods, etc.

A claim was brought under the CPA 1987 in *Richardson v LRC Products Ltd* (2000). After the birth of their second child, the claimant and her husband used condoms, as they did not want any more children. During sex, a condom fractured and the claimant became pregnant. She brought a claim under the CPA 1987, arguing that the condom was a defective product. The court held that, under s 3, in deciding what persons were 'entitled to expect', any instructions and warnings had to be taken into account. The defendants had not claimed that the condoms were 100% effective and evidence showed the inexplicable failure of some condoms. The fracture in the condom did not prove that it was defective. In any event, the claimant could have avoided the pregnancy by taking the 'morning after pill' and her claim failed. More recently, in *XYZ and Others v Schering Health Care Ltd* (2002), the claimants argued that third generation oral contraceptives were defective under the CPA 1987 because they carried a greater risk of causing cardiovascular injuries. However, they were unable to prove the contraceptives were defective on the evidence available.

Section 3 adds that the fact that a safer product is produced does not mean that the earlier version was defective. This last requirement was necessary to allow manufacturers to produce improved products, as, without this exclusion, a person with an earlier version could claim that it was defective.

Damage

This covers death, injury or damage to property. However, it does not cover damage to the actual product or any product supplied with the defective product in it (s 5(2)) or damage not exceeding £275.

Producer

The CPA 1987 renders the 'producer' liable, and this covers manufacturers, producers of raw materials, processors, own branders, importers into the European Union and suppliers. The supplier is only liable if they do not tell the claimant the identity of the producer, own brander or importer. A hospital or health authority could be liable either as a manufacturer, for example, if it produces its own medicines or artificial limbs, or simply as a supplier. It is important that hospitals keep records which enable their suppliers to be identified, so that, in the event of a claim, liability may be passed on. These records should be kept for 10 years, as liability lasts for 10 years from when the product is put into circulation.

Defences

The CPA also provides a number of defences. The most important one is s 4(1)(e) – the defence that the state of scientific and technical knowledge at the relevant time was not such that a producer of products of the same description might be expected to have discovered the defect. Although this imposes an objective test – that of the 'reasonable producer' – it will be interpreted to comply with the Directive, which refers to knowledge that would enable the producer to discover the defect. This defence effectively allows manufacturers to avoid liability if, at the time that the product was produced, the defect could not have been discovered in the light of the scientific knowledge at that time. However, the decision in the following case is significant from the consumer's point of view. In *A v National Blood Authority* (2001), the hepatitis C virus was only identified in May 1989, although no test to screen it was developed until 1991. The defendants therefore argued that under s 4(1)(e) they were not liable because there was no way to test the blood until 1991, so that transfusions given before 1991 could not have been tested. The court said that once the existence of a defect in a product was known, the producer would be liable if they continued to supply the product, irrespective of the fact that the producer could not tell whether a particular 'batch' had the virus. Therefore, the defendants were liable. This decision will have important ramifications as regards blood contaminated with variant Creutzfeldt-Jakob disease (vCJD). The Secretary of State for Health announced in December 2003 that the first patient had died from the disease following a blood transfusion which carried the disease. The problem faced by the NHS is that no test exists to identify vCJD in the blood but the NHS now knows that blood could be infected.

The CPA 1987 amends the Limitation Act 1980 and provides that a claimant must sue within three years of when the damage occurred or the date on which the claimant knew that he had a right of action. This limitation period is subject to a 'longstop' of 10 years from when the product was put into circulation. This 10 year period causes problems with drugs, as their adverse effects may not be realised until many years later.

In medical matters, the main importance of the CPA is with regard to the supply of drugs. Primarily, the manufacturer will be liable for defective drugs, but it is important for hospitals to maintain accurate records and to know who their suppliers are; otherwise, they may be found liable as a 'producer'.

REFORM OF THE SYSTEM OF MEDICAL NEGLIGENCE

Under the present system, patients who have suffered injuries in the course of treatment arising from negligence have to take legal action in the courts. The problems of cost, delay and the effects on the patients has been known for many years. The Woolf Report, *Access to Justice* (1996), led to the introduction of the Civil Procedure Rules 1998, which together with the Pre-Action Protocol for the Resolution of Clinical Disputes have created a more straightforward approach with clear time limits, giving control to the courts and the use of single joint experts providing medical evidence. One alternative system of compensation which has been suggested is a system of 'no fault' liability for medical negligence with the state funding claims. However, worries about the cost and opening the floodgates to claims have meant that such schemes have not been implemented.

In June 2003, the Chief Medical Officer published his report on clinical negligence in the NHS (*Making Amends*). The scale of the problem can be seen from the fact that 10% of inpatients suffer adverse effects and 18% of patients said that they had been given the wrong medication in the previous two years. The two main 'injuries' suffered are death and pain. In the case of primary care (general practitioners, etc), half the claims are for failed diagnosis and one quarter for errors in prescribing medication. In 2001–02, the cost of clinical negligence claims was £446 m. In the case of claims under £45,000, the legal and administrative costs of settling the claims are more than the compensation paid in the majority of cases. The report points out that, despite the above reforms, the system needs to be changed. It identifies the main problems with the present system as being complex, unfair because similar cases have different outcomes, slow, costly, encouraging defensiveness and secrecy and that patients are not given explanations and apologies.

The aims of the proposed new system are:

- to reduce the risks of treatment by analysing and acting on medical errors;
- to provide remedial treatment for patients injured by medical errors;
- fair compensation;
- that the process of compensation should not undermine the relationship between the patient and healthcare staff;
- a clear system for complaining about standards of care; and
- an affordable system of compensation.

Amongst the proposals is a new 'NHS Redress Scheme' for those harmed by negligent hospital care. Compensation up to £30,000 would be paid. If a baby suffered brain damage at birth, a monthly payment would be made for the cost of care (maximum £100,000 yearly) plus lump sums up to £50,000 for adaptations to the home and £50,000 in compensation for pain and suffering. It would not be compulsory to use this scheme.

If patients wished to take their case to court, they would have to use mediation in specified types of cases and more emphasis would be put on periodical payments.

A statute would be passed to impose a 'duty of candour' on healthcare staff and managers to tell patients about actions which resulted in harm. Those reporting medical errors would be exempt from disciplinary action.

The size of the problem of medical negligence claims demands that action should be taken. The Redress Scheme would provide some compensation for many patients who are not presently compensated. Although that scheme might put pressure on patients not to take legal action, it is now up to the government to consider it and the other proposals.

CRIMINAL LIABILITY FOR NEGLIGENCE

If a patient dies as a result of negligent treatment, medical staff could face prosecution for a criminal offence. In criminal offences, the prosecution have to prove two elements: (a) the *actus reus* (guilty act); and (b) the *mens rea* (intention, recklessness or negligence). Possible offences that staff could face include murder and manslaughter.

Murder

Murder is a common law offence and is the unlawful killing of a human being under the Queen's Peace with malice aforethought. The defendant's act must cause the death of the victim. The intention of a doctor is important in deciding whether the act is murder. The *mens rea* is the intention to kill or cause grievous bodily harm. If a doctor gives painkilling drugs, which he knows will shorten the victim's life, is the doctor guilty of murder? In *R v Adams* (1957), the court said that if the purpose was to relieve pain, that was not murder. It is unlikely that a doctor's actions would amount to murder unless the doctor deliberately intended to kill or could foresee that death was highly likely.

Manslaughter

This is a lesser crime than murder and can be divided into two categories:

(a) Voluntary manslaughter – the defendant has the *mens rea* for murder but has one of the defences of provocation, diminished responsibility or suicide pact. It would be extremely unlikely for these defences to be relevant to medical staff.

(b) Involuntary manslaughter – there are two types: constructive manslaughter and gross negligence manslaughter. Constructive manslaughter is where the defendant commits an unlawful act which causes death. Gross negligence manslaughter is where the defendant acts in breach of duty, and it is this type which is relevant to medical care. In *R v Adomako* (1995), the defendant anaesthetist did not notice that, during an operation, the oxygen supply had become disconnected, as a result of which the patient died. The House of Lords said that the defendant had to owe a duty of care to the victim; the death must be caused by breach of that duty; and the breach had to be so bad that it could be described as 'gross'. Here, the oxygen was disconnected for nine minutes and would have been noticed by any reasonably skilled doctor. The defendant was guilty of gross negligence manslaughter. In 2003, Dr Feda Mulhem pleaded guilty to the manslaughter of a young cancer patient through gross negligence. Dr Mulhem had instructed a young doctor at the Queen's Medical Centre in Nottingham to inject an anti-cancer drug into the patient's spine instead of a vein. The Court of Appeal considered *Adomako* in *R v Misra; R v Srivastava* (2004). Both M and S were hospital doctors who were looking after a patient, who had had an operation. The patient caught an infection and died. M and S were charged with gross negligence manslaughter. The court said that they owed a duty of care to the patient. They were in breach of that duty because they did not diagnose the fact that the patient had a severe infection and they did not take adequate steps to treat him. They were convicted. They appealed on the ground that Art 7 of the European Convention on Human Rights requires 'legal certainty' in the definition of a crime and gross negligence manslaughter was not certain because it was difficult to say what was gross. The Court of Appeal said that a jury did not have to decide whether the defendant's act was gross and then whether it was a crime but whether his act was 'grossly negligent' and therefore amounted to a criminal offence. That was a question of fact in each case. The ingredients of the offence of gross negligence manslaughter were clear. The appeal was dismissed.

Mason, McCall-Smith and Laurie have expressed concern that the criminal courts should be used for maintaining standards in operating theatres (*Law and Medical Ethics*, 6th edn, 2002, London: Butterworths). This concern is echoed by Holbrook, who comments on Dr Mulhem, 'He was not seeking to harm his patient; in fact he was intending to further his recovery. His "crime" was that he made a mistake ...' (Holbrook, J, 'The criminalisation of fatal medical mistakes', BMJ, Vol 327, 15 Nov 2003).

THE HUMAN RIGHTS ACT 1998

Article 2 (the right to life) may be used if a health authority fails to make provision for medical care and this failure leads to death or serious injury which could cause death. In *R (on the Application of Khan) v Secretary of State for Health* (2003), K's daughter developed lymphoma and she was given chemotherapy and potassium. She died shortly after this and it was then discovered that she had been given too much potassium. After an investigation, K was told by the Crown Prosecution Service that no prosecution would take place. An inquest into his daughter's death was opened and adjourned to allow K to seek funding for legal representation. K applied for judicial review but the court said that the State had fulfilled its duties under Art 2. On appeal to the Court of Appeal, the court said that the coroner's inquest would be the best place to establish the cause of death.

K needed public funding to play a full part in the inquest and for the State to fulfil its duties under Art 2.

Article 3 (degrading treatment) may provide a basis on which to claim in some circumstances. In *D v UK* (1997), a drug smuggler suffering from AIDS was due to be deported to a country with poor medical facilities and successfully claimed that to deport him would be a breach of Art 3. Article 8 (the right to private life) may have implications for mixed wards.

SUMMARY – MEDICAL NEGLIGENCE

1 *Duty of care*
   - Duty owed: by GP to patients on list; by hospital to patients attending; by ambulance trust (*Kent v Griffiths* (2000)); but not at present outside these relationships.

2 *Breach of that duty*
   - Magnitude of risk: risk of a particular treatment is relevant in determining the standard of care.
   - Cost of avoiding harm: only need do what is reasonable.
   - National Health Service Act 1977: general duties difficult to enforce: *R v Central Birmingham HA ex p Collier* (1988).
   - Professional codes: breach of code relevant to determining negligence but not conclusive.
   - Keeping up to date: medical staff must keep up with the main developments in their field: *Crawford v Charing Cross Hospital* (1953).
   - Following general practice: usually a defence: *Roe v Minister of Health* (1954).
   - Different medical opinions are allowed.
   - New treatments: can be used but failure of existing treatments and medical condition of the patient are important factors in determining if negligent.
   - Misdiagnosis: not necessarily negligence but may be: *Wood v Thurston* (1951).
   - Particular knowledge about the claimant: may create a higher duty of care.
   - Particular characteristics of the patient: may mean a lower standard of care.
   - Failure of communication between staff: it is important to check patient has followed advice if he transfers between hospitals.
   - Newly qualified staff: must reach the *Bolam* standard: *Wilsher v Essex AHA* (1987).

- Alternative medical practitioners: judged by the standard of their particular speciality, but must have an awareness of orthodox medicine.

- Lack of hospital resources: not a defence in negligence: *Bull v Devon AHA* (1993).

- Duty to third parties: medical staff not liable for acts done to third parties as a general rule: *Palmer v Tees HA* (1999).

3 *Causation*

- Causation in fact: the defendant's breach caused the harm: *Barnett v Chelsea Hospital* (1969).

- 'But for' test: would claimant have suffered harm but for defendant's act? Answer must be 'no'; problems in proving this in medical law (*Wilsher* (1987); *Bolitho* (1997)), if so use test of 'material contribution': *Fairchild v Glenhaven Funeral Services Ltd* (2002).

- Causation in law: legal causation is determined by the principle of remoteness.

- Thin skull rule: take your victim as you find them: *Robinson v Post Office* (1974).

4 *Res ipsa loquitur*

- When it is clear the defendant has been negligent, there is no need to prove negligence in the normal way; requirements for *res ipsa loquitur* to apply: (a) no explanation for injury; (b) injury does not normally happen with care; (c) defendant in control of instrument causing harm: *Mahon v Osborne* (1939).

5 *Limitation Act 1980*

- Claims for personal injury: must sue within three years from when right of action arose *or* from when claimant has knowledge of right of action.

6 *Negligence claim for not carrying out statutory duty*

- It is difficult to establish negligence for not carrying out statutory duty: *Smith v Secretary of State for Health* (2002).

7 *Vicarious liability*

- Principle is that one person is liable for the torts of another.

- Hospitals are liable for torts of staff employees: *Roe v Minister of Health* (1954).

- Could be possible direct liability of hospital, but this is not established in English law: see Australian case, *Ellis v Wallsend District Hospital* (1989).

8 *Nervous shock*

- Must be recognised psychiatric illness.

- Primary victims: within range of foreseeable physical harm.

- Secondary victims: requirements of *Alcock* (1991) are: (a) a relationship of love and affection; (b) victim present at accident or aftermath; (c) victim must see or hear event; (d) victim must experience sudden shock: *North Glamorgan NHS Trust v Walters* (2002).

9   *Consumer Protection Act 1987*

- Claims for defective products: important in relation to any 'goods' supplied by a hospital; producer is liable.

- Claimant must prove: (a) product was defective; (b) damage was suffered; and (c) the defect caused the damage: *A v National Blood Authority* (2001) – hepatitis C virus.

10 *Criminal liability*

- Murder: common law offence; need intention to kill or cause GBH and act, causing death;

- Manslaughter: gross negligence manslaughter, where duty is owed and the defendant acts in breach of duty: *R v Adomako* (1995).

CHAPTER 5

CONFIDENTIALITY AND MEDICAL RECORDS

INTRODUCTION

The duty of confidence requires that doctors must keep information about their patients secret. This duty has a long history and is part of the Hippocratic oath:

> All that may come to my knowledge in the exercise of my profession or outside my profession or in daily commerce with men, which ought not to be spread abroad, I will keep secret and will never reveal. [Hippocrates, c 420 BC]

The Declaration of Geneva 1948 (amended at Sydney, 1968) is a modern, international version of the Hippocratic oath and states: 'I will respect the secrets which are confided in me, even after the patient has died.' The main ethical theories also support the duty of confidence. From a utilitarian viewpoint, patients are more likely to give information to doctors if they know that they have a duty of confidence, and this leads to better overall health for the population at large. From a deontological (or duty-based) point of view, the principle of respect for autonomy requires a doctor to keep information about patients confidential. The effect of the Human Rights Act 1998 means that Art 8 of the European Convention on Human Rights (the right to respect for private life) will require a person's medical records to be kept private. Professional codes produced by medical and nursing bodies require members to keep information about patients obtained in the course of their work confidential. The common law rules also require information obtained in certain circumstances to be kept confidential. The common law rules were not developed specifically with regard to medical information but apply generally. In addition, under the Data Protection Act 1998, health professionals must keep health records private, whether they are held on a computer database or in manual files. Under the Freedom of Information Act 2000, which came into force on 1 January 2005, health records are exempt from disclosure.

The duty of confidence is not an absolute duty and even the Hippocratic oath reflects this. The law has had to develop exceptions to the duty, and these will be examined below. The common law on the duty of confidence is trying to maintain a balance between protecting private information about the patient and enabling that information to be revealed if to do so is in the public interest. There are also statutory rules which require medical information to be kept confidential.

THE COMMON LAW RULES

The common law recognises that, in certain circumstances, a duty of confidence may arise. The requirements for bringing a claim for breach of this duty were set out in *Attorney General v Guardian Newspapers (No 2)* (1988). Lord Goff said that there is a duty of confidence if confidential information comes to the knowledge of someone in circumstances where that person has notice that the information is confidential and it would be just not to disclose that information. He went on to say that there was a 'public interest' in maintaining a duty of confidence. The exact legal basis of the duty of confidence is unclear. Sometimes it can arise through a contractual relationship; for example, in a contract of employment an employee may agree to keep the employer's trade secrets confidential. It may also arise through tort or equity in circumstances where it is fair to impose a duty. If personal medical information is given by a patient to a doctor in the course of the doctor-patient relationship, a duty of confidence arises in favour of the patient. This duty arises whether the patient is treated through the NHS, where there is no contractual relationship, or privately, when a contract will exist.

What is the scope of this duty of confidence?

If medical information is given without disclosing the name of the patient, is this a breach of the duty of confidence? In *R v Department of Health ex p Source Informatics Ltd* (2000), SI Ltd wanted information on the prescribing habits of GPs which it could sell to pharmaceutical companies. SI Ltd made an agreement with pharmacists that, for a fee, the pharmacists would provide SI Ltd with information which was taken from prescription forms. This information included the names of GPs and the types and quantities of drugs prescribed, but not the names of the patients. The pharmacists did not give the names of the patients, as SI Ltd was only interested in knowing about the prescribing habits of GPs. The Department of Health issued a policy document stating that, even though this information was anonymous, it could be a breach of the duty of confidence. SI Ltd applied for judicial review, claiming that this policy was wrong. At first instance, the application was dismissed and the court said that the patient would not have consented to the information being passed to SI Ltd, and there was no public interest to override the duty of confidence. In the Court of Appeal, judgment was given by Simon Brown LJ, who set out the requirements for a duty of confidentiality, as established in the judgment of Megarry J in *Coco v AN Clark (Engineers) Ltd* (1969):

(a) the information must have the quality of confidence;

(b) the information must be given in circumstances implying an obligation of confidence;

(c) there must be an unauthorised use of the information.

The court said that the patient had no proprietary right in the prescription form or the information on it and, therefore, had no right to control its use if privacy was not at risk. The patient's privacy was protected here and there was no breach of the duty of confidence by the pharmacists.

If confidential information can be disclosed because it comes within one of the exceptions (see 'Exceptions to the duty of confidence', below), this does not mean the information can be disclosed to anyone. The disclosure may only be made to an appropriate person for particular purposes. In *Woolgar v Chief Constable of Sussex Police* (1999), the claimant nurse had been arrested after the death of a patient, but was later released without being charged with any offence. The nursing regulatory body, the UKCC, also investigated the matter and asked the police for a copy of the statement made by the nurse. The nurse would not consent to this disclosure and, when the police said that they would pass on a copy of the statement, the nurse sought an injunction. The Court of Appeal held that the police could pass this information to the UKCC because the issue of public safety overrode the duty of confidence. In *A Health Authority v X* (2001), during other legal proceedings, the claimant health authority became concerned that a GP may not have been complying with conditions of service as regards prescribing and keeping patient records. The health authority had to decide whether to take disciplinary action and it asked the GP to disclose the medical records of several patients. The GP obtained the consent of some patients but two would not consent. The GP argued that he had a duty of confidence to his patients and did not have to disclose the records to a third party. Under the 'Terms of Service for Doctors', a doctor was required to send medical records of a patient to the health authority when requested. The High Court said that medical records were subject to a duty of confidentiality, but the court had to balance the public interest in such confidentiality against the public interest in health authorities being able to conduct disciplinary proceedings. The terms of service did not give the health authority an unqualified right to have the medical records for any purpose it might choose. However, on balance, the health authority was entitled to disclosure, but the documents were to remain confidential to the health authority, and other public bodies they may properly be given to had to take safeguards against abuse. On appeal to the Court of Appeal, the court confirmed the decision and the fact that conditions had been imposed, and dismissed the appeal.

Medical information given to the doctor by a patient is confidential, but what of other information? In *R v Wilson* (1996), the defendant had branded his wife's bottom with his initials, at her request. He was convicted of actual bodily harm under s 47 of the Offences Against the Person Act 1861. The police obtained the information from a medical report made by the wife's doctor. This would be a breach of the duty of confidence if it was given without consent, because it was information given to the doctor in the course of a medical consultation.

Particular difficulties occur with some categories of patient:

(a) Children: children are owed a duty of confidence, to the extent that their medical records cannot be disclosed to strangers, but what about giving information to their parents? With young children who lack the capacity to consent to treatment, the doctor will need to tell the parents about the treatment which he proposes to give the child, as the doctor must act in the best interests of the child. The parents have a legal duty to look after the child and need to know about the child's health.

But what is the position with older children? A *'Gillick* competent' child can consent to treatment and it may be argued that disclosure of medical information about that child to the parent would be a breach of the duty of confidence. However, if a child refuses treatment, the doctor may ask the parent for consent, and this may mean that medical information about the child is given to the parent. If the child consents to treatment but asks the doctor not to disclose this to his parents then, strictly, the doctor should not tell the parents. The normal exceptions to the duty of confidence apply and, for example, a child may consent to disclosure to their parents.

(b) Incompetent adults: the legal position on disclosing confidential information is unclear. It may be argued that a duty of confidence can be implied from the fact that there is a doctor-patient relationship. Some guidance may be gleaned from *Re F* (1990): with incompetent patients, treatment may be given in the best interests of the patient and, by analogy, medical information may only be disclosed if it is in the patient's best interests to do so.

General Medical Council (GMC) guidance, *Confidentiality: Protecting and Providing Information* (2000), provides:

> 38 Problems may arise if you consider that a patient is incapable of giving consent to treatment or disclosure because of immaturity, illness or medical incapacity. If such patients ask you not to disclose information to a third party, you should try to persuade them to allow an appropriate person to be involved in the consultation. If they refuse and you are convinced that it is essential, in their medical interests, you may disclose relevant information to an appropriate person or authority. In such cases you must tell the patient before disclosing any information, and, where appropriate, seek and carefully consider the views of an advocate or carer.

(c) Dead patients: can medical staff disclose confidential information about a patient after the patient's death? The duty of confidence arises from the personal relationship between the doctor and the patient and, therefore, it can be argued that the legal duty of confidence ends on the patient's death. GMC guidance, *Confidentiality: Protecting and Providing Information* (2000), states:

> 40 You still have an obligation to keep personal information confidential after a patient dies. The extent to which confidential information may

be disclosed after a patient's death will depend on the circumstances. These include the nature of the information, whether the information is already public knowledge or can be anonymised, and the intended use to which the information will be put. You should also consider whether the disclosure of information may cause distress to, or be of benefit to, the patient's partner or family.

The GMC tell their members to keep the duty of confidence even after the patient has died. Some writers share this view:

> It is open to the courts to regard divulgence by a doctor of information supplied in confidence by a patient who has since died as being unconscionable as well as unprofessional. If so, there is no reason in principle why equity should not regard the doctor as owing a duty of confidence to the deceased's estate, consonant with the maxim that equity will not suffer a wrong to be without a remedy ... [Toulson, R and Phipps, C, *Confidentiality*, 1996, London: Sweet & Maxwell]

However, Mason, McCall-Smith and Laurie point out that the death certificate is a public document and it gives the cause of death, which is not then confidential. This can have repercussions for the family if, for example, the patient has died of AIDS (see *Law and Medical Ethics*, 6th edn, 2002, London: Butterworths, p 268).

Exceptions to the duty of confidence

(a) Consent

The patient may consent to disclosure of their medical information. The patient must have the capacity to agree to disclosure and must freely consent. They should also be given sufficient information to know what they are consenting to. However, Mason, McCall-Smith and Laurie (*Law and Medical Ethics*, 6th edn, 2002, London: Butterworths, p 243) point out that such consent is not always given freely:

> What patient at a teaching hospital outpatient department is likely to refuse when the consultant asks: 'You don't mind these young doctors being present, do you?' – the pressures are virtually irresistible and truly autonomous consent is impossible, yet the confidential doctor-patient relationship ... has, effectively, been broken.

The consent to disclosure may be expressly given or may be implied. A patient may expressly consent to relatives being told about their condition. Obviously, any patient going to a hospital for treatment may need a number of medical staff to look at their notes. For example, if the patient has a suspected broken leg, the notes will be passed to a radiologist. Consent to this may be implied. But what limits are there as to whom, within the hospital, should see the information? Professional associations recognise that information must be given to other members of a medical team. The GMC's guidelines allow other healthcare professionals to be given information:

Sharing information with others providing care

7   Where patients have consented to treatment, express consent is not usually needed before relevant personal information is shared to enable the treatment to be provided. For example, express consent would not be needed before general practitioners disclose relevant personal information so that a medical secretary can type a referral letter. Similarly, where a patient has agreed to be referred for an X-ray, physicians may make relevant information available to radiologists. Doctors cannot treat patients safely nor provide continuity of care, without having relevant information about the patient's condition and medical history.

8   You should make sure that patients are aware that personal information about them will be shared within the healthcare team, unless they object, and of the reasons for this. It is particularly important to check that patients understand what will be disclosed if it is necessary to share personal information with anyone employed by another organisation or agency providing health or social care, except where this would put others at risk of death or serious harm.

9   You must make sure that anyone to whom you disclose personal information understands that it is given to them in confidence, which they must respect. Anyone receiving personal information in order to provide healthcare is bound by a legal duty of confidence, whether or not that they have contractual or professional obligations to protect confidentiality.

(b) Public interest

Sometimes, it is in the public interest to breach the duty of confidence. An example of this would be where a patient had committed a serious crime, which was disclosed in the course of medical treatment. As a general rule, a doctor has no legal obligation to tell the police of any crime he becomes aware of through treating a patient. The leading case is *W v Egdell* (1990). W was convicted of killing five of his neighbours and was detained in a secure hospital under the Mental Health Act 1983. Some time later, he applied to a mental health review tribunal to be moved to another hospital. His lawyer obtained a report from Dr E, but this stated that W had an obsessive interest in firearms and explosives and was dangerous. W wished to obtain an injunction to prevent the use of the report. W withdrew his appeal to the tribunal but Dr E sent a copy of his report to both the head of the secure hospital and the Home Office. The Court of Appeal said that Dr E *did* owe a duty of confidence to W. However, here, there were two conflicting public interests. One was that mental patients should be free to seek medical advice and to make full disclosure to doctors. They would only be able to do this if there was a duty of confidence owed to them and they were certain that information divulged would be kept secret. Secondly, there was the public interest in the fact that W was a dangerous patient and, if released, would be a risk to the safety of the public. The court has the task of balancing these interests and, in this case, decided that the disclosure by Dr E was justified. Bingham LJ said:

> There is one consideration which, in my judgment, as in that of the judge, weighs the balance of public interest decisively in favour of disclosure. It may be shortly put. Where a man has committed multiple killings under the disability of serious mental illness, decisions which may lead directly or indirectly to his release from hospital should not be made unless a responsible authority is properly able to make an informed judgment that the risk of repetition is so small as to be acceptable.

Sir Stephen Brown in the same case said that the risk must be 'real, immediate and serious'. It is unclear whether all three of these requirements would have to be met; if so, it limits the circumstances in which disclosure can be made. Once it is accepted that disclosure can be made in the public interest, the disclosure is still limited to those it is necessary to tell, so Dr E could not send a copy of his report to the newspapers.

Issues of public interest arose in *Ackroyd v Mersey Care NHS Trust (MCT)* (2003), which concerned the publication in the *Daily Mirror* of information from the medical records of Ian Brady (one of the 'Moors Murderers') who was detained in a secure hospital. The *Daily Mirror* had obtained the information from A, a freelance journalist who had obtained it from inside the hospital. The question was whether A had to disclose his source in the hospital. The Court of Appeal said that if the hospital source was sued for breach of their duty of confidentiality, they might raise the defence of public interest that the public had a right to know how Brady was treated. If that was the case, it was arguable that Mersey Care NHS Trust would not succeed against A, as there would then be no wrongdoer. There was also an argument over whether the public interest in non-disclosure of medical records should override the public interest in maintaining the confidentiality of A's source inside the hospital. The matter should go for trial.

The courts also take notice of guidelines from the professional medical bodies in making decisions. The GMC's *Confidentiality: Protecting and Providing Information* (2000) states:

Disclosures to protect the patient or others

36 Disclosure of personal information without consent may be justified where failure to do so may expose the patient or others to risk of death or serious harm. Where third parties are exposed to a risk so serious that it outweighs the patient's privacy interest, you should seek consent to disclosure where practicable. If it is not practicable, you should disclose information promptly to an appropriate person or authority. You should generally inform the patient before disclosing the information.

The UKCC's *Guidelines for Professional Practice* (1996) state:

> The public interest means the interests of an individual, or groups of individuals or of society as a whole, and would, for example, cover matters

such as serious crime, child abuse, drug trafficking or other activities which place others at serious risk.

Shortly after *W v Egdell*, in *R v Crozier* (1990), the defendant had been charged with attempted murder and employed a psychiatrist to prepare a report to be used in his case. The report was not used and the defendant was given a prison sentence. The psychiatrist then gave the report to the prosecution and the judge. The defendant was detained under a hospital order. The defendant appealed, claiming that this breach of the duty of confidence meant that he did not have the choice in deciding whether or not to use the report. The Court of Appeal said that there was a public interest in the disclosure of the report and the psychiatrist had acted reasonably.

There are a number of other questions arising from similar circumstances, which remain unresolved. What would the position be as regards the duty of confidence if a patient in the community came to the doctor and it was discovered the patient was dangerous? Is disclosure justified to detect or prevent crime?

What would the position be if the detained person in W's position had committed lesser offences? It would seem that disclosure would not then be justified.

What is the position if a patient has committed a civil wrong? Would this justify breaching a duty of confidence? It seems unlikely that, in normal circumstances, this would override the public interest in a duty of confidence.

(c) Public good

Confidential medical information may be disclosed in circumstances where doing so is for the public good. In *Lion Laboratories v Evans* (1985), confidential documents in the possession of the manufacturers of an intoximeter showed that it was not accurate. The intoximeter readings were used to bring prosecutions for drinking and driving. It was held by the Court of Appeal that there was an important public interest in the disclosure of that information. This case shows that it is not necessary that an offence has been committed, or is likely to be committed, if there is a legitimate public interest which needs protection.

CONFIDENTIALITY AND HIV

The spread of the HIV infection has caused particular problems with regard to the duty of confidence. The fact that there is no known cure and that AIDS sufferers are likely to be ostracised puts the disease in a category of its own. The main dilemma it poses is: should the duty of confidence be strictly maintained for AIDS patients, or should the duty be broken? If confidence is maintained, then others may unwittingly be exposed to the disease but, if others are told about a patient with AIDS, would this result in fewer AIDS sufferers asking for medical help? Although AIDS is not a 'notifiable disease', the Minister of Health has the power under regulations to make sufferers have treatment and, if necessary, be detained. The policy behind this approach is that making AIDS a notifiable disease would make people reluctant to go for treatment. The result of this approach is that the duty of confidence is maintained for AIDS patients.

This dilemma was addressed in *X v Y* (1988). An employee of a health authority wrongly disclosed to a newspaper the names of two GPs who were HIV positive but who continued to practice. The health authority sought an injunction to prevent the newspaper from publishing the names. The court had to balance the competing public interests. On the one hand, there is public interest in knowing which doctors are HIV positive and the freedom of the press. On the other is the public interest that those with HIV should be able to obtain confidential medical help. The court held that the risks to patients from HIV doctors were very small and that the interest in publication was outweighed by the special need for confidentiality with HIV positive patients. Rose J said:

> The public in general and patients in particular are entitled to expect hospital records to be confidential and it is not for any individual to take it upon himself or herself to breach that confidence whether induced by a journalist or otherwise.

More recently, in *H (A Healthcare Worker) v Associated Newspapers Ltd and H (A Healthcare Worker) v N (A Health Authority)* (2002), a number of issues fell to be decided. H, a healthcare worker, developed HIV whilst working for the 'N' health authority. When H was diagnosed, he told N and stopped working. Under Department of Health guidelines then in place, patients who had been treated by H needed to be told. N asked H for details of these patients and their medical records. H refused to disclose private patients he had treated because he believed that the risks to them were minimal. ANL (the *Mail on Sunday*) also wanted to publish a story about the matter. H sought injunctions to stop N telling patients or disclosing his identity (right to private life under Art 8) and to stop ANL (Associated Newspapers Ltd) disclosing his name, clinical specialty or health authority. The main issue facing the Court of Appeal was balancing the public interest in freedom of the press (and freedom of expression under Art 10) and the public interest in keeping confidential the fact that a healthcare worker was HIV positive (private life, Art 8). The story which ANL wanted to publish contained matters of public interest. Although publication of H's identity was not allowed, details of his specialty was, as a ban would restrict public debate on the matter. As regards the patient records, H should hand these to the health authority so that the position of the patients could be evaluated. The Department of Health produced new guidelines for infected healthcare workers.

GMC guidance provides: 'Only in the most exceptional circumstances, where the release of the doctor's name is essential for the protection of patients, may a doctor's HIV status be disclosed without his or her consent' (*HIV Infection and AIDS: The Ethical Considerations* (revised 1993)).

The Department of Health issued new guidelines in 2002 on dealing with health staff with AIDS: *Guidance for Clinical Health Care Workers: Protection Against Infection with Blood-borne Viruses.* These guidelines were produced after advice from the Expert Advisory Group on AIDS, which recommended that it is no longer necessary to notify every patient who has had an exposure prone procedure by an infected healthcare worker. This is because of the low risk to the patient and the anxiety caused to patients and the public. A decision about informing is now made on a case by case basis.

Particular problems with the duty of confidence occur where a patient is HIV positive. Can the doctor tell the patient's sexual partner? The GMC's *Serious Communicable Diseases* (1998) gives the following guidance:

Giving information to close contacts

22 You may disclose information about a patient, whether living or dead, in order to protect a person from risk of death or serious harm. For example, you may disclose information to a known sexual contact of a patient with HIV where you have reason to think that the patient has not informed that person, and cannot be persuaded to do so. In such circumstances you should tell the patient before you make the disclosure, and you must be prepared to justify a decision to disclose information.

23 You must not disclose information to others, for example relatives, who have not been, and are not, at risk of infection.

The advice to medical staff when dealing with a patient who has the HIV virus is to try to persuade them to tell their sexual partner. If they refuse then, under the above guidance, the doctor can tell the partner if he knows the specific individual at risk. However, legally, the matter has not been decided and it could be seen as a breach of the duty of confidence. The court would have to consider the balance between the two private interests: the patient's right to confidence and the sexual partner's right not to be exposed to the risk of a fatal disease. The court would probably be in favour of disclosure but the issue has not been decided.

Can the doctor tell other health staff?

The GMC guidance when dealing with a patient with HIV or other communicable disease is to tell the patient the full implications of having HIV, how to protect others from the disease and the importance of other health staff knowing about the disease in order to provide proper care.

Serious Communicable Diseases states the following:

19 If patients still refuse to allow other healthcare workers to be informed, you must respect the patients' wishes except where you judge that failure to disclose the information would put a healthcare worker or other patient at serious risk of death or serious harm. Such situations may arise, for example, when dealing with violent patients with severe mental illness or disability.

In order to provide the most appropriate treatment, it is important that the patient's GP knows that the patient has HIV but, if the patient does not want them to be told, that confidence must be respected by the hospital unless the GP is exposed to a serious risk by not knowing.

Is there a duty to disclose confidential information to a third party?

If a doctor knows that the patient has HIV or that the patient has threatened to kill someone, is the doctor under a duty to warn that third party? This point has been decided in the US in *Tarasoff v Regents of the University of California* (1976). In August 1969, P told his psychologist, Dr M, that he intended to kill T, another student, who had rejected his sexual advances. Dr M asked the campus police to detain P, which they did for a short time and then released him. In October 1969, P killed T and her parents claimed negligence for failing to warn and failing to detain. The court said that, as a general rule, there was no duty to control another's conduct or to warn third parties about such conduct. But there are exceptions if the defendant has a 'special relationship' with the person who needs to be controlled or the foreseeable victim.

The public interest in effective treatment of mental illness and confidentiality had to be balanced against the public interest in protection from violence:

> We recognise the public interest in supporting effective treatment of mental illness and in protecting the rights of patients to privacy ... and the consequent public importance of safeguarding the confidential character of psychotherapeutic communication. Against this interest, however, we must weigh the public interest in safety from violent assault. [Tobiner J]

Here, the balance was in favour of protection from violence. There was a special relationship between Dr M and P, and the doctor knew that P was a serious danger to T. The doctor was under a duty to take reasonable care to protect the victim. This could be by a warning to the victim, or to friends of the victim or to the police. Here, Dr M was in breach of that duty and the defendants, his employers, were liable.

A more recent example is *Garamella v New York Medical College* (1999). In 1985, Dr DeMasi, a psychiatrist employed by the first defendants, enrolled to study psychoanalysis at the first defendants' college. As part of the course, Dr DeMasi was required to undergo 'training psychoanalysis', which was carried out by Dr Ingram (the second defendant), one of the first defendants' staff. Dr Ingram was under a contractual duty to tell the first defendants if Dr DeMasi was having the required personal psychoanalysis and whether he was ready to be certified as a psychoanalyst. During the psychoanalysis, Dr DeMasi disclosed to Dr Ingram that he was a paedophile. Dr Ingram ended the sessions but did not tell the first defendants either this or the fact that Dr DeMasi was unsuitable to work with children. In 1986, the claimant, a child who attended the hospital for treatment, was sexually assaulted by Dr

DeMasi, who was later convicted for this offence. The claimant sued for personal injury. The court said that Dr DeMasi had threatened to harm children and would be working with them. Dr Ingram was responsible for certifying Dr DeMasi's fitness on the training programme and, therefore, had a duty to warn the New York Medical College that the training psychoanalysis was not progressing satisfactorily. The claimant was one of a foreseeable class of victims and Dr Ingram owed the child a duty of care. Although there was a conflict between the public policies of confidentiality and reporting child abuse, a psychiatrist had a duty to disclose when harm to identifiable victims was reasonably foreseeable.

The English courts would be reluctant to impose such a duty. The general rule in negligence is that a person is not liable for the acts of a third party. In *Palmer v Tees HA* (1999), an outpatient who was being treated for mental illness by the defendants had threatened to kill a child. The claimant's four year old daughter was abducted and murdered by the patient and the claimant suffered nervous shock. Three days later, she saw the body of her daughter. The Court of Appeal considered whether a duty could be owed to the claimant. First, the claimant victim had to be identified and here the defendants did not know whom the patient would attack. Secondly, what precautions could the defendant have taken? The powers to detain outpatients are limited and the best thing to do would have been to warn the victim, but the defendants did not know who to warn; therefore, no duty was owed.

If a doctor discovers in the course of a consultation that a woman patient is being physically abused by her partner, can the doctor inform the police? This would be a clear breach of the duty of confidence. The doctor may only persuade the patient to tell the appropriate authorities. If a doctor discovers that a child patient is suffering abuse, the doctor may tell a third party. The GMC's *Confidentiality: Protecting and Providing Information* (2000) provides:

> 39 If you believe a patient to be a victim of neglect or physical, sexual or emotional abuse and that the patient cannot give or withhold consent to disclosure, you should give information promptly to an appropriate responsible person or statutory agency, where you believe that the disclosure is in the patient's best interests.

STATUTORY EXCEPTIONS TO THE DUTY OF CONFIDENCE

A number of statutes provide that the duty of confidence may be broken in certain circumstances. The reasons for this vary, from protecting public health to collecting statistics.

Public Health (Control of Disease) Act 1984

Section 10 of this Act lists notifiable diseases, including cholera, plague, relapsing fever, smallpox and typhus. Further diseases have been added by regulations. Under s 11(1):

If a registered medical practitioner becomes aware, or suspects, that a patient whom he is attending within the district of a local authority is suffering from a notifiable disease or from food poisoning, he shall ... send to the proper officer of the local authority for that district a certificate stating –

(a) the name, age and sex of the patient and the address of the premises where the patient is;

(b) the disease or, as the case may be, particulars of the poisoning from which the patient is, or is suspected to be suffering and the date, or approximate date, of its onset ...

The National Health Service (Venereal Diseases) Regulations 1974 provide that any information which would identify an individual who has been examined or treated for any sexually transmitted disease shall not be disclosed. Disclosure may be made to inform a doctor, or someone acting under the direction of a doctor, in the treatment of the patient or prevention of the spread of the disease.

The Abortion Regulations 1991, made under the Abortion Act 1967, require that notice of termination of pregnancy must be given to an officer of the Department of Health and to other authorised persons for a variety of reasons. The latter include a police officer not below the rank of superintendent for the purposes of investigating whether an offence has been committed under the Abortion Act; to a court for the purposes of criminal proceedings; for scientific research, etc. Disclosure in breach of the regulations is a summary offence.

There is no general duty on medical staff to assist the police in enquiries by disclosing confidential information, but some statutes create particular obligations.

Health Act 1999

This Act created the Commission for Health Improvement (CHI). Under s 23 of the Act, the Secretary of State may make regulations allowing the CHI to enter and inspect NHS premises and take copies of patient records. Under s 23(2), the circumstances in which information may be obtained are limited and regulations may not make provision for disclosure of confidential information which identifies a living individual unless one or more of the following conditions are met: (a) the information is in a form in which the identity of the individual cannot be ascertained; (b) the individual consents; (c) the individual cannot be traced despite taking all reasonable steps; (d) where the Commission is exercising its functions under s 20(1)(c) (investigating the management and quality of healthcare) (i) it is not practicable to disguise the identity of the individual; (ii) the Commission considers there is a serious risk to the health of patients; and (iii) the Commission considers the matter is urgent and the information should be disclosed without the individual's consent.

Road Traffic Act 1988

Section 172(2) of this Act states:

Where the driver of a vehicle is alleged to be guilty of an offence to which this section applies – ...

(b) any other person shall if required as stated above give any information which it is in his power to give and may lead to identification of the driver.

In this sub-section references to the driver of a vehicle include references to the person riding a cycle.

(4) A person who fails to comply with the requirement of sub-s (2)(b) above is guilty of an offence.

Consequently, a doctor who suspects that a patient has been involved in a traffic accident is under a duty to give information to the police to identify the driver. In *Hunter v Mann* (1974), the court held that this duty was limited to disclosing information which would lead to identification.

Police and Criminal Evidence Act 1984

If the police are investigating a serious offence, they may obtain a warrant to obtain material which would be of use. Under s 9, certain material is 'excluded material' and this would include a patient's medical records, samples of tissue, fluids, etc. In order to gain access to this, the police must apply to a circuit judge.

Misuse of Drugs Act 1971

The Misuse of Drugs (Notification of Supply to Addicts) Regulations 1973, made under the Act, require doctors to inform the Home Office about patients they treat for drugs within seven days.

REMEDIES FOR BREACH OF THE DUTY OF CONFIDENCE

The two main legal remedies for breach of the duty of confidence are damages and an injunction to prevent the disclosure of confidential medical information. If a doctor breaches the duty of confidence, the patient may have an action in tort or in contract. A claim in contract may only be brought if there is an existing contract between the doctor and the patient, for example, where the patient is paying for private treatment. This would exclude NHS patients, whose only claim would be in tort. If the claim were in contract, then damages would only be awarded for financial loss, for example, if the patient had lost their job as a result of the breach. As a general rule, a claim for distress or mental harm cannot be made in contract but would have to be made in tort. An injunction could stop disclosure of information, as in *X v Y* (1988) but, if the breach has already happened, an injunction would be too late.

In addition to the legal remedies, a healthcare worker who breached their duty of confidence would face disciplinary action from their professional body, for example, the GMC in the case of doctors.

ACCESS TO MEDICAL RECORDS

Originally, a patient had no right to see their medical records unless disclosure was obtained in the course of a legal claim against the hospital. It was argued against such disclosure that the contents could cause distress to patients, for example, if they had cancer. If records were disclosed, this would stop medical staff from putting in full comments, which would be detrimental to patient health and, even if disclosure was made, patients would not understand the records. The demand for access to medical records increased in the 1980s and the first step was the Data Protection Act 1984, which gave a right of access to computerised records. This Act has been replaced by the Data Protection Act 1998.

Data Protection Act 1998

This Act was passed to implement European Council Directive 95/46 on the Protection of Individuals in Respect of the Processing of Personal Data. It came into force in March 2000. One important change made by the 1998 Act is that it also governs manually held information, which was not covered by the Data Protection Act 1984. The 1998 Act defines 'data' to include manual data which is part of a 'relevant filing system' from which information is readily accessible. An example of this would be an alphabetical filing system for patients' records. A patient will therefore have access to both computer-held information about them and handwritten medical notes. The Act sets out eight data protection principles, which include the following:

- personal data will be processed fairly and lawfully;
- personal data shall be obtained only for one or more lawful purposes;
- personal data shall be adequate, relevant and not excessive in relation to the purpose for which it is processed;
- personal data shall be accurate and, where necessary, kept up to date.

Section 7 of the Act gives the data subject the right of access to the data, which includes:

- a description of the data;

- the purposes for which it is being processed; and
- to whom it may be given.

There is also a right to a copy of the data in an intelligible form if a written request is made and a fee paid.

The data subject has the right to change inaccurate data and to claim compensation if damage is suffered as a result of breach of the Act. In addition, breach of the Act is a criminal offence.

Under s 2, 'sensitive personal data' includes information about health (including medical records) and the consent of the data subject is needed to process this data or, if consent cannot be given, processing is necessary to protect the 'vital interests' of the data subject. This exception covers mentally incapacitated adults and children.

The Act applies to existing patient information and not just to data kept after the Act came into force.

Regulations provide that access can be denied if it would cause serious harm to the physical or mental health of the applicant or any other person (Data Protection (Subject Access Modification) (Health) Order 2000).

A patient may ask the data controller to stop processing their records if this is causing harm or distress. If the Act is breached, the patient may also claim damages. Additionally, the patient may have their records altered.

The Information Commissioner (formerly the Data Protection Commissioner) is responsible for enforcing the Act.

Access to Medical Reports Act 1988

If someone wants access to a medical report on a person, they must obtain the consent of that person (s 3). This consent must be in writing. This Act gives a patient the right to a copy of a report, which is made for employment or insurance purposes, before it is sent to the appropriate person. The report will usually be made by the patient's GP. The patient has the right to correct any errors in the report or, if the doctor refuses to change the report, the patient may add their objections to the report. If disclosure of the report would cause serious harm to the physical or mental health of the patient, it can be refused.

Access to Health Records Act 1990

This statute gave patients the right to access medical information kept in manual files. It covers a wide range of health professionals, including doctors, dentists, opticians, chemists, nurses, midwives and physiotherapists. Parents may apply for access to their children's medical records but this will only be granted if the child consents or, if the child does not understand the nature of the application, if access is in the best interests of the child.

A child under 16 who is capable of understanding the nature of such an application may obtain access (s 4(1)). The patient is entitled to a copy of the record on payment of a fee. Access may be refused if it would cause serious harm to the physical or mental health of the patient. The patient has the right to change the record if it is not accurate or, if the holder refuses to change it, he may add a comment to the record. The Act does not apply to any records made before 1 November 1991, when the Act came into force. In 1995, a Code of Practice on Openness was introduced in the NHS, which allows access to all records made before or after 1 November 1991.

As the Data Protection Act 1998 now covers the manual records covered by the Access to Health Records Act 1990, the only real relevance is for the records of dead people. The Data Protection Act 1998 only applies to information about living persons.

THE HUMAN RIGHTS ACT 1998

Article 8

1   Everyone has the right to respect for his private and family life, his home and his correspondence.

2   There shall be no interference by a public authority with the exercise of this right except such as is in accordance with the law and is necessary in a democratic society in the interests of national security, public safety or the economic wellbeing of the country, for the prevention of disorder or crime, for the protection of health or morals, or for the protection of the rights and freedoms of others.

Article 8 is a qualified right and may be restricted in accordance with the provisions of Art 8(2). Medical records are part of someone's private life and disclosure of a patient's records would be a breach of Art 8. In *McGinley v UK* (1999), two ex-servicemen, involved in nuclear testing in the Pacific in the 1950s, wanted the release of their medical records in order to establish a connection between the testing and cancer. The European Court of Human Rights held that there was no breach of Art 8 on the facts, but it said that, in the circumstances of the government carrying out dangerous activities with serious consequences for peoples' health, those affected had a right to the information. This creates a positive duty of disclosure.

In *R v Secretary of State for the Home Department ex p Belgium, Amnesty International and Others* (1999), the question arose as to whether the Home Secretary could disclose the medical report on Senator Pinochet, which stated that he was medically unfit for trial. Disclosure would be to Belgium, France, Spain and Switzerland, but Senator Pinochet refused. The report had been shown to the Chief Medical Officer, who said that the four countries would not be able to prove that it was wrong and therefore there was no reason for disclosing it. The Court of Appeal said that, in such a case, openness was paramount and disclosure was necessary for the prevention of disorder or crime, and they agreed to disclosure. The court considered that disclosure of the medical report was within the exceptions in Art 8(2).

The courts now take Art 8 into account, as can be seen from *A Health Authority v X* (2001) and *H (A Healthcare Worker) v Associated Newspapers Ltd* (2002).

SUMMARY – CONFIDENTIALITY

1   *Duty of confidence*
   - Common law duty of confidence to a patient where information is given to a doctor in the course of treatment.
   - Giving anonymous information is not a breach of duty: *R v Department of Health ex p Source Informatics Ltd* (2000).
   - Disclosure within the exceptions must only be to the appropriate person for the particular purpose: *A Health Authority v X* (2001).
   - Problem cases: children – distinguish between children who lack capacity to consent to treatment and *Gillick* competent children; incompetent adults: information may be disclosed in best interests; dead patients: legal duty ends on death but GMC guidance still requires it.

2   *Exceptions to duty*
   - Patient consents to disclosure.
   - Public interest: *W v Egdell* (1990) – serious crime; but note, there is often a balance of competing public interests: *Ackroyd v Mersey Care NHS Trust* (2003).

3   *Confidentiality and HIV*
   - AIDS patients: keep duty of confidence or disclose? Cases have said maintain confidence.
   - May tell known sexual partner of patient under GMC guidelines; but legally this may be a breach of the duty of confidence.
   - Cannot tell other health staff if patient refuses unless there is a serious risk to healthcare workers or other patients.
   - No duty to disclose confidential information to third parties: *Palmer v Tees HA* (1999), but contrast US position: *Tarasoff v Regents of the University of California* (1976).

4   *Statutory exceptions to the duty of confidence*
   - Notifiable diseases can be disclosed.
   - Sexual diseases: may be disclosed to doctor to prevent spread.
   - Abortions must be notified to Department of Health or police if there is an offence under the Abortion Act 1967.

- Patient records may be disclosed under the Health Act 1999 for certain purposes.
- If a patient is suspected of being the driver involved in a road accident.
- When police investigating serious offences, can obtain medical records with a court order.
- If treating a patient for use of illegal drugs.

5   *Access to medical records*
- Main provision of the Data Protection Act 1998: patient has right to copy of medical records.

6   *Human Rights Act 1998*
- Most relevant provision is Art 8, right to respect for private life.

CHAPTER 6

INFERTILITY

INTRODUCTION

'Infertility' means that a person is unable to have children. This can have a profound effect on both men and women and it is not an uncommon problem – estimates say that one in 10 couples are infertile. Originally, nothing could be done about infertility but medical advances have brought *in vitro* fertilisation (IVF) treatment and the possibility of using surrogate mothers (substitute mothers). The term *'in vitro'* simply means 'in glass', and refers to activities carried out in glass dishes or flasks, hence the phrase 'test tube baby'. The first 'test tube baby', Louise Brown, was born in Britain in 1978. Although this was seen by some as a great breakthrough, many others were against such developments and saw them as interfering with nature. A committee was set up in 1982 under Mary Warnock, 'To consider recent and potential developments in medicine and science related to human fertilisation and embryology; to consider what policies and safeguards should be applied, including consideration of the social, ethical and legal implications of these developments; and to make recommendations'. The committee produced the Warnock Report (*Report of the Committee of Inquiry Into Human Fertilisation and Embryology*, Cmnd 9314, 1984) which recommended that reproductive services should be regulated. The Report was followed by the Human Fertilisation and Embryology Act (HFEA) 1990, which set up a legal framework for infertility treatment and a system of licensing for providers of that treatment. Although there are now approximately 8,000 babies born each year in the UK through IVF treatment (*HFEA 12th Annual Report, 2002–2003*, p 2), the law has struggled to keep up with medical developments and the debate on infertility has raised many novel ethical and legal questions. What is the legal status of the embryo? Do people have a right to have children? Do single sex couples have a right to have children? What age limit should be put on women having infertility treatment? Do couples have a right to choose the sex of their baby? What rights do children born as a result of such treatment have? Do children born through IVF following sperm donation have a right to know the father? Who are the legal parents? The Human Rights Act 1998 also has a significant effect in this area, particularly Arts 12 (the right to marry and have a family) and 8 (the right to respect for private and family life).

THE HFEA 1990 SCHEME – OUTLINE

Section 5 of the HFEA 1990 provided for the creation of the Human Fertilisation and Embryology Authority to license clinics for the purpose of treatment under the 1990 Act, to supervise the services they provide, to license storage of material and to supervise research. As regards the provision of infertility services, activities may be divided into:

- those which are a criminal offence unless carried out under a licence, such as creating an embryo outside the body;
- those which are not covered by the Act and are perfectly legal, such as artificial insemination by the husband; and
- those which are criminal offences and cannot be licensed, for example, cloning.

Section 1 defines what is meant by embryo: 's 1(1)(a) embryo means a live human embryo where fertilisation is complete ... s 1(2) of this Act, so far as it governs bringing about the creation of an embryo, applies only to bringing about the creation of an embryo outside the human body.' With the development of cell nuclear replacement (CNR), the question arose whether this came within s 1(1)(a) of the HFEA 1990. With CNR, the nucleus from a cell is transplanted into an egg, from which the nucleus has been removed. This then develops into an embryo without the need for fertilisation. This question fell to be decided in *R (on the Application of Quintavalle) v Secretary of State for Health* (2003). It was argued that 'fertilisation' in s 1(1)(a) meant the Act applied to embryos created by fertilisation, not CNR. The High Court had decided that this procedure was outside the HFEA 1990 but the Court of Appeal reversed this decision. The House of Lords said that the purpose of the Act was to protect live human embryos. Taking a purposive approach to interpretation of the HFEA 1990, it applied to embryos whether created by fertilisation or by CNR. The process was within the Act. Parliament could not have intended to distinguish between embryos produced by fertilisation and by CNR because the latter was only a possibility at the time the Act was passed. The appeal was dismissed.

Section 3 prohibits the creation, keeping or using of an embryo outside the body without a licence. Section 3(3) prohibits placing an embryo in an animal, or replacing the nucleus of a cell of an embryo with another nucleus from a person or embryo (cloning). Section 4 prohibits the storage and use of any gametes without a licence (a gamete is a reproductive cell, the male cell is sperm and the female an ova). Breach of s 4 is a criminal offence. In summary, if the treatment involves creating an embryo outside the body or the use of stored material, the Act applies. Control over what is done with donated sperm or eggs is given to the owners, because the 1990 Act requires the consent of the owner for any use of the gametes.

Schedule 3: consents to use of gametes or embryos

Under para 1 of Sched 3 to the 1990 Act, consent must be in writing and, to be effective, it must not have been withdrawn. The issue of consent arose in *Mrs U v Centre for Reproductive Medicine* (2002). Mrs U married in 1993 but her husband had had a vasectomy in 1978. They opted for surgical retrieval of Mr U's sperm for use in IVF treatment. Under s 4 (1)(a), no one shall store gametes except with a licence and breach is a criminal offence. Under s 11, although the Human Fertilisation and Embryology Authority can grant licences for storage of gametes and embryos, the provisions of Sched 3 concerning consent must be met. The day before treatment, Mr U signed the consent form, which provided that sperm would only be used during his lifetime but he also marked 'no' in the box for allowing the sperm to perish. The sperm was then retrieved and stored. Some time after this, the couple attended a meeting about treatment at the clinic. Mr U was asked by the nurse to change his form to comply with the centre's policy of not allowing posthumous use. Mr U changed the form to allow the sperm to perish on death. The first course of treatment failed and Mr U then died unexpectedly. The clinic sought a court ruling on whether the sperm could be allowed to perish or be destroyed. The Court of Appeal said that in order to continue storing the sperm, the clinic needed consent to comply with Sched 3. Mrs U claimed undue influence but the court said that although Mr U was put under pressure to change his mind, he could have asked for more time and the pressure did not amount to undue influence. Therefore, there was no effective consent and continued storage or use was unlawful.

In *Evans v Amicus Healthcare Ltd and Others* (2004), the Court of Appeal dealt with a claim by Natalie Evans who wished to use a frozen embryo created with her former partner. Her partner had withdrawn his consent to use it when the relationship ended. The court said it had no power to override the withdrawal of consent.

Paragraph 2(1) provides that consent to the use of any embryo must specify one or more of the following: (a) use for treatment services to the person giving consent or that person with another specified person together; (b) use for treatment to other persons; or (c) use for research. The consent must also state both the maximum period of storage (the maximum allowed under the 1990 Act is 10 years (s 14(3))) and what is to be done with the gametes or embryo if the person giving consent dies or is incapacitated and cannot alter the consent.

Paragraph 3 provides that before someone gives consent, they must be given relevant information and the opportunity for proper counselling. Paragraph 4 allows consent to be withdrawn by notice by the person who gave the consent. But consent cannot be withdrawn after the embryo has been used. Paragraph 5 provides that a person's gametes must not be used for treatment services unless there is an effective consent and they are used in accordance with that consent. Paragraph 6(1) provides that gametes must not be used for the creation of an embryo *in vitro* unless there is an effective consent. Paragraph 6(3) provides that an embryo created *in vitro* must not be used unless there is effective consent by each person whose gametes were used to create the embryo. Paragraph 8 provides that a person's gametes must not be stored unless there is consent for that purpose.

ARTIFICIAL INSEMINATION

If the man is infertile (that is, unable to produce sperm), this problem may be overcome by use of artificial insemination by donor (AID). This method involves semen from the donor being injected into the woman. If the man is impotent (that is, unable to have normal sexual intercourse), his sperm may be injected into his wife artificially, known as artificial insemination by husband (AIH).

(a) By husband (or partner)

This method may or may not involve the help of a doctor. Using this method is not regarded as consummation of the marriage, which may therefore be annulled. If the marriage is annulled, any child born as a result of AIH would be regarded as legitimate, because the parents were married at the time of conception.

One particular problem arises from the practice of 'sperm banking', where sperm may be frozen for future use. This may be used if the husband is going to have a vasectomy or is about to undergo chemotherapy, which could damage his sperm. If the husband dies, the question arises of who then owns the sperm. Originally, s 28(6)(b) of the HFEA 1990 provided that, where sperm was used after a man's death, the man was not to be treated as the father of the child. This stopped the child from making any claim against the dead man's estate. However, it is not illegal to use sperm from a dead man. Following the case of Diane Blood, the law was changed (see below).

(b) By donor

This involves the woman being impregnated with sperm from another man, as her partner is infertile. The introduction of a third party raises the question of their legal status in the arrangements. Although the law could not control any private arrangements of this nature, it does control public arrangements, that is, where services are provided to the public. Control of donors is important because of the possibility of passing on genetic defects or disease. A licence is needed under the HFEA 1990 to provide AID services. A man's sperm may only be used if there is an effective consent to that use.

Problems and developments

A number of problems have arisen under the HFEA 1990, as seen in the case of *R v Human Fertilisation and Embryology Authority ex p Blood* (1997). Mr and Mrs Blood wanted to start a family but, before Mrs Blood could become pregnant, Mr Blood caught meningitis and went into a coma. Sperm was taken from Mr Blood and stored and, shortly after this, he died. Mrs Blood then wanted to use the sperm to have a baby, but the Human Fertilisation and Embryology Authority refused to allow this because, under s 4(1)(a) of the 1990 Act, there was no licence to store the sperm and, under Sched 3, Mr Blood had not consented in writing to the use of his sperm. Mrs Blood's claim for judicial review failed. She then appealed, claiming that:

- under s 4(1)(b) of the 1990 Act, treatment was allowed without written consent for 'the woman and the man together'; and

- the Authority's refusal to allow export of the sperm for treatment abroad was a breach of European Union law, which allowed citizens to have medical treatment in any Member State.

The Court of Appeal held that, under s 4(1)(b), treatment could not be regarded as being provided for a woman and man together once the man who had provided the sperm had died. In any case, the exception to written consent only applied if the sperm was used immediately and did not need to be stored, so s 4(1)(b) did not apply. Without a written consent from the husband, the applicant's treatment and storage of the sperm were prohibited under the 1990 Act. However, under the EC Treaty, the applicant had a right to receive medical treatment in another Member State and refusing export of the sperm made fertilisation treatment impossible. The court said that the Human Fertilisation and Embryology Authority had failed to take into account the fact that there was unlikely to be any similar cases in the future and the appeal was allowed. The Authority then allowed Mrs Blood to take the sperm abroad.

As regards the legal position of the child born as a result of AID, s 28(2) of the HFEA 1990 provides that if the parties are married and the embryo was not created with the sperm of the other party to the marriage, that other party shall be treated as the father of the child, unless he did not consent to the insemination. This makes the husband the legal father of the child. Under s 28(3), if the couple are unmarried and treatment services are provided by a licensed clinic 'for her and a man together', and the embryo was not created with sperm from her partner, her partner will be treated as the father of the child. The interpretation of s 28(2) fell to be considered in the unusual case of *The Leeds Teaching Hospitals NHS Trust v Mr and Mrs A and Others* (2003). Mr and Mrs A, and Mr and Mrs B were having fertility treatment at the same clinic. Mr and Mrs A were white and Mr and Mrs B were black. Due to a mistake, Mrs A's eggs were fertilised with Mr B's sperm and Mrs A had black twins. The main question was who was the legal father of the twins? Under s 28(2), if the parties are married and the embryo was not created with the sperm of the other party, that other party shall be treated as the father unless he did not consent to the insemination. Under s 28(3), if no man is treated as the father under s 28(2), but in the course of treatment together the embryo was not created by the sperm of that man, that man is treated as the father of the child. Mr A argued that he was the father under s 28(2) or alternatively under s 28(3). The court said that the common law presumption was that a child born to a mother during marriage was legitimate. Under s 28(5), this applied to s 28(2) and 28(3). But on the facts of this case, this presumption was rebutted by tests that showed that Mr B was the biological father of the twins. As regards consent under s 28(2), Mr A had consented to his sperm being mixed with Mrs A's eggs but not to donated sperm being mixed. Because of the mistake which was made he could not be regarded as consenting and could not be presumed to be the father under s 28(2). Mr B was the legal father of the twins. The court's interpretation of s 28 infringed Mr and Mrs A's right to private life under Art 8, but this interference was necessary to protect the rights of others, here the twins, and anyway could be remedied by adoption.

The effect of s 28(3) was considered in *U v W (Attorney General Intervening)* (1997). Miss U and Mr W lived together for four years in an 'on-off' relationship. Miss U wanted a child and, because Mr W's sperm was weak, they went to a special clinic in Rome for fertility treatment. They agreed to use donor sperm and signed a form accepting maternity and paternity of the unborn child. Mr W then returned to the UK and Miss U had the treatment. Later, Miss U had twins and claimed that Mr W was the father. The court considered whether s 28(3) of the 1990 Act applied to Mr W. It was argued for Miss U that the requirement for a licence under the 1990 Act was a restriction on the right to medical treatment under Art 59 of the EC Treaty (now Art 49 since the re-numbering of the Treaty, brought about by the Treaty of Amsterdam). It was held that the licensing system did not infringe Art 59 and, although the couple had been treated together, the doctor was not licensed. Therefore, s 28(3) did not apply and Mr W was not the father. The courts have further considered what treatment 'together' means in *Re R (Parental Responsibility: IVF Baby)* (2003). The man was infertile and both he and his partner signed a consent for IVF treatment. The man agreed that although his sperm would not be used, they were being treated together and he would be the father of any resulting child. The first embryo placement did not work. The woman returned for a second attempt, without telling the clinic that they had separated. This treatment resulted in the birth of a child. The man was granted a declaration of paternity and the court said that under s 28(3) the embryo had been placed in the mother 'in the course of treatment services provided for her and the man together'. The Court of Appeal said that the important point in time when the services were provided was the point when the embryo was placed in the mother. At that point, the couple were separated and the treatment could not be regarded as being provided for the woman and man together. If the circumstances of the couple changed dramatically, then new counselling should be offered before a new attempt was made. It would be easy for clinics to check the relationship between the man and woman at that time.

Section 28(4) provides that 'Where a person is treated as the father of the child by virtue of sub-section (2) or (3) above, no other person is to be treated as the father of the child'. This means that the sperm donor cannot be treated as the father if there is already deemed to be a father.

Section 28(6) originally provided that (a) where the sperm of a man was used for a purpose for which consent was required and was given; or (b) sperm was used after his death, he was not to be treated as the father of the child. This meant that, under s 28(6)(a), a sperm donor was not the legal father, as long as the sperm was used in accordance with his consent. Under s 28(6)(b), the man was not treated as the legal father and consequently the child would not have a claim against the dead man's estate.

Following the *Blood* case, the High Court ruled in March 2003 that the restriction in s 28(6)(b) was incompatible with Art 8 of the European Convention on Human Rights. The McClean Report, *Review of the Common Law Provisions Relating to the Removal of Gametes and of the Consent Provisions of the Human Fertilisation and Embryology Act 1990*, in 1998 recommended that where children were born after the death of their father, they should be able to put their father's name on the birth certificate. The Human Fertilisation and Embryology (Deceased Fathers) Act 2003 received the Royal Assent on 18 September 2003. The Act came into force on 1 December 2003.

The HFE(DF)A 2003 provides for certain deceased men to be registered as fathers. Section 1(1) inserts an addition (5A) to s 28(5) of the HFEA 1990, stating that a deceased man may be registered as a father if:

(a) a woman has a child as a result of placing in her an embryo or sperm and eggs or artificial insemination;

(b) the embryo was created using the sperm of a man after his death, or the embryo was created before his death but placed in the woman after his death;

(c) the woman was married to the man immediately before his death;

(d) the man consented in writing, and did not withdraw his consent, to the use of his sperm after his death and to being treated as father of the child for the purposes of registration as father under s 5I;

(e) the woman has agreed in writing not later than 42 days from the day the child was born for the man to be treated as father; and

(f) no one else is to be treated as the father under s 28(2) or (3) or by adoption, then the man shall be treated as the father of the child for the purpose in s 5I (that is, registration).

Section 5B deals with the position where the woman is not married to the man but treatment services were being provided 'for the woman and man together before his death' by a person with a licence (s 5B(c)). If the relevant above provisions are met (a, b, d, e and f), then the man shall be treated as the father of the child.

Section 5C deals with the position where the man and woman were married when the embryo was created but the sperm was not from the other party to the marriage (that is, donor sperm was used). If the above relevant provisions are met (a, c, d, e and f), then the other party to the marriage shall be treated as the father of the child.

Section 5D deals with the situation where the woman was not married but treatment services were being provided for the woman and man together, but the embryo was not created using the sperm of that man. If the above relevant provisions are met (a, d, e and f), then the man shall be treated as the father of the child.

The new sections, 5F and 5G, provide that an election after 42 days may be treated as valid with the consent of the Registrar General if the applicant can show a 'compelling reason'.

Section 1(2) inserts the following after s 29(3) of the HFEA 1990: 3B provides that where ss 5A, 5B, 5C and 5D apply, the deceased man (a) is to be treated in law as the father of the child for the purpose in that section, but (b) is to be treated in law as not being the father for any other purpose.

Section 3 makes provision for existing cases. It provides that the Act applies to cases where sperm was used after 1 August 1991 and a child was born before s 1 of the Act came into force (1 December 2003). The woman may agree in writing, within six months of this section coming into force, that the other party to the marriage or her partner should be treated as the father of the child.

The issue of withdrawal of consent arose in two cases which were heard together by the High Court. In *Evans v Amicus Healthcare Ltd; Hadley v Midland Fertility Services Ltd* (2003), the two claimant women had IVF treatment with their male partners. The male partners had signed consent forms agreeing to the treatment. Following treatment, embryos were created and stored. Later, the couples separated and the male partners withdrew their consents to the use of the embryos. The two women wanted a declaration that it would be lawful to treat them using the embryos. Under Sched 3, para 6(3) of the HFEA 1990, an embryo could not be used unless there was a consent by each person whose gametes had been used to create it, and that consent must not have been withdrawn. A number of questions arose for decision. Could the two women be given treatment on their own? There was also an argument based on promissory estoppel, as the second claimant argued that her partner was estopped from going back on his original promise. There were also questions whether there was a breach of Arts 2 and 8 of the European Convention on Human Rights (see below, 'The Human Rights Act 1998'). The court held that the consents had been given originally for 'treatment together'. The time of treatment would be when the embryos were transferred. As the couples had now separated, they were not being treated together. There was no consent by the male partners for the women to be treated on their own; *Re R (A Child)* (2003) applied. As regards estoppel, the requirements for consent to treatment provided by the HFEA 1990 envisaged that people may wish to change their minds if circumstances changed, and the HFEA 1990 provided for withdrawal of treatment. Given that it was not possible to succeed on the basis of estoppel, the claims were dismissed. Natalie Evans appealed to the Court of Appeal. In *Evans v Amicus Healthcare and Others* (2004), the court dismissed the appeal stating that her partner was entitled to withdraw his consent and that future treatment of Natalie Evans would not be 'treatment together' as they had separated. The statutory scheme required bilateral consent.

If a single woman requests AID, there are no legal rules to apply and the decision will have to be made on ethical grounds.

INFERTILE WOMEN

A woman may be infertile because of problems in producing ova (eggs) or because of anatomical problems, such as blocked fallopian tubes. The development of IVF means that the ovum may be fertilised in the laboratory and the embryo may then be transferred to the woman's uterus. If the couple are married and the wife's ovum is fertilised with her husband's sperm, the status of the mother, father and child are the same as with a natural birth.

In vitro fertilisation

This process involves taking eggs from the woman, fertilising them with the husband's sperm in the laboratory and then inserting them into the woman's uterus. The first child born in this way was Louise Brown, in 1978. The legal consequences as regards the status of the parties are the same as with AIH, above. The process needs a high level of medical skill and care and it is argued by some that it wastes resources, as the success rate is quite low. The process also requires the transfer of a number of eggs to be successful and sometimes the result is a multiple pregnancy. This in turn may result in the babies dying or the mother being at risk of complications, or the mother ending up with several babies to look after.

Ovum donation

If a woman is unable to produce fertile ova, this problem may be overcome by the donation of an ovum by another woman. The donated ovum is fertilised using the husband's (or partner's) sperm and the resultant embryo is then placed in the wife's womb. Under s 27(1) of the 1990 Act, the woman who carries a child as a result of the placing in her of an embryo or sperm and eggs, and no other woman, is to be treated as the mother of the child.

Embryo donation

If both the woman and her husband are infertile, it is possible for donated sperm and ovum to be used to create an embryo *in vitro*. The embryo may then be implanted in the woman. The child born as a result of this procedure is not genetically related to the husband and wife. Legally, the husband will be the father (s 28) and the wife will be the mother, under s 27.

Gamete intra fallopian transfer

Gamete intra fallopian transfer (or GIFT) involves taking eggs from an infertile woman and sperm from her husband (or partner). These are mixed together and inserted in the fallopian tubes of the woman to allow fertilisation to take place inside the body. Therefore, under s 1(2) of the 1990

Act, the Act does not apply, as the embryo is not created outside the body. If either the sperm or eggs were donated, then the Act would apply.

PRE-IMPLANTATION GENETIC DIAGNOSIS

The technique of pre-implantation genetic diagnosis enables an embryo to be tested for a genetic disease and, if one is found, the embryo is not used. The Human Fertilisation and Embryology Authority licences treatment on this basis. The development of such techniques has raised the spectre of test tube babies produced to be used for helping others. In August 2000, the first such case occurred in America. Adam Nash was born after tissue matching of an embryo, in order to save the life of his sister Molly. Blood containing stem cells was taken from his umbilical cord to be used in treating Molly's condition, fanconi anaemia. A similar situation recently arose in the UK. In *R (Quintavalle) v HFE Authority* (2003), Mr and Mrs H's fourth son was born with a life-threatening blood disorder (beta thalassaemia major). The couple wished to have another child who was free of that disease but with a tissue type to match their sick son. Stem cells could be taken from the new baby to treat the sick son. Mrs H wished to have IVF treatment using an embryo with a tissue type that matched her sick son. The Human Fertilisation and Embryology Authority agreed to grant a licence for IVF treatment which included pre-implantation genetic diagnosis and tissue typing. This decision was challenged by Quintavalle acting on behalf of a group called CORE (Comment on Reproductive Ethics) on the basis that the HFE Authority had no power to issue a licence for tissue typing to select between healthy embryos. The applicant sought judicial review. The High Court said that the Authority had acted *ultra vires* and quashed their decision. The Court of Appeal considered whether the treatment was covered by the term 'treatment services' within s 2(1) of the HFEA 1990, which provides that it means medical, surgical or obstetric services provided for the purpose of assisting women to carry children. The court said that whether the treatment was to produce a child without genetic defects or with stem cells to match a sick sibling, it was still treatment to assist women to have children. Whether it was the first or the second, the purpose was to make sure that the embryos were in a suitable condition for placing in the womb. The HFEA 1990 allowed licensing for embryo research to detect genetic abnormalities in embryos and it would be strange if the Act was interpreted to prevent the use of embryos free from abnormalities. The appeal was allowed.

This decision leaves open how far the Human Fertilisation and Embryology Authority will now go in licensing treatment. Some are concerned that this enables licences for screening for purely social purposes.

The technique of pre-implantation genetic diagnosis also enables embryos of a particular sex to be selected. The Authority does not allow selection on the basis of sex. It conducted a review on whether to allow clinics to provide such a service, including an opinion poll, but 80% were against it (*Sex Selection: Choice and Responsibility in Human Reproduction*, 2003, Human Fertilisation and Embryology Authority). The Authority has recommended to the government that clinics should not be allowed to provide sex selection of embryos for non-medical reasons.

AVAILABILITY OF INFERTILITY TREATMENT

Should infertility treatment be available for everyone who wants it? If the answer to this question is no, then who should be eligible for treatment? The first restriction is that most types of treatment for infertility are expensive. Additionally, the success rates are not high; for example, only 15% of IVF treatments are successful. Another factor is the age of the woman. The older the woman, the greater the risks in pregnancy and the lower the chances of successfully giving birth to a child. In *R v Sheffield HA ex p Seale* (1994), Seale was a 37 year old woman who wanted IVF treatment but was turned down by the defendant health authority because of their policy of not providing the treatment for women over 35 years of age. The claimant argued that choosing 35 years as the cut off point was irrational. It was held that this policy was not unreasonable, given the finite resources of the defendants. The policy of the defendant health authority was based on the fact that treatment was less likely to be successful in women over 35 years old and it had to balance demand for infertility treatment against other demands for its services.

Another consideration is provided in s 13(5) of the 1990 Act:

> A woman shall not be provided with treatment services unless account has been taken of the welfare of any child who may be born as a result of the treatment (including the need of that child for a father), and of any other child who may be affected by the birth.

This provision attempts to make the welfare of any child born an important factor in deciding whether someone should be provided with treatment. Kennedy and Grubb point out (*Medical Law, Text with Materials*, 3rd edn, 2000, London: Butterworths) that 'If there is an option to bring about the birth of a child, it can never (or almost never) be in its welfare or interests not to be born. Existence for the child is preferable to non-existence'. They argue that the section is about the suitability of the parents. Gillian Douglas informs us that when the 1990 Act was passing through Parliament, unsuccessful attempts were made to limit treatment to heterosexual couples and s 13(5) was inserted to prevent the creation of single parent families. In a case before the 1990 Act, a claim for judicial review was brought after someone was refused IVF treatment. The applicant was refused treatment after it was discovered that she had a criminal record, including conviction for prostitution. The court held that the criteria applied by the hospital (those used for assessing suitability for adoption) were suitable and that she had had the opportunity to appeal to the hospital against the refusal; therefore, her claim failed (*R v St Mary's Hospital Ethical Committee ex p Harriott* (1998)).

The Human Fertilisation and Embryology Authority has produced a *Code of Practice* (6th edn, 2004) which provides guidance on assessing the welfare of the child. Paragraph 3.14 provides:

Where the child will have no legal father the treatment centre is expected to assess the prospective mother's ability to meet the child's/children's needs and the ability of other persons within the family or social circle willing to share responsibility for those needs.

Many argue that single parents and same sex couples should not be refused treatment. The case of Barrie Drewitt and Tony Barlow in 1999 is examined below, p 127.

ANONYMITY OF THE DONOR

There seems to be a deep-seated psychological desire for people to know their origins, as evidenced by adopted children trying to trace their natural parents. An adopted child has the legal right to trace their natural parents on reaching 18 years old (s 51 of the Adoption Act 1976). Should a child have the right to know who their genetic parents are? It has been argued in the past that the identity of donors should be kept secret because, if they were to be made liable for the child who is born, there would be a shortage of sperm donors. How has the law dealt with this conflict? Under s 28(6)(a) of the 1990 Act, where the sperm of a man is used in accordance with the consent he has given, he is not to be treated as the father of the child. The Act makes certain provisions about the anonymity of the donor. Section 31(2) requires the Human Fertilisation and Embryology Authority to keep a register of anyone who provides gametes or who receives treatment services, or anyone who is born as a result of such services.

Under s 31(3), if the applicant has reached the age of 18, they may ask the Authority to comply with a request under sub-s (4) and the Authority shall do so if the register shows that the applicant was, or may have been, born as a consequence of treatment services, and the applicant has been given the opportunity to have proper counselling about the effect of the Authority meeting their request.

Under s 31(4), the applicant may ask the Authority to give information about whether the register shows that someone other than a parent of the applicant would or might be a parent of the applicant but for ss 27–29. (Section 27 provides who shall be the mother, s 28 provides who shall be the father and s 29 provides that those so treated are to be the legal mother and father for all purposes.) If the information shows that the applicant might have been born as a result of donated sperm or eggs, the applicant must be told that fact. The applicant cannot be told the name of the donor. The Warnock Committee (1984) recommended that information about the donor should not be given. Similarly, the applicant must be told whether someone named, whom they intend to marry, is genetically related to the applicant. Under s 31(5), regulations cannot make the Authority give information about identity prior to those regulations coming into force. See the 2004 Regulations below. Under s 35, disclosure may be made for the purpose of bringing proceedings under s 1 of the Congenital Disabilities (Civil Liability) Act 1976. A child born disabled as a result of something done in the course of selection, keeping or use outside the body of the embryo or gametes used to form the embryo may sue.

There has been an ongoing debate over whether sperm donors should or should not be anonymous. Jonathan Glover examines the arguments both for and against in the Glover Report, *Fertility and the Family* (1989). 'Some adopted children find they come to care very much who their biological parents are, and may go to great lengths to find out. Our sense of who we are is bound up with the story we tell about ourselves. A life where the biological parents are unknown is like a novel with the first chapter missing.' Glover points out that some sperm donors did not want to be identified in case they had to pay child maintenance or the child wanted contact with them. However, on the other hand, from the child's point of view, knowledge of their origin was important: '... it can be better for a child to be born without the right to know the biological father than for the child not to be born at all. But if the donor programmes can be kept up, best of all might be to be born with the right to know.' In 2002, Baroness Warnock said that it was time to remove anonymity from donors. The courts have also contributed to the debate. In *Rose v Secretary of State for Health and Human Fertilisation and Embryology Authority* (2002), the two claimants had been born by artificial insemination by an anonymous donor. They wanted the Secretary of State to provide non-identifying information about the donors, or a contact register or identifying information about the donors. The court said that Art 8 (right to respect for private and family life) had been interpreted by the European Court of Human Rights to include the right to establish details of his or her identity and the right to obtain information about a biological parent. The court granted a declaration that the HFEA 1990 was incompatible with Art 8. A consultation exercise was carried out by the Department of Health in 2001–02 on providing information about sperm, egg and embryo donors. Points in favour of providing donor information included that it was a basic human right of the child to know their origin, that society should not keep such information secret and that more openness is needed to remove the stigma that still attaches to this method of conception. The arguments against giving donor information included reducing the number and choice of donors, reducing the impact on the social family by having a third party who could be contacted (the donor) and a possible move to unregulated treatment.

In January 2004, the Minister for Public Health announced that the government was going to remove anonymity for those donating sperm, eggs or embryos in the future. The Human Fertilisation and Embryology Authority (Disclosure of Donor Information) Regulations 2004, which came into force on 1 July 2004, provide for the Human Fertilisation and Embryology Authority to provide information to someone over 18 years who may have been born as a result of treatment services provided under the HFEA 1990. The information may be about sperm, eggs or embryos. However, the donor will not be legally or financially responsible for the child. The regulations will not be retrospective and anyone donating before April 2005 will remain anonymous. The chairman of the Human Fertilisation and Embryology Authority, Suzi Leather, said of the proposals: 'Although it is right to respect the guarantees of anonymity that have been given to donors in the past, it also seems to me wrong that the state has information about someone's origin which they want and cannot have. Secrecy on adoption has been discredited and secrecy in assisted reproduction will come to be too.' When the law is changed, it is likely that the number of donors will go down. However, the Glover Report explains the experience in Sweden that the decline is temporary:

> The effect of abolishing anonymity in Sweden seems to have been an initial decline in numbers of donors. This may suggest that many donors prefer to be anonymous, quite apart from the fear of paternity suits. But this must be linked to two other effects of the new law. There was a decline in demand: couples felt less comfortable at the thought that the child might eventually wish to contact the donor. And physicians in some AID centres refused to continue offering AID under the new law. In the centres still continuing with AID, the number of donors have returned to normal, although they are now more often older and more often married ...

SURROGACY

The word 'surrogate' means 'substitute' and a surrogate mother is someone who has a child for another woman. Surrogacy was defined in the Warnock Report: 'Surrogacy is the practice whereby one woman carries a child for another with the intention that the child should be handed over after birth.' It went on to say, 'The use of artificial insemination and the recent development of *in vitro* fertilisation have eliminated the necessity for sexual intercourse in order to establish a surrogate pregnancy' (Warnock: para 8.1).

The basic idea of surrogacy is that one woman (the surrogate) has a baby for a husband and wife (or partners), where the wife is infertile. The surrogate is artificially inseminated with the husband's sperm. When the baby is born, the surrogate mother gives it to the husband and wife (the commissioning parents). In this case, the child is genetically half related to the husband and wife but there is also a genetic relationship with the surrogate mother, and this is known as a *partial surrogacy*.

Another possibility is that an embryo is created *in vitro*, using the sperm and egg from the husband and wife, and then the embryo is placed in the surrogate mother. When the child is born, it is given to the husband and wife. Here, the child is genetically related to the husband and wife in the same way as a natural birth. The surrogate mother has no genetic relationship with the child. This is known as a *complete surrogacy*. There are many other combinations; for example, the commissioning mother may provide the egg or the sperm may be provided by an anonymous donor.

The practice of surrogacy has raised many ethical and legal problems. The Warnock Report (*Report of the Committee of Inquiry Into Human Fertilisation and Embryology*, Cm 9314, 1984) made a number of points about surrogacy: that introducing a third party into the process of procreation was an attack on marriage; the intrusion involved was worse than AID, because the carrying mother made a greater contribution than the sperm donor; a woman should not use her uterus for financial profit (para 8.10). Also, the practice distorts the relationship between the mother and child, because the carrying mother becomes pregnant with the intention of giving away the child; it damages the child, who will have a strong bond with the carrying mother; a surrogacy agreement is degrading for the child, as effectively the child is bought for money (para 8.11). The possibility of surrogacy for convenience, where the commissioning mother does not want to go through pregnancy, is ethically unacceptable and is simply treating someone as a means to an end (para 8.17).

The Warnock Report concluded that the main worry was the commercial exploitation of surrogacy, and it recommended:

... that legislation be introduced to render criminal the creation or the operation in the United Kingdom of agencies whose purposes include the recruitment of women for surrogate pregnancy or making arrangements for individuals or couples who wish to use the services of a carrying mother. [para 8.18]

The Report also said: 'We recommend that it be provided by statute that all surrogacy agreements are illegal contracts and therefore unenforceable in the courts' (para 8.19). However, the Report did not want to make private surrogacy arrangements illegal. It pointed out that, from a deontological (duty) viewpoint, the practice of surrogacy was using the surrogate mother as a means to an end. The Report (para 8.17) also condemned the practice from a utilitarian viewpoint: 'Even in compelling medical circumstances the danger of exploitation of one human being by another appears to the majority of us far to outweigh the potential benefits, in almost every case.'

Arguments for and against surrogacy

For surrogacy:

- It helps childless couples.
- It encourages altruism, for example, having a child for a friend.
- Women should be allowed to do what they want with their own bodies (autonomy).
- It gives life to a child.
- Women have a right to make a surrogacy arrangement if they wish.
- Separating mother and child is practised in adoption.

Against surrogacy:

- It is an unnatural practice.
- It may be seen as selling babies.
- It may be used for convenience, for example, a woman who does not want the 'bother' of pregnancy.
- It splits up the mother and baby.
- Women should not sell their bodies for money.
- Risks of pregnancy to the surrogate mother.
- Harm caused if the surrogate mother keeps the child.
- A child has a right to be brought up by his own parents.
- It exploits women.
- It brings a third party into the relationship between two people.
- The carrying mother has a more intimate role than the semen donor does.
- The purpose of the agreement is to give the child away to the commissioning couple.
- People should not be treated as a means to an end.

The *Brazier Report* (1998) also examined the above arguments and identified the main concerns as: (a) the welfare of the child; (b) should the law protect the surrogate mother, her family and the commissioning couple; and (c) whether payment to the surrogate mother is acceptable.

The legal position

The practice of surrogacy raises many legal questions. What is the role of the law in relation to surrogacy? What is the legal status of surrogacy agreements? Should payments be allowed to the surrogate mother? How should the law deal with disputes over the child who is born? As regards the role of the law, the Warnock Report (1984) argued that private surrogacy arrangements should not be subject to legal control and, clearly, it would be impossible for the law to control such activity. But the Report was also keen to stop the commercial development of surrogacy.

The first case involving surrogacy was heard in 1978, although it did not appear in the law reports until some years later. In *A v C* (1985), Mr A and his partner, who could not have any more children, made an agreement with C that C would have a child using Mr A's sperm in return for £3,000. C refused to give up the baby. It was held at first instance that the agreement was unenforceable but Mr A could have access to the child. The judge said: 'The agreement between the parties I hold as being against public policy. None of them can rely upon it in any way or enforce the agreement in any way. I need only give one of many grounds for saying this, namely that this was a purported contract for the sale and purchase of a child' (Comyn J). On appeal by C, the Court of Appeal described it as 'a bizarre and unnatural arrangement' and said that A should not have access to the child. In the later case of *Re C (A Minor) (Wardship: Surrogacy)* (1985), an American couple wanted a child and, as the woman was unable to bear children, they sought a surrogate mother through an agency. Kim Cotton, a mother in the UK, agreed to have a baby through artificial insemination with the commissioning father's sperm. The local council obtained a place of safety order for the child and the genetic father started wardship proceedings to obtain the child. The court considered that Kim Cotton had given up all rights to the baby and said that 'the moral, ethical and social considerations are for others and not for this court in its wardship jurisdiction'. The court focused on what was in the best interests of the child and said that the couple should look after it.

At the time that these cases were heard, the courts were clearly against the idea of surrogacy arrangements and their views reflected the public view. The government's response was to pass the Surrogacy Arrangements Act 1985. The aim of the Act is to prevent agencies from making money from surrogacy arrangements. Under s 2(1), it is a criminal offence to do any of the following on a commercial basis: (a) initiate or take part in negotiations with a view to making a surrogacy arrangement; (b) offer or agree to negotiate the making of a surrogacy arrangement; or (c) collect information to use in making or negotiating a surrogacy arrangement. It is also an offence to cause another person to do any of these acts.

However, it is not an offence for anyone who wishes to be a surrogate mother to do the above acts (s 2(2)) or receive payment (s 2(3)). Similarly, someone wishing to be a commissioning parent does not commit an offence in these circumstances and may make payments to the surrogate mother. But one effect of s 2 is that doctors and lawyers could not be paid for any help or advice they would give in such matters, which falls within s 2(1), for example, a lawyer who draws up a surrogacy agreement. However, a doctor providing medical help, such as IVF treatment, will not commit an offence.

The British Medical Association in their guidance on surrogacy, *Considering Surrogacy? Your Questions Answered*, states:

> Because surrogacy involves another person taking on the risks of pregnancy, it is only acceptable as a last resort, where it is impossible or very dangerous for the intended mother to carry a child herself. Sometimes people speculate about women taking part in surrogacy arrangements, although capable of bearing children themselves, because they wish to avoid the physical, social, psychological or financial drawbacks of bearing a child themselves. There is no evidence to suggest that this happens in Britain and it would not be seen as an acceptable use of a surrogacy arrangement.

However, the surrogate and the commissioning couple have to be careful that they do not commit an offence under the Adoption Act 1976, which provides that it is an offence to give or receive a payment for the adoption of a child unless it is approved by a court.

Section 3(1) provides that any advertisement (a) that someone is willing to make a surrogacy arrangement or negotiate such an arrangement; or (b) that anyone is looking for a woman to be a surrogate mother or for persons wanting a woman to be a surrogate, where the newspaper is published in the UK, the proprietor, editor or publisher is guilty of an offence (s 3(2)). Under s 3(2) it is the proprietor, editor or publisher of the newspaper containing the advertisement who is guilty of an offence. The section also makes it an offence to advertise through the means of a 'telecommunications system' (that is, radio and television (s 3(3))). The position of the person placing the advertisement is unclear.

The Surrogacy Arrangements Act 1985 was amended by s 36(1) of the HFEA 1990, which added a new s 1A to the Surrogacy Arrangements Act 1985, and made all surrogacy arrangements unenforceable. The new s 1A provides: 'No surrogacy arrangement is enforceable by or against any of the persons making it.' However, private surrogacy arrangements are not illegal and there is, therefore, an ambivalence in the law. Although a private surrogacy arrangement can be made, it cannot be enforced in the courts. The two main issues which could arise are: (a) trying to enforce the terms of a surrogacy 'contract' during the pregnancy; and (b) trying to enforce the agreement after the birth by making the surrogate mother give up the baby.

In the US case of *Re Baby M* (1987), the court had to consider an agreement under which a surrogate mother, Mary Whitehead, consented to artificial insemination with the sperm of a husband and agreed to give the baby to the husband and his wife, Mr and Mrs Stern. It was also agreed that the surrogate mother would be paid $10,000 'for surrogate services and expenses' and she agreed to 'terminate all parental rights to said child', and that the wife, Mrs Stern, would adopt the child. When the baby was born, the surrogate mother refused to give up the child. The court said at first instance that the contract was valid and had been broken, but the Supreme Court of New Jersey said that the contract was invalid, as it broke laws forbidding payment for adoption and the adoption of the child was void. It was also against public policy for the surrogate mother to give up all rights to the child. 'This surrogacy contract violates the policy of this State that the rights of natural parents are equal concerning their child.' However, as the baby had lived with the husband and wife for 18 months, the court allowed it to remain with them.

The English courts have had similar difficulties in dealing with surrogacy agreements. In *Re P (Minors) (Wardship: Surrogacy)* (1987), a divorced woman, Mrs P, made an agreement to have a child for Mr and Mrs B, in return for payment. Twins were born and Mrs P refused to hand them over. The court said that the welfare of the children was the important factor. In deciding on this matter, the court looked at the two families the twins could end up with. One family, Mr and Mrs B, had two parents, were better off financially and provided a more stimulating environment, but the other family had their natural mother, Mrs P, with whom they had bonded over a period of five months. The court had to carry out a balancing exercise and awarded care of the twins to the mother.

A novel situation arose in December 1999, when a homosexual couple, Barry Drewitt and Tony Barlow, had twins using the sperm of one of them and eggs from a woman donor, which were carried by a surrogate mother. The twins were born in California and the two men were registered as the parents. In English law, the surrogate mother is the legal mother and her husband is the legal father. The question arose as to whether they could be admitted to the UK, as the twins were not British citizens. They were allowed into the country, as this was considered to be more in their best interests than returning to their surrogate mother. The homosexual couple cannot apply for a parental order under s 30 of the 1990 Act because they are not parties to a marriage. The Home Office later announced that the twins could stay in the UK.

It would seem that the commissioning couple are at a disadvantage compared to the mother in gaining control of the child. However, the mother in both of the above cases has been the genetic mother, that is, there is a partial surrogacy. If the commissioning couple provide the embryo, so that the surrogate mother merely carries the child (full surrogacy), the couple may have a stronger claim, although, legally, under s 27(1) of the 1990 Act, the surrogate mother is the legal mother in both cases.

As regards enforcing the agreement before birth, it would not be possible to force the surrogate mother to attend a clinic for medical treatment or to change her habits, for example, give up smoking cigarettes during pregnancy.

The problems caused by differing laws on surrogacy were highlighted in *(1) W (2) B v H* (2002) and *(1) W (2) W v H* (2002), which consisted of two hearings to determine the issues. The defendant went to California and made a legal surrogacy agreement under Californian law with the applicants. The defendant later found that she was pregnant with twins and was concerned that the applicants did not want two children. She returned to England and the twins were born here. The first hearing dealt with the question of whether the defendant's refusal to return to California was a breach of the applicants' rights of custody of the twins. The court said that although a surrogacy agreement was enforceable in California, under the Surrogacy Arrangements Act 1985 it was not binding in English law. The defendant was treated as the mother under s 27(1) and 27(3) of the HFEA 1990 and the applicant husband was the father under s 28(3). The court dismissed the applicants' claim. At the second hearing, the court said that the twins should return to California for the courts there to determine the position. The Californian courts would have regard to the welfare of the twins.

Who are the legal parents of a child born to a surrogate mother?

At common law, a woman who gives birth to a child is the mother and, if she is married, her husband is presumed to be the father. If the woman is not married, then she has parental responsibility under s 2(2) of the Children Act 1989 but the father does not have parental responsibility. However, the father can acquire parental responsibility by making an agreement with the mother that he should have parental responsibility, or parental responsibility may be granted to a father by the court (s 4 of the Children Act 1989). Under s 111 of the Adoption and Children Act 2002, any father named on the child's birth certificate also acquires parental responsibility. These rules have caused problems when applied in cases of assisted reproduction. For example, if an embryo is placed in an infertile woman who gives birth to a child, she is the mother, even though she is not genetically related to the child. In *Re W (Minors) (Surrogacy)* (1991), a married woman agreed to be implanted with an embryo created *in vitro* from the commissioning father's sperm and commissioning mother's egg. The surrogate mother agreed to hand over the child, which she did at birth. In law, the surrogate mother was treated as the mother and her husband would be treated as the father if he had agreed to the procedure.

In the light of this case, a new section (s 30) was added to the HFEA 1990, which was at that time going through Parliament. Under s 30(1), the court may make an order (parental order) for a child to be treated as the child of a commissioning couple who are married, if the child has been carried by another woman as the result of the placing in her of an embryo or sperm and eggs or her artificial insemination and the gametes of one or both of the commissioning couple were used to create the embryo. Certain conditions, set out in sub-ss (2)–(7), must be met:

(2) the application must be made within six months of the birth;

(3) at the time of the application the child's home is with the husband and wife;

(4) the husband and wife are both over 18 years;

(5) the father of the child, (if he is not the husband) and the woman who carried the child have agreed to the making of the order;

(6) in (5) no agreement is needed if the person cannot be found and the woman's agreement is not valid if given under six weeks from the child's birth;

(7) no money or other benefit, other than for reasonable expenses, has been given or received by the husband and wife in relation to the making of the order unless authorised by a court.

This section restricts obtaining a parental order to heterosexual married couples and has been widely criticised as discriminatory against others who may wish to have such rights. In *Re Q* (1996), an unmarried surrogate mother gave birth to a child created from the egg of the wife and donated sperm provided through a licensed clinic. The commissioning couple applied for a parental order under s 30 of the 1990 Act and the question arose as to who was the father for the purpose of giving consent. It was held that, under s 28(6) of the Act, a man who donated sperm for the purpose of licensed treatment was not to be treated as the father of the child. If the surrogate mother had been married, the embryo had not been created with her husband's sperm and he had consented to the procedure, he would have been treated as the father under s 28(2). This did not apply so, under s 28(3), if the embryo was placed in the woman or she was artificially inseminated, if the course of treatment provided for 'her and a man together' was by a licensed clinic and the embryo was not created using the sperm of that man, that man should be treated as the father. But this did not apply here, as the section envisaged medical treatment for the man. The result was that there was no man who could be treated as the father and whose consent was necessary.

When an application is made under s 30 of the HFEA 1990, the court must be satisfied that no money or other benefit, other than reasonable expenses, has been given or received by the commissioning parents. The question of payment to the surrogate mother raises difficult ethical and legal questions. Should the surrogate mother be paid for the use of her body? Could such a payment be seen as buying a child? In *Re C (A Child)* (2002), the applicants, a childless couple, were introduced to a surrogate mother through COTS (Childlessness Overcome Through Surrogacy). This is a non-profit making organisation that facilitates surrogacy arrangements. The applicants and the surrogate mother signed an 'agreement' under which the surrogate mother would give up the child at birth and be paid £12,000 expenses. These arrangements were followed, but when the applicants applied for a parental order, it was discovered that the surrogate mother received income support. The question for the High Court was whether the £12,000 was for expenses reasonably incurred. It was held that the surrogate mother had not incurred expenses and loss of earnings of £12,000. But the court found that the applicants had acted in good faith and had been told a figure by COTS that was not much less. It was in the best interests of the child that she should be treated as the child of the applicants and that they should have parental responsibility. The payment of £12,000 was authorised by the court and a parental order was made under s 30.

Future developments

The history of surrogacy shows that, initially, there was widespread antipathy to the practice, both from the general public and the legal and medical professions. In *A v C* (1985), a surrogacy arrangement was described as 'most extraordinary and irresponsible'. The impact of the Warnock Report and the Surrogacy Arrangements Act 1985 was to stop the development of commercial agencies for surrogacy, and, although private surrogacy was not banned, it was not encouraged. Over time, attitudes have changed and a more liberal view has been taken. The British Medical Association (BMA), in *Conceptions of Motherhood: The Practice of Surrogacy in Britain* (1996), shows an acceptance of the practice in focusing on the welfare of both the baby born and the surrogate mother, although the BMA considers that surrogacy is a 'last resort' for infertile women. There has also been the establishment of organisations which operate on a non-commercial basis to help those wishing to have children through surrogacy or to be surrogate mothers, for example, COTS.

In 1998, a Committee under the chairmanship of Professor Margaret Brazier produced its Report, *Surrogacy: Review for Health Ministers of Current Arrangements for Payments and Regulation* (Cm 4068). The Committee considered whether payments should be made to surrogate mothers, whether surrogacy arrangements should be regulated and whether any changes were required as a result to the Surrogacy Arrangements Act 1985 and the HFEA 1990. The Committee made the following recommendations:

(a) Payments: payments to surrogate mothers should cover only genuine expenses associated with the pregnancy; further payments should be prohibited to stop such arrangements from being made for money; legislation should define expenses in broad terms of principle, leaving details to be given through regulations.

(b) Regulation: agencies involved in surrogacy arrangements should be registered with the Department of Health, which should draw up a Code of Practice.

(c) Legislation: the Surrogacy Arrangements Act 1985 and s 30 of the HFEA 1990 should be repealed and replaced by a new Surrogacy Act, which should set out the main legal principles governing surrogacy arrangements. These would include the following:

- surrogacy contracts should be non-enforceable;
- prohibition of commercial agencies;
- new statutory provisions in relation to payments to surrogate mothers;
- a Code of Practice;
- registration of non-profit making surrogacy agencies;
- prohibition of unregistered agencies;
- a revised s 30 parental order, under which applicants must prove that they have followed the Surrogacy Act. Further parental orders should only be available in the High Court and the commissioning couple must be resident in the UK, Channel Islands or the Isle of Man.

These recommendations seek to bring all the rules into one Act of Parliament and to make improvements as regards payment and regulation. The Brazier Committee saw surrogacy as a special and distinct form of fertility treatment, requiring its own special regulations under which the welfare of the child must be paramount. This was because a woman was carrying a child who was given to others and all parties in the process were vulnerable. As a step forward, the Committee suggested that, as an interim measure, a voluntary code should be drawn up.

In January 2004, the Minister for Public Health announced a review of the HFEA 1990. The Minister said that, since the Act had been brought in, over 73,000 babies had been born as a result of treatment under the Act:

The nature of assisted reproduction and embryology is such that new procedures and technologies are being developed that could not have been envisaged when the Act was first drafted. It is also important to consider to what extent the Act is able to take account of changes over time in the public perception of ethical issues it covers. The Act is, after all, based on debate that took place in the 1980s. [Melanie Johnson MP, Minister for Public Health, January 2004]

The review will also be conducted in the light of the EU Tissues and Cells Directive, which was adopted by the Council in March 2004 and Member States are required to comply with the provisions by 7 April 2006. The aim of the Directive is to provide common standards of safety and quality throughout the European Union for the use of tissues and cells, including human gametes. The Human Fertilisation and Embryology Authority intends to conduct a consultation exercise of centres and interested parties on how the new provisions will be implemented.

THE HUMAN RIGHTS ACT 1998

The Articles which have proved to be useful in this area are Art 12, the right to marry, and Art 8, the right to respect for private life. Article 12 provides that 'Men and women of marriageable age have the right to marry and to found a family, according to the national laws governing the exercise of this right'. Originally, this Article was held to apply only to the opposite sexes and, in *Cossey v UK* (1990), a man who had had a sex change was not allowed to marry.

Article 8(1) provides that 'Everyone has the right to respect for his private and family life'. This is subject to the qualification in Art 8(2):

There shall be no interference by a public authority with the exercise of this right except as is in accordance with the law and is necessary in a democratic society in the interests of national security, public safety or the economic well being of the country, for the prevention of disorder or crime, for the protection of health or morals, or for the protection of the rights and freedoms of others.

It has previously been held that the right to family life does not include life with a transsexual partner (*X, Y and Z v UK* (1997)), but this may be within private life. In *X, Y and Z v UK*, X was a female to male transsexual who had lived with a woman, Y, for some years. In 1992, Y gave birth to Z, who had been conceived through artificial insemination by donor. X was refused permission to be registered as the father of Z. X, Y and Z claimed that the refusal to register X as Z's father was an infringement of their right to respect for family life under Art 8 of the European Convention on Human Rights. The European Court of Human Rights said that the issue was the relationship between a child conceived by AID and the person who had the role of the father, and how the law should treat them. There was no general agreement between States on such issues and the UK was not in breach of Art 8 by not recognising X as Z's father.

There have been developments in both the English courts and the European Court of Human Rights since the above cases. Attitudes have slowly changed and this has been reflected in the decisions of the courts. In *I v UK* (*sub nom Goodwin v UK*) (2002), I had gender reassignment surgery and lived as a woman. She was unable to obtain a birth certificate showing that she was a female. She claimed a breach of Arts 8 (right to private life) and 12 (right to marry). The government argued that it had struck a balance between the rights of the individual and the interest of the community, even though it accepted that there were situations where a person had to disclose their sex change. The government further argued that the right to marry did not include the right to marry someone of the same biological sex. Evidence was given that there was a move amongst European States to give legal recognition following gender reassignment. It was held by the European Court of Human Rights that, with respect to Art 8, this gave a right to each individual to establish their identity. The unsatisfactory situation of post-operative transsexuals as neither one gender nor the other was no longer acceptable. The UK government was in breach of Art 8. As regards Art 12, the right to marry, it was artificial to say that such a post-operative transsexual had not been deprived of the right to marry because they were able to marry a woman, because the applicant was now living as a woman and would only want to marry a man. There was also a breach of Art 12.

Following this decision, the government announced that it would introduce legislation dealing with marriage and acquired gender. Another case then reached the House of Lords. *Bellinger v Bellinger* (2003) concerned a man, the appellant, who had gender reassignment surgery to become a woman. She then went through a marriage ceremony in 1981. The appellant now sought a declaration that the 'marriage' was valid and that s 11(c) of the Matrimonial Causes Act 1973 was incompatible with Arts 8 and 12. It was held by the court that this was a complex matter and it was for Parliament to determine. The court would not make a declaration that the marriage was valid. Section 11 of the Matrimonial Causes Act 1973 provided that a marriage shall be void if '(c) the parties are not respectively male and female'. The court said that this was incompatible with Arts 8 and 12. The Gender Recognition Act 2004 provides for people to change gender by applying to a Gender Recognition Panel, who may grant a gender recognition certificate. Certain requirements must be met but not that the applicant undergoes gender reassignment surgery. Although the Act received the Royal Assent on 1 July 2004, only a few sections came into force on that date and most of the Act is not in force at the time of writing.

In *Evans v Amicus Healthcare and Others* (2004), the Court of Appeal considered whether the statutory requirements of the HFEA 1990 were incompatible with her right to respect for her private life under Art 8. The court said that the statute required both parties to consent to implantation.

To change that requirement in the interests of proportionality would create more difficulties and hence there was no breach of Art 8.

SUMMARY – INFERTILITY

1   *HFEA 1990 scheme*
   - As regards embryos, the Act only deals with embryos created outside the body; question of cell nuclear replacement: *R (on the Application of Quintavalle) v Secretary of State for Health* (2003).
   - Consent to use of gametes and embryos: must be in writing and not been withdrawn: *Evans v Amicus Healthcare and Others* (2004).

2   *Artificial insemination*
   - By husband: if the husband dies and his sperm is used, he may now be registered as the father: *R v Human Fertilisation and Embryology Authority ex p Blood* (1997); the Human Fertilisation and Embryology (Deceased Fathers) Act 2003.
   - By donor: there must be effective consent for use of sperm; if couple married, husband is treated as father of child unless he did not consent, s 28(2); if couple not married and treatment 'together', partner is treated as father, s 28(3): *Leeds Teaching Hospitals NHS Trust v Mr and Mrs A and Others* (2003); if someone is treated as the father under sub-s (2) or (3), no other person can be the father, s 28(4).

3   *Infertile women*
   - *In vitro* fertilisation: legal position same as for natural fertilisation.
   - Pre-implantation genetic diagnosis: allows selection of embryos and must be licensed by Human Fertilisation and Embryology Authority: *R (Quintavalle) v HFE Authority* (2003).
   - Issue of sex selection.
   - Who is eligible for treatment? Requirement of s 13(5) of the HFEA 1990 – need of child for a father; Human Fertilisation and Embryology Authority Code of Practice (2004) – where child has no legal father, the treatment centre must assess mother's ability together with other members of the family to meet child's needs.

4   *Anonymity of donor*
   - Section 28(6)(a) of the HFEA 1990: sperm donor is not treated as father.
   - Person born as a result of AID can obtain certain information when they reach 18 years.
   - Courts have said that HFEA 1990 is incompatible with Art 8, respect for private and family life, which includes the right to establish biological parents: *Rose v Secretary of State for Health and*

HFE Authority (2002); the government will change the law for children born after 1 April 2005.

5 *Surrogacy*
- Partial surrogacy: another woman receives AI (by husband or partner) for commissioning couple; complete surrogacy: baby created *in vitro* from husband and wife (or couple) and then implanted in surrogate mother.
- Arguments for and against.
- Legal position: Surrogacy Arrangements Act 1985 creates certain criminal offences for acting for commercial gain; but it is not an offence to be a surrogate mother or to be a commissioning parent.
- Surrogacy Arrangements Act 1985 amended by s 36(1) of the HFEA 1990, making surrogacy arrangements unenforceable; *Re P (Minors) (Wardship: Surrogacy)* (1987).
- Legal parents: at common law – woman who gives birth and her husband.
- Section 30 of the HFEA 1990: court can order child to be treated as child of commissioning couple if they are married; subject to conditions.
- Payment of surrogate mothers: s 30 provides no money must be given or received by the commissioning couple, except reasonable expenses: *Re C (A Child)* (2002) – £12,000 OK.
- Future changes: Brazier Report 1998 – need one Act to deal with surrogacy.

6 *Human Rights Act 1998*
- Most important Articles: Art 8, respect for private and family life, and Art 12, right to marry; decisions of the courts have led to the Gender Recognition Act 2004.

CHAPTER 7

ABORTION

INTRODUCTION

Abortion means ending a pregnancy by destroying the foetus. There were 175,600 abortions performed for women resident in England and Wales in 2002. Additionally, there were 9,400 abortions for non-residents. Three quarters of the abortions were for single women. The issue of abortion raises some of the most profound questions in medical law and ethics. When does human life begin? When does a 'person' come into existence? Does a foetus have a right to life? Does a woman have the right to do what she wants with her own body? The debate on abortion has polarised between those who claim that the foetus has a right to life (pro-life) and those who argue that a woman has the right to do what she wants with her own body (right to choose). A deontological (duty) approach would argue that there is a duty to maintain life (sanctity of life) and would not allow abortions. The utilitarian view would consider whether the consequences of having abortions were better for the overall good of society than not having them, with no particular concern for the foetus. Many of the issues cannot be solved and the law often has to take a pragmatic line, at the risk of pleasing neither side.

DEVELOPMENT OF THE LAW ON ABORTION

Abortion was a misdemeanour at common law. Various Acts of Parliament were passed in the 19th century which made abortion a criminal offence, culminating in the Offences Against the Person Act (OAPA) 1861. Section 58 of this Act provides that it is an offence for a pregnant woman to give herself poison or to unlawfully use an instrument or other means with intent to procure a miscarriage. The section also provides that anyone else who unlawfully gives a woman poison or unlawfully uses an instrument to procure a miscarriage commits an offence. In the case of someone apart from the woman herself carrying out the act, they may be convicted, whether the woman is pregnant or not, but they must have had a belief that she was pregnant. In *R v Dhingra* (1991), a doctor fitted a coil (IUD) to a woman 11 days after she had intercourse. He was charged under s 58. The court held that he should be acquitted because medical evidence was given that implantation could not have taken place.

Section 59 provides that it is an offence to supply poison or instruments in the knowledge that they will be used to procure the miscarriage of a woman, whether she is pregnant or not. This section covers supplying things to a woman to enable her to bring about a miscarriage. Glanville Williams, in his *Textbook of Criminal Law* (3rd edn, 1996, London: Stevens), notes that it would be extremely unlikely for a woman to be prosecuted for procuring an abortion on herself because it would be something done in distress and she would be likely to injure herself in doing so.

The OAPA 1861 protected the foetus *in utero* and once the child was born it was protected by the law of homicide. However, while the baby was in the process of being born, it was not protected by the law. The Infant Life (Preservation) Act (IL(P)A) 1929 was passed to fill this gap in the law. Section 1 provides:

(1) ... any person who, with intent to destroy the life of a child capable of being born alive, by any wilful act causes a child to die before it has an existence independent of its mother, shall be guilty of felony, to wit, of child destruction ... Provided that no person shall be found guilty of an offence under this section unless it is proved that the act which caused the death of the child was not done in good faith for the purpose only of preserving the life of the mother.

(2) For the purposes of this Act, evidence that a woman had at any material time been pregnant for a period of 28 weeks or more shall be *prima facie* proof that she was at that time pregnant of a child capable of being born alive.

The IL(P)A 1929 therefore creates the offence of child destruction. The Act applies to any child 'capable of being born alive' and this covers any child from 28 weeks' gestation onwards. There is some overlap with the OAPA 1861, which protects the foetus up until the start of birth. It is not an offence if the foetus is killed in the course of saving the mother's life. This defence was included because, before the development of Caesarean operations, if normal delivery of the foetus was not possible, the doctor would have to crush the skull of the foetus to save the mother's life. The OAPA 1861 did not have this defence and the question was whether a doctor who ended a pregnancy before the 28 week point was guilty of an offence under the OAPA 1861.

In *R v Bourne* (1938), a 14 year old girl became pregnant after being raped and the defendant doctor carried out an abortion with the consent of her parents. He was charged with procuring a miscarriage under s 58 of the OAPA 1861. The court said that the word 'unlawfully' as regards the use of any instrument to procure a miscarriage was not meaningless, but could be given the meaning found in s 1(1) of the IL(P)A 1929. The court then considered the phrase 'for the purpose of preserving the life of the mother' in s 1(1), and said that it included both the physical and mental health of the mother and was not limited to situations where her life was in immediate danger. Here, the girl's life was not in danger but her mental health was. MacNaghten J said:

It is not contended that those words mean merely for the purpose of saving the mother from instant death. There are cases we are told, where it is reasonably certain that a pregnant woman will not be able to deliver the child which is in her womb and survive. In such a case where the doctor anticipates, basing his opinion on the experience of the profession, that the child cannot be delivered without the death of the mother, it is obvious that the sooner the operation is performed the better. The law does not require the doctor to wait until the unfortunate woman is in peril of immediate death. In such a case he is not only entitled, but it is his duty to perform the operation with a view to saving her life.

The court said that the burden of proof was on the prosecution to prove that the defendant had not carried out the abortion in good faith to preserve the life of the mother. The jury acquitted the defendant.

Even after this case, however, doctors were unsure about the circumstances in which they could carry out an abortion. 'The extent of the defence available to doctors was unclear. Some doctors interpreted this defence liberally to include the mother's mental health and even happiness. Others would intervene only to prevent a life-threatening complication of pregnancy endangering the woman' (Brazier, M).

MODERN METHODS OF CONTRACEPTION

Some methods of contraception, such as the 'morning after pill' and the intra-uterine device (coil), could be seen as causing an abortion if they take effect after fertilisation. If this is the case, then the requirements of the Abortion Act 1967, that two doctors agree that one of the grounds under the Act is complied with (see below), would have to be met. It has been generally accepted that anything done before implantation is legal and does not come within the phrase 'to procure a miscarriage' under ss 58 and 59 of the OAPA 1861. If a method of contraception does affect the fertilised egg after implantation, a prosecution could be made under s 58 or 59 of the 1861 Act on the basis that it was procuring a miscarriage. A number of commentators have argued that use of the morning after pill could be an offence. Does the meaning of 'miscarriage' only cover the destruction of a fertilised implanted egg or does it have a wider meaning to include destruction of a fertilised egg that has not implanted in the womb? This was the question facing the court in *The Queen (on the Application of SPUC) v Secretary of State for Health* (2002). The Society for the Protection of the Unborn Child (SPUC) applied for judicial review to challenge the statutory instrument which allowed the sale of emergency contraception ('morning after pill') to women aged 16 years and over, that was provided under the supervision of a pharmacist. The morning after pill worked by preventing fertilisation of the egg by the sperm and by preventing implantation of the fertilised egg in the womb. It did not affect a fertilised egg that was implanted. SPUC argued that the pill was an abortifacient (a drug which brings about an abortion) and was given to procure a miscarriage and was therefore an offence under s 58 and/or s 59 of the OAPA 1861. SPUC argued that in 1861 'miscarriage' included preventing implantation of the fertilised egg. The medical evidence showed that the morning after pill, intra-uterine devices and sometimes the pill prevented a fertilised egg implanting in the womb. If the morning after pill was found to be an abortifacient, it could only be used legally if prescribed by two doctors. It was held by the High Court that the word 'miscarriage' in ss 58 and 59 of the OAPA 1861 presupposed implantation of the fertilised egg. Using the morning after pill was not an offence under s 58 or 59. The word miscarriage had not been defined in the OAPA 1861 and should be interpreted as it was currently understood, in the light of current medical knowledge. Munby J said:

> Whatever it may or may not have meant in 1861 the word 'miscarriage' today means the termination of an established pregnancy, and there is no established pregnancy prior to implantation. There is no miscarriage if a fertilised egg is lost prior to implantation. Current medical understanding of what is meant by 'miscarriage' excludes result brought about by the pill, the mini-pill or the morning after pill. That is also, I should add, the current understanding of the word 'miscarriage' when used by lay people in its popular sense.

The judge went on to add that he did not accept SPUC's argument about the meaning of 'miscarriage' in 1861, as medical works of the time supported the belief that it was only possible after implantation. The court also pointed out that using contraceptives seemed to be within Art 8, respect for private and family life, and was up to the individual to decide.

THE ABORTION ACT 1967

The Abortion Act 1967 provided that abortion would be legal if carried out under certain conditions. One of the reasons behind the Act was to end the practice of 'back street' abortions, which often caused injury to women. The Abortion Act 1967 was amended by the Human Fertilisation and Embryology Act 1990. The new s 1(1) of the Abortion Act provides that a person will not be guilty of an offence if a pregnancy is terminated in accordance with the following provisions. A registered medical practitioner (doctor) may terminate a pregnancy if *two* doctors are of the opinion formed in good faith that one of the grounds specified in the Act are complied with:

(a) the pregnancy has not exceeded 24 weeks and continuing it would involve greater risk to the physical or mental health of the pregnant woman or her existing children than if the pregnancy was ended; or

(b) termination is necessary to prevent grave permanent injury to the physical or mental health of the pregnant woman; or

(c) continuing the pregnancy would involve greater risk to the life of the pregnant woman than ending it; or

(d) there is a substantial risk that if the child were born, it would suffer such physical or mental abnormalities that it would be seriously handicapped.

Section 1(2) provides that in determining the risk to health in paras (a) and (b), the pregnant woman's 'actual or reasonably foreseeable environment' may be taken into account.

Section 1(4) provides that sub-s (3) and so much of sub-s (1) as relates to the opinion of two doctors shall not apply to a termination by a doctor where he is of the opinion formed in good faith, that it is immediately necessary to save the life or prevent grave permanent injury to the physical or mental health of the pregnant woman.

Ground (a) is often known as the 'social' ground for abortion, because the effect of s 1(2) is to allow such matters as home and family circumstances to be considered. The risk to the woman of continuing the pregnancy until birth must be greater than ending the pregnancy by having an abortion. Abortions in the first 12 weeks of pregnancy are a lesser risk than continuing the pregnancy, so there is no problem with such early terminations. The doctor has to make a decision that, on balance, termination has less risk than continuing the pregnancy. This ground covers risk to the mother's health and the health of her existing children. It may also be argued that this ground would cover having an abortion because the foetus is female, as in Asian cultures, where male children are favoured and female children are seen as a burden. Having a female baby could, therefore, affect the mental health of the mother. The British Medical Association in its guidance, *The Law and Ethics of Abortion* (revised 1999), states that 'Fetal sex is not one of the criteria for abortion listed in the Abortion Act 1967 and therefore termination on this ground alone has been challenged as outwith the law. There may be circumstances, however, in which termination of pregnancy on grounds of fetal sex would be lawful'. It goes on to explain that this may be lawful under s 1(1)(a), before adding:

> The association believes that it is normally unethical to terminate a pregnancy on the grounds of fetal sex alone except in cases of severe x-linked disorders. The pregnant woman's views about the effect of the sex of the fetus on her situation and on her existing children should nevertheless be carefully considered. In some circumstances doctors may come to the conclusion that the effects are so severe as to provide ethical justification for a termination.

Ground (a) has a 24 week time limit, which in practice is measured from the first day of the woman's last period.

Ground (b) allows an abortion to prevent grave permanent injury to the pregnant woman. There is no time limit for this ground. Also, note s 1(4), which provides that one doctor who forms the opinion, in good faith, that termination is immediately necessary to prevent grave permanent injury, may authorise the abortion. This would cover a situation where the mother is likely to suffer damage to her heart or kidneys if the abortion is not carried out.

Abortion is allowed under ground (c) only if the risk to the life of the pregnant woman by continuing with the pregnancy is greater than terminating the pregnancy. There is no time limit under this ground. Again, s 1(4) allows one doctor to authorise an abortion.

Ground (d) allows an abortion if two doctors believe, in good faith, that there is a 'substantial risk' that, if a child was born, it would suffer such physical or mental abnormalities as to be 'seriously handicapped'. These rather vague phrases are open to interpretation. What amounts to a 'substantial risk' has been described as follows:

> A further problem is in deciding what amounts to a 'substantial' risk. The Royal College of Physicians describe a risk of more than 10% of producing a seriously abnormal child as a 'high' risk. Presumably, where the abnormality is less severe, a greater degree of probability would be classed as high. A one in 10 chance of a foetus carrying spina bifida may indeed be regarded as a substantial risk, but a further complication is that it is not generally possible to determine from pre-natal screening the degree of handicap an affected foetus may suffer. Parents may therefore be faced with the possibility of aborting a normal, or mildly affected foetus. [Douglas, G, *Law, Fertility and Reproduction*, 1991, London: Sweet & Maxwell]

The Act does not define what is meant by 'seriously handicapped' and this could allow a wide interpretation leading to abortion for relatively minor handicaps, for example, if the foetus had a withered hand. In *R (on the Application of Jepson) v Chief Constable of West Mercia* (2003), the Reverend Joanna Jepson brought a claim for judicial review of a decision by the defendant not to prosecute two doctors who carried out a late abortion because of a cleft palate. She argued that such an abortion is outside s 1(1)(d) of the Abortion Act 1967 and is a breach of the rights of the foetus under Arts 2, 3 and 8 of the Convention. The 2002 Abortion Statistics show that 1% were under s 1(1)(d) and of these Down's syndrome, at 20%, was the most common.

Another difficulty with the interpretation of ground (d) is the matter of whether the handicap has to exist when the child is born or at some later point. If the handicap must exist at birth, then an abortion could not be carried out for a disease that does not develop until later life.

There is still argument over whether the Abortion Act 1967 gives a right to 'abortion on demand'. As the vast majority of abortions are carried out under s 1(1)(a) – the 'social' ground – it is argued that this is effectively 'on demand'. The 2002 Abortion Statistics show that 94% were under s 1(1)(a). However, a woman seeking an abortion on the NHS, rather than privately, is dependent on finding a doctor to agree and there is wide variation in practice in different parts of the country, even within the NHS. This leads to the argument that the laws on abortion are too restrictive and give doctors the control over whether to give an abortion. However, even if a doctor keeps within the rules laid down in the Act, there seems to be a wide scope for allowing abortions.

Incompetent patients

An incompetent adult or a child cannot consent to an abortion. In the case of a girl under 16 years old, can she consent to an abortion? In *Gillick v West Norfolk and Wisbech AHA* (1986), the House of Lords said that children under 16 years old could consent to medical treatment if they had a sufficient understanding of the treatment. A girl under 16 could consent to an abortion if she understood what was involved. If there is a conflict between a *Gillick* competent girl and her parents, such that the girl does not want an abortion but the parents do want her to have an abortion, the parents' consent is valid (*Re W (A Minor) (Medical Treatment)* (1992)).

In the case of an incompetent adult, an abortion could be performed in her best interests. In *T v T* (1988), the patient was a woman aged 19 who was pregnant but was incompetent. It was proposed that she have an abortion, but she would not understand what was going on and was incapable of consenting. It was held that an abortion could be carried out if this was in her best interests. In cases where an adult is incompetent, it is up to the courts to decide. More recently, in *Re SS (Medical Treatment: Late Termination)* (2002), a 34 year old woman was detained in a psychiatric hospital. When she was 14 weeks pregnant she asked for an abortion but then changed her mind a number of times. Two doctors decided that she did not have the capacity to consent. She said that if she had the child she would not care for it. The patient sought declarations (a) that she lacked capacity to make a decision about abortion; and (b) that it was in her best interests to have an abortion, even though by the time of the case she was over 23 weeks pregnant (the legal limit is 24 weeks). The court said that there was no medical evidence that an abortion was in her best interests and at such a late stage the procedure would be traumatic and would need her help. The alternative was for the patient to have the child and it could be taken into care. On balance, continuing the pregnancy carried fewer risks and an abortion was not in her best interests. The court gave further guidance on when it was necessary to obtain a court declaration to terminate a pregnancy in *An NHS Trust v D* (2004). The pregnant patient was mentally incapacitated and had severe schizophrenia. The court set out the following guidelines: (a) an application was not necessary if there was no doubt about capacity and best interests; (b) an application should be made if there was any doubt about either capacity or best interests; (c) applications should normally be made where: (i) there was a realistic prospect of the patient regaining capacity during or shortly after pregnancy; (ii) there was disagreement between medical staff about the patient's best interests, or the patient, her family or the father were against termination; (iii) procedures under the Abortion Act 1967 had not been followed; or (iv) there was an exceptional situation, for example, it was the patient's last chance to have a baby; (d) a termination in accordance with the Abortion Act 1967 in the best interests of an incapacitated patient was not a breach of Art 8 (private and family life) but was a legitimate interference with that right under Art 8(2).

The Abortion Act 1967 in practice

Section 1(1) of the Abortion Act 1967 provides that the termination should be carried out by a 'registered medical practitioner'. Originally, abortions were carried out surgically, by a doctor. New methods were developed which enabled abortions to be carried out using drugs that caused the foetus to be expelled from the mother. Although the doctors set up the apparatus and inserted a catheter (tube) into the womb, it was usually nurses who administered the drugs. The Department of Health and Social Security (DHSS) issued a circular which stated that nurses who terminated a pregnancy by such a method committed no offence under the Abortion Act 1967. In *Royal College of Nursing v DHSS* (1981), the House of Lords considered the issue. The Abortion Act 1967 provides, under s 1(1), 'Subject to the provisions of this section, a person shall not be guilty of an offence under the law relating to abortion when a pregnancy is terminated by a registered medical practitioner'. The court held that the interpretation of the phrase had to be seen in the light of the purpose of the Act – that abortions should be carried out with proper skill. This particular process was authorised by a doctor and was carried out under the supervision of a doctor; therefore, it fell within the provisions of the Act. On the question of whether the procedure was carried out by a 'registered medical practitioner', Lord Keith said:

> In my opinion, this question is to be answered affirmatively. The doctor has responsibility for the whole process and is in charge of it throughout. It is he who decides that it is to be carried out. He personally performs essential parts of it which are such as to necessitate the application of his particular skill. The nurse's actions are done under his direct written instructions. In the circumstances, I find it impossible to hold that the doctor's role is other than that of a principal, and I think he would be very surprised to hear that the nurse was the principal and he himself only an accessory. It is true that it is the nurse's action which leads directly to the introduction of abortifacient drugs into the system of the patient, but that action is done in a ministerial capacity and on the doctor's orders.

However, the decision was by a narrow majority of 3:2 and Lord Wilberforce, in a dissenting judgment, said that allowing nurses to carry out the procedure was extending the law, a task which should be left to Parliament. The decision of the House of Lords means that staff involved in the process of treatment are acting legally if they act under the supervision of a doctor.

The Abortion Act 1967 provides a 'conscientious objection' clause. Section 4 reads as follows:

> (1) ... subject to sub-section (2) of this section, no person shall be under any duty, whether by contract or by any other legal requirement, to participate in any treatment authorised by this Act to which he has a conscientious objection; provided that in any legal proceedings the burden of proof of conscientious objection shall rest on the person claiming to rely on it.

(2) Nothing in sub-section (1) of this section shall affect any duty to participate in treatment which is necessary to save the life or prevent grave permanent injury to the physical or mental health of a pregnant woman.

Therefore, no person is under a duty to 'participate in any treatment' if they have a conscientious objection, and s 4(2) provides that the exception does not apply if there is an emergency and treatment is necessary to save the life or prevent grave permanent injury to the pregnant woman. If a doctor had to carry out an abortion in an emergency, he could not rely on the exception. In *Janaway v Salford HA* (1989), J was a Catholic who objected to abortion. She worked as a medical secretary and was asked to type a letter referring a patient for the termination of a pregnancy. She refused to do this on the ground of conscientious objection and was subsequently dismissed. She brought a claim for unfair dismissal. She argued that, under s 4(1) of the Abortion Act 1967, she could refuse to type the letter referring the patient to the consultant because it would lead to the termination of a pregnancy and was therefore participating in treatment. The health authority argued that the meaning was limited to the actual procedure of the abortion. The House of Lords held that the phrase 'participate in any treatment' meant the actual medical process of the abortion and J was not justified in refusing to type a letter.

This is quite a narrow interpretation of 'participate in any treatment' and means that administrative duties in connection with abortion, or merely giving advice about abortion, would not be covered by s 4.

Place of treatment

Section 1(3) of the Abortion Act 1967 provides:

Except as provided by sub-section (4) of this section, any treatment for the termination of pregnancy must be carried out in a hospital vested in a Primary Care Trust or the Secretary of State for the purposes of his functions under the National Health Services Act 1977 ... or in a place approved for the purposes of this section by the Secretary of State.

Thus, under s 1(3), abortions must be carried out in an NHS hospital or other place approved by the Secretary of State. Private clinics must be licensed by the Department of Health. The object of specifying where abortions took place was to ensure that they took place in suitable conditions.

Section 1(3A) provides for other places to be approved in the case of medicines used to effect abortions. This covers the use of drugs such as RU486 (Mifepristone), known as the abortion pill, which must be used in the first two months of pregnancy. RU486 effectively stops implantation of the fertilised ovum or causes it to be discharged. In the latter case, it works as an abortifacient and so the requirements of the Abortion Act 1967 must be met. The drug can only be given at an NHS hospital or other approved place.

The rights of the foetus

An enduring problem in connection with abortion is trying to determine the moral status of the foetus and to decide when a foetus becomes a person. A wide range of suggestions have been made about what constitutes 'personhood'. Tooley has argued that self-awareness is necessary for personhood, but this would exclude newborn babies. Kant, arguing from a deontological viewpoint, said that rational agents were persons. This is an even higher threshold and would exclude young children and some adults. Ronald Dworkin has said that, from conception, the foetus is a form of human life. The Catholic Church's position is that a human being is created from the moment of conception. Suggestions for the exact point at which personhood occurs include conception, implantation of the embryo, viability, birth, or some later point.

English law has considered the rights of the foetus in a number of cases. In *Paton v British Pregnancy Advisory Service Trustees* (1979), a wife wished to have an abortion and obtained the permission of two doctors without consulting her husband. The husband applied to the court for an injunction to stop the abortion. The High Court held that the husband had no rights under the Abortion Act 1967 to stop an abortion. Sir George Baker P said, as regards any possible rights of the foetus, 'The foetus cannot, in English law, in my view, have any right of its own, at least until it is born and has a separate existence from the mother'. In *Paton v UK* (1980), the husband took his case to the European Commission on Human Rights, claiming that the foetus had rights under Art 2 (the right to life) of the European Convention on Human Rights, but this was rejected. By allowing a woman to have an abortion, English law was protecting the life of the woman, which meant limiting the rights of the foetus. The Commission said:

> If Article 2 were held to cover the foetus and its protection under this Article were, in the absence of any express limitation, seen as absolute, an abortion would have to be considered as prohibited even where the continuance of the pregnancy would involve a serious risk to the life of the pregnant woman. This would mean that the 'unborn life' of the foetus would be regarded as being of a higher value than the life of the pregnant woman.

The Court of Appeal also considered the rights of the foetus in *Re F (In Utero)* (1988). A mother who had a history of mental illness and drug abuse and had led a nomadic existence around Europe was 38 weeks pregnant when she disappeared from her flat. The local authority wished to make the unborn child a ward of court. The court held that it did not have jurisdiction and said that it is the interests of the child which are predominant, but this would cause a conflict with the interests of the mother. This, in turn, would lead to difficulties if an order was made against the mother and she refused to comply with it. Only minors can be made wards of court and a minor can only be a person if they have been born. In *St George's Healthcare NHS Trust v S* (1998), the court said that 'an unborn child is not a separate person from its mother. Its need for medical assistance does not prevail over her rights'. The court went on to say that a pregnant woman could refuse treatment even though her own life and that of her unborn child depended on it.

In *Attorney General's Reference (No 3 of 1994)* (1998), the defendant stabbed his pregnant girlfriend in the stomach. A baby was born but died three months later from injuries caused by the stabbing. The House of Lords said that a conviction for constructive manslaughter would be possible. The House of Lords rejected the argument of the Court of Appeal that the foetus should be treated as an integral part of the mother. Lord Mustill stated that:

> The mother's leg was part of the mother; the foetus was not ... I would, therefore, reject the reasoning which assumes that, since (in the eyes of English law) the foetus does not have the attributes which make it a 'person', it must be an adjunct of the mother. Eschewing all religious and political debate, I would say that the foetus is neither. It is a unique organism.

The European Court of Human Rights considered whether a foetus was protected by Art 2 in *Vo v France* (2005). Due to a mix up, the pregnant applicant was subjected to a medical procedure which damaged the amniotic sac around the foetus and led to her needing an abortion. The French court held that the doctor could not be convicted of unintentional homicide because a foetus was not a person under French criminal law. The applicant argued that Art 2, the right to life, applied to the foetus. The court said that the question of when the right to life begins was up to individual countries to decide. There was no consensus within Europe on when life begins. It was therefore impossible to decide whether an unborn child was a person. Even if it was assumed that Art 2 did apply here, where a death was not caused intentionally, the requirement in Art 2 to provide a remedy did not necessarily mean a remedy in criminal law. Here, the parents could have made a civil claim for damages. Consequently, there was no breach of Art 2.

The rights of the pregnant woman

The Abortion Act 1967 does not give the pregnant woman a legal right to demand an abortion. Montgomery (*Health Care Law*, 1997, Oxford: OUP) says that doctors control access to abortions and this varies widely throughout the country. In the US, the Supreme Court in *Roe v Wade* (1973) said that the constitutional right to privacy in the US Constitution included a woman's right to abortion up to the time that the foetus was viable. After this, the State had a right to intervene on behalf of the foetus, unless the life or health of the mother was threatened.

There is growing awareness of the fact that tobacco, alcohol and drugs, when taken by the mother, can have an effect on the unborn baby. But can, or should, the actions of the mother be controlled? The Law Commission has said that the foetus should not have a right of action against the mother, as this would compromise the mother-child relationship. In the Canadian case of *Winnipeg Child and Family Services (Northwest Area) v G* (1997), the mother, a glue-sniffing addict, was five months pregnant and the court ordered that she should be detained to protect the unborn child. The Supreme Court set this judgment aside and said that the foetus' existence was dependent on the body of the woman and any intervention on behalf of the foetus could conflict with the mother's interests. It was not appropriate for a court to extend the law in such a way.

This conflict between mother and foetus is also seen in cases where the mother refuses medical treatment which could lead to harm to the foetus. In the US case of *Re AC* (1987), a woman who was 26 weeks pregnant was dying of cancer but refused a Caesarean section. The court ordered the operation to be carried out but both the baby and the mother died two days later. An appeal court later reversed the decision and said that a decision of a competent patient should prevail, unless there are compelling reasons to override it. The English courts have dealt with numerous cases involving this conflict between a pregnant woman and her foetus. In *Re S (Adult: Refusal of Medical Treatment)* (1992), the pregnant woman refused a Caesarean section on religious grounds but the court granted a declaration allowing the operation to save the life of the mother and the child.

In *Re MB (Medical Treatment)* (1997), the woman was 40 weeks pregnant and the foetus was in the breach position; natural delivery would risk brain damage or death to the child. The mother agreed to a Caesarean section but, due to a fear of needles, refused the anaesthetic. The local health authority applied for a declaration that treatment would be lawful. It was held by the Court of Appeal, in overruling *Re S* (1992), that a competent woman may refuse treatment for any reason or no reason, even though the consequences may be death or serious handicap for the child or her own death. The court said that the woman was temporarily incompetent and allowed the Caesarean section. In *St George's NHS Trust v S* (1998), the Court of Appeal said that an unborn child's need for medical assistance does not prevail over the rights of the mother: 'She is entitled not to be forced to submit to an invasion of her body against her will, whether her own life or that of her unborn child depends on it.'

The rights of the father

The husband in *Paton v British Pregnancy Advisory Service Trustees* (1979) had claimed an injunction to stop the mother from having an abortion. The court considered the fact that the provisions of the Abortion Act 1967 had been complied with and said:

> The 1967 Act gives no right to a father to be consulted in respect of the termination of a pregnancy. True, it gives no right to the mother either, but obviously the mother is going to be right at the heart of the matter consulting with the doctors if they are to arrive at a decision in good faith ... The husband, therefore, in my view, has no legal right enforceable at law or in equity to stop his wife having this abortion or to stop the doctors from carrying out the abortion ...

The father then took the case to the European Commission on Human Rights in *Paton v UK* (1980), arguing that his right under Art 8 of the European Convention on Human Rights, the right to respect for family life, had been broken. The Commission, in applying Art 8(2) ('There shall be no interference by a public authority with the exercise of this right except such as is in accordance with the law and is necessary ... for the protection of the rights and freedoms of others') said that, here, the rights of the mother had to be protected and dismissed his claim. In the later case of *C v S* (1998), C's girlfriend was 18 weeks pregnant and wanted to have an abortion. C claimed that the foetus was 'a child capable of being born alive' under s 1(1) of the IL(P)A 1929 and having an abortion would be an offence of child destruction under that section. Section 1(2) provides 'evidence that a woman had at any material time been pregnant for a period of 28 weeks or more shall be *prima facie* proof that she was at that time pregnant of a child capable of being born alive'. C argued that a foetus of 18 weeks was capable of being born alive. The Court of Appeal was given medical evidence that at that stage of development such a foetus would not be able to breathe naturally or with the aid of a ventilator and the court confirmed that a father had no right to stop an abortion:

> ... if it has reached the normal stage of development and so is incapable ever of breathing, it is not in our judgment 'a child capable of being born alive' within the meaning of the 1929 Act and accordingly the termination of this pregnancy would not constitute an offence under that Act. [Sir John Donaldson MR]

In the Scottish case of *Kelly v Kelly* (1997), the court held that a father could not stop his wife from having an abortion. Although a father has responsibilities and rights after a child is born, before that time he has no rights in English law.

LIABILITY FOR INJURIES IN RELATION TO BIRTH

If a foetus suffers an injury whilst it is in the womb (*in utero*) and as a result is born disabled, does it have a right of action against the person causing the injury? Under the Congenital Disabilities (Civil Liability) Act 1976, a child born after 21 July 1976 has a statutory right to claim damages. Under s 1, if a child is born disabled as a result of a negligent act before its birth, the child will have a claim. It must be proved that the negligent act affected:

- the ability of either parent to have a healthy child; or
- the mother during pregnancy; or
- the mother or child during birth,

and the child would not otherwise have been disabled.

Under s 4(1), the mother cannot be liable under the Act except for injuries caused to the foetus as a result of her negligent driving. This claim was allowed because the mother will have compulsory insurance against liability. The Law Commission said, before the Act was passed, that a claim should not be allowed by the child against the mother because of the effect this would have on the relationship between them. The child must be born alive to bring a claim (s 4(2)). The Act replaces the common law for those children born after the Act was passed (s 4(5)). The duty to the child is owed through the parent, so the defendant must be in breach of a duty owed to the parents (s 1(3)), although the parents do not have to suffer injury themselves.

The common law position on such a claim was unclear until *Burton v Islington HA* (1992). A pregnant woman had a routine operation but the hospital had not tested to see whether she was pregnant. As a result of the operation, the foetus was damaged. The child was born disabled in 1967. Obviously, this all happened before the 1976 Act. The defendant claimed that it was not liable because, at the time of the operation, the claimant was not a living person and had no legal rights. The Court of Appeal held that a duty of care was owed to the foetus because it was foreseeable that the foetus could be damaged. If the child was born alive, this duty crystallised and the child could sue for negligence. However, since the Act was passed, the common law rules only apply to those born before the Act, as provided in s 4(5).

Claim for wrongful life

This is a claim that the child who is born disabled as a result of negligence would have been better off if they had not been born at all. This type of claim may arise, for example, if a hospital fails to tell a woman, before she becomes pregnant, that, because of a genetic defect, she may have a disabled child; or where a hospital negligently screens a pregnant woman and misses an abnormality in the foetus and, consequently, a disabled child is born. The claim is brought by the child.

In *McKay v Essex AHA* (1982), a pregnant woman suspected that she had German measles and was given a blood test by the defendants. She was negligently told that she did not have the disease, continued with the pregnancy and the baby was born disabled in 1975. The Court of Appeal considered what the effect would be if the child's claim was allowed and said that it would be imposing a duty on doctors to carry out an abortion in all cases where abnormality was suspected:

> To impose such a duty towards the child would, in my opinion, make a further inroad on the sanctity of human life, which would be contrary to public policy. It would mean regarding the life of a handicapped child as not only less valuable than the life of a normal child, but so much less valuable that it was not worth preserving, and it would even mean that a doctor would be obliged to pay damages to a child infected with rubella before birth who was in fact born with some mercifully trivial abnormality. These are the consequences of the necessary basic assumption that a child has a right to be born whole or not at all, not to be born unless it can be born perfect or 'normal', whatever that may mean.

The court also said that it could not measure the loss to the child as the difference between its present condition and its condition if it had not been born, as a court of law could not evaluate non-existence. Therefore, the claim failed. Ackner LJ said that no claim for wrongful life could be made under the Congenital Disabilities (Civil Liability) Act 1976 because the Act dealt with claims for being born disabled as a result of negligence, and not claims that the child should not have been born.

Although a claim for wrongful life by a child will fail, the parents may claim for the extra expense of bringing up a disabled child.

Claim for wrongful birth

Originally, a claim for wrongful birth could be made if a healthy child was born as a result of negligence (also known as wrongful conception) or a handicapped child was born as a result of negligence. Claims could be made either in contract or negligence.

The courts have not been consistent in dealing with these cases and have varied their approaches between following legal principles and following public policy. What if a healthy child is born because of a negligently performed sterilisation or because the parents are not warned about the possibility of reversal of a sterilisation? In *Udale v Bloomsbury HA* (1983), the claimant became pregnant after a sterilisation was carried out negligently. She claimed damages for the pain of childbirth and the cost of bringing up the child. The court said that it would be 'highly undesirable' for a child to know that a court has declared his life a mistake; the mother's joy would cancel out the inconvenience and financial disadvantage of having a child; and, in our culture, a child is regarded as a blessing. The court said that it would be against public policy to award damages for the cost of bringing up the child and rejected that claim. However, damages were given for the pain and suffering of childbirth.

This case was followed by *Emeh v Kensington AHA* (1985), which also involved a negligently performed sterilisation which led to the birth of a child with congenital abnormalities. The Court of Appeal said that the courts should follow legal principle and rejecting such claims as a matter of policy was wrong. It was unreasonable to expect the woman to have an abortion, and damages were awarded for the cost of bringing up the child. In *Thake v Maurice* (1986), the Thakes had five children and did not want any more. Mr Thake paid for a vasectomy operation and his wife later became pregnant after the vasectomy was naturally reversed. The Court of Appeal held that it was negligent not to warn of this risk. Mrs Thake did not realise she was pregnant until it was too late to have an abortion, but, if she had been warned, she would have been alert to the possibility and could have had an abortion. The court awarded damages for bringing up the child. In the High Court, Pain J had said that 'Every baby has a belly to be filled and a body to be clothed'.

The law was changed by the House of Lords in *McFarlane v Tayside Health Board* (2000). Mr M had a vasectomy and was later told that he could dispense with contraception. Mrs M later became pregnant and gave birth to their fifth child, a healthy baby. The parents claimed damages for the pain and suffering of childbirth and the cost of bringing up the child. The court said that, as a matter of principle, the parents of a healthy child that was born because of a failed sterilisation were not entitled to claim the cost of bringing up the child. It was not fair, just and reasonable to impose a duty on the doctor for the consequential responsibilities imposed on or accepted by the parents to bring up the child. As a matter of justice, the law did not allow the parents of a healthy but unwanted child to claim the cost of bringing it up, but the mother was entitled to damages for the pain and suffering of pregnancy and giving birth.

Following *McFarlane*, claims for wrongful conception and wrongful birth resulting in the birth of a healthy child will not succeed. The effect on claims for the birth of a handicapped child is uncertain. (See Maclean, A, *McFarlane v Tayside Health Board*: a wrongful conception in the House of Lords?' [2000] Web JCLI.)

If a claim is made because a handicapped child is born as a result of negligence by the hospital, the parents would have to establish that if they had known the true facts, the mother would have had an abortion. This is necessary to establish causation because, if the mother would have continued with her pregnancy, then the hospital would not have caused the loss. In *Salih v Enfield HA* (1991), the defendants had negligently failed to warn the pregnant mother of the risk of rubella. The mother contracted the disease and, as a result, her child was born disabled. The Court of Appeal said that the parents were entitled to the cost of bringing up the child. However, in *Rand v East Dorset HA* (2000), which was decided after *McFarlane v Tayside Health Board*, Mrs Rand was not told that a scan taken during her pregnancy showed abnormalities and later she had a child with Down's syndrome. In a claim for wrongful birth, the claimants were awarded damages only for the loss arising as a result of the child's disability and not for the cost of bringing up the child.

But should a distinction be made between healthy and disabled children or does this reflect a view that a disabled child is somehow worth less than a healthy child? In *Parkinson v St James and Seacroft University Hospital NHS Trust* (2001), the claimant was sterilised at the defendant's hospital. The operation was carried out negligently. Subsequently, she had a child which was born disabled, although it was accepted that the disability was not caused by any negligence by the defendant. The Court of Appeal said that in the period between *Emeh* up to *McFarlane*, parents were entitled to damages for the whole cost of bringing up either a healthy or disabled child. It would not be fair, just and reasonable to award damages which were more than the extra costs of bringing up a child with a significant disability. She was therefore entitled to claim those extra costs of bringing up a disabled child.

The High Court of Australia refused to follow *McFarlane* in *Cattanach v Melchior* (2003). The Melchiors had two children and did not want any more. Mrs Melchior was sterilised by the appellant surgeon but later gave birth to a healthy child. It was held by a majority of 4:3 that the surgeon had been negligent in not warning her of the risk that the sterilisation might not work, and she was awarded the costs of bringing up the child. A further qualification has been added to the law by the House of Lords in *Rees v Darlington Memorial Hospital* (2003). The claimant suffered from a severe and progressive visual disability and believed that as a result she would not be able to look after a child. She arranged to be sterilised but the operation was carried out negligently. She later became pregnant and gave birth to a healthy son. She initially claimed the costs of bringing up the child but the High Court rejected her claim. On appeal to the Court of Appeal, she only claimed the extra costs of bringing up the child caused by her disability. The Court of Appeal allowed her appeal by a majority of 2:1 and awarded her the extra costs attributable to her disability. She appealed, arguing that this decision was inconsistent with *McFarlane*. The House of Lords said that the policy considerations behind *McFarlane* were that it was wrong to regard an unwanted child as a financial liability; the rewards of being parents cannot be quantified; and awarding large sums to parents of a healthy child against the NHS would offend the public view of allocating resources. The arguments that *McFarlane* was wrong were not persuasive and it remained good law. Nonetheless, the claimant was the victim of a legal wrong. Refusing any compensation except for damages for the pregnancy and birth was unfair and did not recognise the loss to the parent of the opportunity of life as she had wished without the child. It was appropriate to award a conventional award of £15,000. This was not compensation but showed some measure of recognition of the wrong done. The court added that the same approach should be taken in all cases, without distinction between those where the parties were healthy or the child or the parent were disabled. The decision by the House of Lords was by a majority of 4:3. The dissenting judges argued that on the facts the case could be distinguished from *McFarlane*. Lord Hope said: 'The fact that the child's parent was a seriously disabled person provided a ground for distinguishing *McFarlane* and it would be fair, just and reasonable to hold that such extra costs as could be attributed to the disability were within the scope of the tortfeasor's duty of care and were recoverable.'

THE HUMAN RIGHTS ACT 1998

The relevant Articles to abortion issues are Arts 2 and 8, and to a lesser extent Art 10.

Article 2(1) provides 'Everyone's right to life shall be protected by law'. In *Paton v UK* (1980), the husband argued that allowing the abortion was a breach of Art 2 as it allowed the foetus to die. The European Commission on Human Rights said that in allowing abortion, English law was protecting the life of the mother. The 'life' of the foetus was intimately connected with that of the pregnant mother and therefore had to be limited by the mother's interests. The Commission rejected the claim that a foetus had protection under Art 2. The Court of Appeal, in *Re F (In Utero)* (1988), heard an application to make a foetus a ward of court to protect it from the mother. The court said that it could not make the foetus a ward of court, as to do so would create conflict between the legal interests of the mother and those of the unborn child.

Article 8(1) states that 'Everyone has the right to respect for his private and family life...'; 8(2) states that 'There shall be no interference by a public authority with the exercise of this right except such as is in accordance with the law and is necessary in a democratic society in the interests of ... health or morals, or for the protection of the rights and freedoms of others'. In *Paton v UK* (1980), the husband also claimed that to allow the abortion was a breach of his right to family life. The Commission said that this was necessary to protect the health of the mother, as the abortion was to protect her health. The interference was justified. In *The Queen (on the Application of SPUC) v Secretary of State for Health* (2002), the court said that, although no argument had been put forward on the matter, personal choice about contraception seemed to be a right which was protected under Art 8 and part of 'respect for private and family life'. The court also considered Art 10(1). This provides that 'Everyone has the right to freedom of expression'. This arose in the context that costs were awarded against SPUC for both the Secretary of State for Health and the other defendants. The court was concerned that if this meant the insolvency of SPUC, which was 'a voice central to this debate', that could have implications for freedom of speech.

SUMMARY – ABORTION

1 *Development of the law of abortion*
   - Section 58 of the OAPA 1861: offence for pregnant woman (or anyone else) to use poison or an instrument to procure a miscarriage: *R v Bourne* (1938).
   - Infant Life (Preservation) Act 1929 created offence of child destruction to protect the baby while being born if 'capable of being born alive'.

2 *Modern methods of contraception*
   - A method of contraception which took effect after fertilisation could be within the Abortion Act 1967: *The Queen (on the Application of SPUC) v Secretary of State for Health* (2002) – miscarriage means terminating established pregnancy.

3 *Abortion Act 1967*
   - Doctor may end pregnancy if two doctors agree that one of grounds is met: (a) s 1(1)(a), not after 24 weeks and continuing

with the pregnancy is a greater risk to the woman than ending it; (b) to prevent grave injury to the physical or mental health of the woman; (c) continuing the pregnancy would create a greater risk to the woman than ending it; (d) there is a substantial risk that the child may be seriously handicapped.

- Only one doctor needed for (b) and (c).
- Problems over interpretation of 'seriously handicapped'.
- Question whether abortion on demand exists because of s 1(1)(a).
- Incompetent adult or child cannot consent to an abortion; *Gillick* competent child could consent; with an incompetent adult abortion could be carried out in her best interests.
- Practical working of the Abortion Act 1967: must be carried out by a registered medical practitioner: *Royal College of Nursing v DHSS* (1981); no need for staff to participate in any treatment if they have a conscientious objection: *Janaway v Salford HA* (1989).

4   *Rights of those involved*
- Foetus: consider moral status; legal status – no rights until birth; pregnant woman can refuse treatment: *Re F (In Utero)* (1988).
- Pregnant woman: cannot be controlled to protect foetus: *Re MB (Medical Treatment)* (1997).
- Father: no right to stop an abortion: *Paton v British Pregnancy Advisory Service Trustees* (1979).

5   *Liability for injuries in relation to birth*
- Congenital Disabilities (Civil Liability) Act 1976: liable if child born disabled because of negligent act; must be born alive; no claim against mother unless involves her negligent driving.
- Wrongful life: if a child born disabled claims it would have been better off if not born; cannot succeed: *McKay v Essex AHA* (1982).
- Wrongful birth: no claim for cost of bringing up a healthy child as a result of negligence: *McFarlane v Tayside Health Board* (2000); if child is disabled, parents can claim extra costs; if parent is disabled, can claim extra costs: *Rees v Darlington Memorial Hospital* (2003).

6   *Human Rights Act 1998*
- Main Articles are Art 2, right to life – but has not helped foetus; and Art 8, respect for private and family life – which included right to contraception.

CHAPTER 8

MEDICAL RESEARCH

INTRODUCTION

The issue of medical research was brought into the public spotlight by the reports on Bristol Royal Infirmary and Alder Hey Children's Hospital which revealed that body parts had been taken from dead children without consent, for the purposes of research. Although this may have turned many people against research, the importance of medical research needs to be re-emphasised. Medical progress in the fight against major diseases like cancer will be hampered without research involving human subjects. Medical research raises many important issues, such as the consent of the research subject, the impact of the duty of confidence and what redress the research subject may have if they suffer harm as a result of taking part in the research.

One important question is to determine what is meant by 'medical research'. First, a distinction can be made between 'research', which is closely defined and will have a particular purpose, and 'experimentation', which is rather more open ended and general. As regards research, there are various ways in which it is categorised. A distinction is made between therapeutic research and non-therapeutic research. Therapeutic research is aimed at helping an individual patient or group of patients; non-therapeutic research is carried out on patients but is unlikely to be of benefit to them directly, although the aim of the research is to increase knowledge generally. Research may also be divided into non-invasive and invasive. With non-invasive research, the research subject is not given any treatment but, for example, their medical history is used as part of a research project. With invasive research, the research subject is given drugs or a medical procedure is carried out on their body and this creates a risk.

There are various international and professional codes dealing with medical research and the European Clinical Trials Directive, which has been implemented by the Medicines for Human Use (Clinical Trials) Regulations 2004, deals with clinical trials for medicines. However, the fact remains that in the UK there is no comprehensive legal framework dealing with medical research on human beings which requires a specific legal permission.

ETHICS AND RESEARCH

The two main ethical theories provide different answers to medical research. From a duty based (or deontological) approach, the researcher would owe a duty to the research subject not to harm them in carrying out the research. The duty is not to sacrifice one individual for the sake of others. This raises the dilemma that an individual research subject should not be used as a means to an end, that of greater medical knowledge. A duty based approach also gives the research subject the right to have their autonomy respected.

A utilitarian approach looks at the consequences of the research. The overall harm and benefit needs to be considered. The harm to the individual research subject may be outweighed by the overall benefit to future patients. Thus, there is a conflict with the duty based approach not to harm the research subject. Clause 5 of the Declaration of Helsinki 1964 provides: 'In medical research on human subjects, considerations related to the wellbeing of the human should take precedence over the interests of science and society.' This clearly overrules the utilitarian view.

ETHICAL CODES

The need for an international ethical code on medical research arose from the evidence at the Nuremberg Trials following the Second World War. Evidence showed that Nazi doctors had carried out medical research on the inmates of concentration camps, often with great cruelty and resulting in the death of the inmates. The judges at Nuremberg set out 10 basic principles in the Nuremberg Code 1947, to be followed in all cases of medical research, for example, that the voluntary consent of the subject was absolutely essential. This was followed by the Declaration of Helsinki in 1964, which was drawn up by the World Medical Association. This sets out, in more detail, guidance on the ethical principles to be followed in carrying out medical research. It has been amended several times, most recently in Edinburgh in 2000. Some examples of the principles from the Declaration are set out below:

5   In medical research on human subjects, considerations relating to the wellbeing of the human subject should take precedence over the interests of science and society.

    ...

10 It is the duty of the physician in medical research to protect the life, health, privacy, and dignity of the human subject.

    ...

20 The subjects must be volunteers and informed participants in the research project.

    ...

24 For a research subject who is legally incompetent, physically or mentally incapable of giving consent or is a legally incompetent minor, the investigator must obtain informed consent from the legally authorised representative in accordance with applicable law. These groups should not be included in research unless the research is necessary to promote the health of the population represented and this research cannot instead be performed on legally competent persons.

The General Medical Council issued *Research: The Role and Responsibilities of Doctors* in 2002. This sets out guidance on consent, confidentiality, adults lacking capacity and children.

The Council of the European Union issued a Directive on research into the development of new medicinal products, Directive 2001/20/EC of 4 April 2001, which has been implemented by the Medicines for Human Use (Clinical Trials) Regulations 2004, which came into force on 1 May 2004. The aim of the Directive is to standardise clinical research trials across the European Union but it only covers the development of new medicines and not medical research in general.

RESEARCH ETHICS COMMITTEES

In the UK, since the 1960s, the Department of Health has required health authorities to establish local research ethics committees. These are independent committees with both medical and lay members that give advice on any research involving NHS patients or facilities. Since October 2002, the responsibility for the local research ethics committees has been under the control of the Strategic Health Authority for that particular area. The Department of Health also set up the Central Office for Research Ethics Committees (RECs) to co-ordinate the operation of local research ethics committees. In 2001, the Central Office issued *Governance Arrangements for NHS Research Ethics Committees*, which sets out rules for research ethics committees to follow:

6   **Composition of an REC**

6.1 An REC should have sufficient members to guarantee the presence of a quorum (see 6.11) at each meeting. The maximum should be 18 members. This should allow for a sufficiently broad range of experience and expertise, so that the scientific, clinical and methodological aspects of a research proposal can be reconciled with the welfare of research participants, and with broader ethical implications.

The arrangements go on to provide for a range of 'expert' members with experience in clinical research, research methods, hospital medicine and general practice, and for 'lay' members, who are to be independent of the NHS and who should make up one third of the membership of the committee.

As to the role of such committees, this is set out in the next regulation:

3   **The remit of an NHS REC**

3.1 Ethical advice from the appropriate NHS REC is required for any research proposal involving:

a   Patients and users of the NHS. This includes all potential research participants recruited by virtue of the patient or user's past or present treatment by, or the use of, the NHS. It includes NHS patients treated under contracts with private sector institutions.

b   Individuals identified as potential research participants because of their status as relatives or carers of patients and users of the NHS, as defined above.

c   Access to data, organs or other bodily material of past and present NHS patients.

d   Fetal material and IVF involving NHS patients.

e   The recently dead in NHS premises.

f   The use of, or potential access to, NHS premises or facilities.

g   NHS staff – recruited as research participants by virtue of their professional role.

The responsibilities of RECs are to safeguard the rights of the research subjects.

Research ethics committees must consider proposals for research and balance the risks and inconveniences against the benefits for the participants and communities. Approval is not required for non-NHS research, although in practice approval will usually be obtained from a local REC. If the Department of Health guidelines were not followed by a researcher and a research subject suffered injury, this would not necessarily lead to a claim in negligence against the researcher. However, if a researcher was employed by the NHS, they could face disciplinary action in such a situation.

Sometimes, a research project may apply to a wide area of the country and need approval of a number of local RECs in different authorities. This could cause problems if different committees had different views of the proposed research. The Department of Health therefore set up a number of multi-centre research ethics committees (MREC). A research proposal would go to the appropriate MREC and the local RECs affected would only consider local issues arising.

Under the Medicines for Human Use (Clinical Trials) Regulations 2004, regs 5–10 provide for ethics committees to be responsible for giving opinions on clinical trials of medicinal products. Regulation 5 establishes the UK Ethics Committees Authority. The Authority is given power to set up ethics committees for the purposes of giving opinions on clinical trials, to recognise existing ethics committees and to monitor the work of ethics committees. This Authority can therefore authorise existing ethics committees for the purposes of the Regulations. The Regulations therefore put ethics committees on a statutory basis. The power to monitor the work of the ethics committees is a new and welcome development. In due course, it is likely that existing committees will come within this framework.

RANDOMISED CONTROLLED TRIALS

Medical research frequently involves a randomised controlled trial. The principle behind such a trial is simple. To decide if a new drug is better than the existing one, the new drug is given to one group of patients with the same condition, and a similar group is given the existing standard drug. The effects are then monitored. The use of randomised controlled trials raises a number of important concerns. First, the consent of the patient must be obtained to the trial, in order to have her autonomy respected. Obtaining a legally valid consent from the patient would require an explanation of the nature of the trial and the fact that allocation of treatment is random. If this is not done, the patient would have a claim in battery. Secondly, a doctor is under a duty to give the patient the best treatment. This is not compatible with entering the patient in a trial where treatment is allocated randomly. Only if the doctor is genuinely unsure about which treatment is most effective can the trial be ethical. Thirdly, the patients allocated to the group given the new drug will be exposed to new risks. The patient must be told of these risks in order to obtain a valid consent. Fourthly, at what point should the trial be stopped? Should this be when evidence emerges that a new drug is better than an existing one, or conversely if evidence emerges that the new drug is causing harm to the research subjects? From a duty based viewpoint the answer would be 'yes' in both cases.

Trials of new drugs are now governed by the Medicines for Human Use (Clinical Trials) Regulations 2004. The licensing authority is the Medicines and Healthcare products Regulatory Agency (MHRA). Any trial involving healthy volunteers needs authorisation from the MHRA. Under reg 12, no one may start or conduct a clinical trial unless this has been authorised by the licensing authority and approved by an ethics committee. Provision is also made for trials to be stopped if something goes wrong.

CONSENT TO RESEARCH

The need for the research subject to consent to a trial was set out in the Nuremberg Code. The legal principles which apply are similar to the position where medical treatment is given to a patient. It may be argued that a patient taking part in medical research should be given more information than when being given medical treatment because of the additional risk involved. There are a number of difficulties arising with consent to research. These include the fact that the nature of a clinical trial means there are unknown factors about it, so the amount of information will be limited. The nature of the patient's condition is also important, as they may be so ill the very fact of being entered in a trial would make their condition worse. The individual views and beliefs of the patient may be significant. For example, a woman with breast cancer who does not want to be disfigured should not be put forward for a trial between mastectomy (removal of the breast) and lumpectomy (removal of the growth from the breast).

The requirements for a valid consent are put neatly by Mason, McCall-Smith and Laurie (*Law and Medical Ethics*, 6th edn, 2002, London: Butterworths) as follows: 'It is widely agreed that the patient's consent must be based on four main lines of explanation: the purpose of the experiment;

the benefits to the patient and society; the risks involved; and the alternatives open to the subject.'

A useful decision to consider is the Canadian case of *Halushka v University of Saskatchewan* (1965). The claimant student agreed to undergo a test involving a new drug at the hospital for $50. He was told that a catheter would be inserted in a vein and that the test would last a couple of hours and that it was a 'safe test and there was nothing to worry about'. In fact, the drug was a new anaesthetic that had not been used before. During the test the catheter was advanced towards his heart and his heart stopped. Although it was restarted, he was in a coma for four days. He sued for trespass and negligence. The Saskatchewan Court of Appeal said that the duty owed by a researcher to a research subject is 'at least as great as, if not greater than, the duty owed by the ordinary physician or surgeon to his patient'. There are no exceptions to disclosure as with medical treatment. The researcher does not have to balance the lack of treatment against the risk of the treatment. The research subject is entitled 'to full and frank disclosure of all the facts, probabilities and opinions which a reasonable man might be expected to consider before giving his consent'. The claimant had not been told that the catheter would be advanced towards the heart and even though this was not the cause of the heart stopping, it may have meant the claimant refused to consent. His consent was invalid and the defendants were liable in trespass. Even though this case is about non-therapeutic research, rather than research to benefit a patient, it provides clear guidance that in such circumstances a research subject should be given full information about the nature of the procedure and the risks. With therapeutic research, other considerations have to be taken into account and such a full disclosure may not be required.

The General Medical Council (GMC) have also issued guidance on research, *The Role and Responsibilities of Doctors* (2002):

Para 16 Participants' consent is legally valid and professionally acceptable only where participants are competent to give consent, have been properly informed, and have agreed without coercion.

Para 19 You must ensure that any individuals whom you invite to take part in research are given the information which they want or ought to know and that it is presented in terms and a form that they can understand.

Paragraph 20 sets out what that information should include, for example, the aims of the research, why the patient has been asked to take part, if the project involves randomisation, information about possible benefits and risks, that the patient can withdraw at any time and the compensation available if they suffer harm.

Another issue with consent is that it must be a voluntary consent. A doctor treating a patient must ensure that the patient entering a trial does not feel compelled to enter it. This problem is more pronounced in the case of non-therapeutic research where volunteers are used and sometimes given payment. It is important in such circumstances to make sure that the volunteers are not subject to any pressure to take part in the research.

As regards trials of drugs, Sched 1, para 3 of the Medicines for Human Use (Clinical Trials) Regulations 2004 provides that a person only gives an informed consent if it is given freely after that person is told of the nature, implications and risks, and either it is evidenced in writing, dated and signed or, if unable to sign it, is given orally in the presence of one witness.

CHILDREN AND RESEARCH

The question of when children can consent to research poses even more problems than with adults consenting to research. If a child is not capable legally of consenting, can a parent consent for the child? The starting point is the *Gillick* case, which provided that a child can consent to medical treatment when they reach a sufficient age and understanding to make a judgment about a particular treatment. If a child is a patient and the research is aimed at providing therapeutic treatment, it can be argued that a *Gillick* competent child could consent to take part in the research. With therapeutic treatment, a parent would be able to give a valid consent for a child who was not *Gillick* competent. However, if the child was to be entered in a randomised controlled trial, that would change the picture. The child may not then receive treatment, for example, if the child was given a placebo, or may not receive the best treatment, and it could be argued that entering the child in the trial would not be acting in their best interests. Even if consent is given by a parent, it is good medical practice for the doctor to obtain the consent of the child where the child has some understanding of what is involved. The Royal College of Paediatrics and Child Health have issued guidance which provides that the consent of the child should be obtained from the age of five years.

But what is the position with non-therapeutic research? Can a child consent to research that will not provide an immediate benefit to them? Section 8 of the Family Law Reform Act 1969 allows children over 16 years to consent to medical treatment but this would only cover therapeutic treatment. Resort must then be had to the *Gillick* case. If the child is considered to have sufficient understanding to appreciate the risks and the fact that the child would not benefit, the child could consent. Parents can consent to experimental treatment even if the effects are unknown if the circumstances are such that there is no alternative. In *Simms v Simms* (2003), the parents of two 16 year old victims of variant Creutzfeldt-Jakob disease (vCJD) wished to consent to experimental treatment which carried no significant risk to the victims. The victims were too ill to consent. The court said that taking into account the fact that there was no cure and the treatment would not make the condition worse, the parents could give a valid consent. However, it is difficult to see how a parent could give a valid consent for a child when the research is not for their benefit.

The Medicines for Human Use (Clinical Trials) Regulations 2004, which apply in the case of trials of drugs, set out conditions which apply in the case of minors, in Sched 1, Pt 4. A minor is anyone under 16 years old. A person with parental responsibility or, if it is an emergency, a legal representative, may give consent for a minor to take part in a trial. The person consenting must be told that the minor may withdraw at any time. The minor must be given information about the risks and benefits according to his capacity to understand. No incentives or financial inducements must be given to the minor. The trial must relate directly to a condition from which the minor suffers or the trial is such that it can only be carried out on minors.

INCOMPETENT ADULTS

Should research ever be carried out on an incompetent adult? Such a person cannot give a valid consent and no one can consent on their behalf. The Law Commission in their report, *Mental Incapacity* (Report No 231, 1995, London: HMSO), have said that as regards non-therapeutic research any touching of the person is a battery, unless it can be justified on the basis of necessity. The Law Commission accepted that non-therapeutic research does take place on incompetent adult patients. The Commission recommended that such research should be lawful if the research is into a condition from which that person suffers.

Guidance can be found from the Draft Additional Protocol to the Convention on Human Rights and Biomedicine, released for consultation in 2001. It proposes that research may be carried out on persons without capacity to consent if:

(a) the results of the research have the potential to produce real and direct benefit to the subject's health;

(b) research of comparative effectiveness cannot be carried out on persons able to consent;

(c) where possible, the persons undergoing the research have been informed of their rights and the safeguards prescribed;

(d) the necessary authorisation has been given specifically and in writing by the legal representative or an authority, person or body provided for by national law, taking into account any previously expressed wishes or objections by the subject; and

(e) the person concerned does not object to taking part.

This Convention has not been ratified by the UK. The law needs to address the issues arising in the case of incompetent adults being used in research.

The Medicines for Human Use (Clinical Trials) Regulations 2004 apply to trials involving drugs. Under Sched 1, certain conditions are set out for the protection of incapacitated adults. Under Pt 1(5), any adult unable to give an informed consent due to physical or mental incapacity and before that incapacity refused to take part, cannot be included in a trial. As regards other incapacitated adults, Pt 5 sets out certain conditions, which include the following: an informed consent may be given by someone with a relationship to that person or by a 'legal representative' or from their doctor, if the doctor is independent of the trial; the person giving the consent must be told about the objectives and the risks of the trial; they must be told that the research subject may be withdrawn at any time; the research subject must be given information about the risks and benefits according to their capacity; the trial must relate to a life threatening or debilitating condition from which the subject suffers. Enabling someone to give consent for an incapacitated adult is a new step, as up to now no one has had authority to make decisions for an incapacitated adult.

The Mental Capacity Bill makes various provisions for research on a person lacking capacity (see cll 30–33).

CONFIDENTIALITY AND RESEARCH

At common law, a doctor is under a duty to keep information about a patient obtained in the course of treatment confidential. Likewise, a doctor conducting research has a duty of confidence to the patient. However, there is a difference with research in that the results of the research need to be published for the benefit of others. Does such publication amount to a breach of confidence or can it be justified as being in the 'public interest'? When the patient agrees to take part in the research, they may agree to disclosure of information and this would be a good defence. Alternatively, disclosure would have to be in the public interest. Doctors may be asked for information about patients for research and a doctor would only be able to give this information with the consent of the patient or if the information was anonymised; otherwise it would be a breach of the duty of confidence.

The GMC has given guidance in *Research: The Role and Responsibilities of Doctors* (2002). Paragraph 30 provides that doctors should obtain consent to disclosure, anonymise the data where this will serve the purpose, and keep disclosures to the minimum necessary. Paragraph 31 provides that patient records should not be disclosed unless express consent has been obtained, wherever that is practicable. Paragraph 32 provides that if it is not practicable to obtain consent or anonymise records, the patient must be told about access to their records and given the opportunity to object and any objection must be respected. This reflects the common law position.

The other important consideration with confidentiality is the Data Protection Act 1998, which came into force on 1 March 2000. The Act covers all personal data whether kept in a manual file or electronically. Under the Act, the Information Commissioner keeps a register of data controllers. A data controller is someone who determines the purpose or way in which data is processed and this would include a researcher. Each organisation must have a data controller to see that the requirements of the Act are followed. Information about a patient's health is within the definition of 'sensitive personal data', which can only be used subject to certain conditions.

The first data protection principle is that data shall be processed 'fairly and lawfully'. To fulfil this requirement, one requirement of Sched 2 and one requirement of Sched 3 must be met. Under Sched 2, the requirements include if the patient has given 'explicit consent', and if it is in the 'legitimate interests' of the data controller, unless this would prejudice the data subject. Under Sched 3, the requirements include medical purposes 'including preventative medicine, diagnosis, research, care, treatment and management of healthcare services'.

The Data Protection Act 1998 does not apply if the data has been anonymised, as it is not then personal data. In *R v Department of Health ex p Source Informatics Ltd* (2000), pharmacists sold information on prescriptions about drugs to SI Ltd but they removed the name of the patients. The Court of Appeal held that this was not a breach of the duty of confidence at common law and neither was it a breach of the Data Protection Act 1998.

COMPENSATION

If the research subject suffers injury during the trial as a result of something going wrong, can they claim compensation? It may be possible to bring a claim in negligence. This claim could be against the researchers for the way in which they devised or conducted the trial. Alternatively, a claim could conceivably be made against the local REC in approving the trial.

There are strong arguments that healthy volunteers for non-therapeutic research should be entitled to compensation without proving negligence because they take risks which may lead to benefits for all. In 1978, the Pearson Commission recommended that if any volunteer for medical research suffered harm, the authority carrying out the research should be strictly liable. Since then, various similar recommendations have been made. The Department of Health makes *ex gratia* payments to those injured but this is hardly satisfactory and the law needs to be changed.

Under the Medicine for Human Use (Clinical Trial) Regulations 2004, applications for testing new drugs have to be approved by an ethics committee and, under reg 15, in considering its opinion, the committee must consider a long list of matters including provision for compensation in the event of injury or death resulting from the trial; the insurance cover of the sponsor; and the amounts for compensating subjects. This makes compensation an important factor and this could be used as a model for all clinical trials.

SUMMARY – MEDICAL RESEARCH

1 *Ethics*
   • Duty based: do not harm research subject.
   • Utilitarian: main consideration is overall benefit to society.

2   *Ethical codes*
  • Declaration of Helsinki 1964: interests of research subject take precedence over science, etc.
  • GMC: *The Role and Responsibilities of Doctors*, 2002: need to give information and obtain consent.

3   *Research ethics committees*
  • Need approval for research involving NHS patients or facilities.
  • Drugs trials: need approval of committee and the MHRA (Medicine for Human Use (Clinical Trial) Regulations 2004).

4   *Randomised controlled trials*
  • Standard surgical procedure used for one group and new procedure for second group.
  • Problems with consent, best treatment, extra risks, stopping trial.
  • Drug trials now need authority of MHRA and ethics committee.

5   *Consent to research*
  • Must be told benefits and risks, and alternatives.
  • Therapeutic research.
  • Non-therapeutic research: *Halushka v University of Saskatchewan* (1965).
  • Drug trials: need signed consent.

6   *Children*
  • Therapeutic research: *Gillick* competent child could consent; parent could consent for child without capacity.
  • Problems if a randomised controlled trial.
  • Non-therapeutic research: may be able to consent if *Gillick* competent.
  • Non-therapeutic research: parents could consent in extreme situations: *Simms v Simms* (2003).
  • Drug trials: parents can consent for child under 16 years.

7   *Incompetent adults*
  • Cannot consent and no one can consent for them.
  • Law Commission: research should be lawful if on condition from which adult suffers.
  • Drug trials: consent may be given by others and research on something from which the subject suffers.

8   *Confidentiality*
  • Duty of confidence, but exceptions: consent and public interest.
  • Data Protection Act 1998: need explicit consent or be in interests of data controller; but if data anonymised it may be used: *R v Department of Health ex p Source Informatics Ltd* (2000).

9   *Compensation*
  • Possible claim in negligence.
  • Arguments for strict liability.

CHAPTER 9

DEATH

INTRODUCTION

Death is a taboo subject in contemporary society and it raises many difficult ethical and legal issues. Medical advances mean that more people can be kept alive for longer, and this merely highlights the problems. When does someone die? Is the principle of the sanctity of human life paramount and should all means be used to keep people alive, whatever the cost, or should there be limits on the use of scarce medical resources to keep people alive? This question is particularly relevant to babies born with severe brain damage: should they be allowed to die? Is there a right to life and a right to die? Are there legal and moral differences between killing and letting die? How should the criminal law deal with 'mercy killing'? There are also the difficult questions about the 'quality of life' of patients with terminal illnesses. What of the position of patients in a 'persistent vegetative state'; should treatment be withdrawn? To what extent does the Human Rights Act 1998 help to protect peoples' rights? This chapter will examine these issues. However, there are no simple resolutions to most of them.

DEFINING 'DEATH'

Forty years ago, if someone's heart stopped, they would have been pronounced dead, but, fortunately, that is no longer the case, as it is now possible to resuscitate people. Deciding when someone is dead has changed over the years, as medical understanding and technology has advanced. In 1976, the Conference of Royal Colleges and their Faculties published a report that brain death could be diagnosed with certainty. It has been accepted by the medical profession that if a patient is diagnosed as 'brain stem dead', this means that the patient is dead. Certain tests can be carried out to determine if this has happened, and, once it is established, the process is irreversible, even though a patient may still be able to breathe using a ventilator. The Department of Health Code of Practice endorses this:

> Death entails the irreversible loss of those essential characteristics which are necessary to the existence of a living human person. Thus, it is recommended that the definition of death should be regarded as 'irreversible loss of the capacity for consciousness, combined with irreversible loss of the capacity to breathe'.

The courts have accepted this practice of the medical profession. In *R v Malcherek; R v Steel* (1981), M stabbed his wife, who was put on a ventilator. It was later discovered that she had irreversible brain damage and the ventilator was switched off. M argued that he had not caused the death but that it was the doctor, by switching off the ventilator. It was held by the Court of Appeal that the original act by M was a substantial and continuing cause of death. The doctor switching off the ventilator did not break the chain of causation, because the victim was already dead. The court did not give a definition of death but accepted the practice of doctors, who had concluded that the patient was, 'for all practical purposes', dead.

The courts confirmed in a later case that brain stem death means that someone is dead. In *Re A* (1992), a badly injured child was put on a ventilator but was later diagnosed as brain stem dead. The parents wanted the ventilator to be kept on. The court made a declaration that someone certified as brain stem dead was dead for all legal, as well as medical, purposes. If a doctor switched off the ventilator, the doctor was not acting illegally. The court added that the child could not be made a ward of court, as the court did not have jurisdiction over a dead child.

One problem with brain stem death is that it does not give a time of death; it tells us only that the patient is dead when the tests are carried out. This could cause legal problems if the exact time of death was important. This might be necessary to determine who should inherit property under a will, whether inheritance tax is payable on a lifetime gift or whether payment should be made on a life insurance policy in the case of suicide.

There has also been some concern that patients could be diagnosed as brain stem dead simply so that their organs can be used for transplants.

Another issue is whether there should be a legal definition of 'death'. Those in favour of having a definition argue that this would bring certainty to the law, but the argument against is that any rigid definition would soon be out of date. Following a Code of Practice enables new developments in medicine to be taken into account without having to change a legal definition.

A problem also arises in the case of babies born with part of their brain missing (anencephalic), as the test of brain stem death cannot be used to determine if the baby is dead. If the organs are required for transplant, should the baby be treated as dead?

Knowledge that you are dying

Does a patient who is dying have the right to know that fact? In practice, doctors will frequently not tell a dying patient that they are dying. This may be justified on the basis that knowing might make the patient's condition worse and the doctor can rely on 'therapeutic privilege'. The patient will have access to their notes but the information that they are dying may lawfully be withheld if it is likely to cause distress. However, the duty to respect the patient's autonomy would require a patient to be told whether they were dying, if the patient asked.

SUICIDE

Originally, suicide was a crime at common law. The Suicide Act 1961 changed the law and it is not now a criminal offence to take your own life. However, s 2(1) of that Act makes it an offence if someone 'aids, abets, counsels or procures the suicide of another, or an attempt by another to commit suicide'. In *Attorney General v Able* (1984), the Voluntary Euthanasia Society distributed a leaflet setting out ways to commit suicide. The question arose as to whether this was an offence under s 2. Woolf J said that, in order to prove that distributing the booklet was assisting suicide under s 2(1), three things had to be proved: (a) that the defendant intended the booklet to be used by someone contemplating suicide; (b) that the defendant distributed the booklet to such a person; and (c) that such a person was assisted or encouraged to commit suicide by reading the booklet. The court applied the three requirements and said that: (a) the defendant would know that some of those the booklet was sent to would be contemplating suicide; and (b) that the defendant had distributed the booklet. But as regards (c), the defendants would not necessarily know that the booklet was to be used to assist a member to commit suicide. It could have been obtained for information or research purposes. The accessory would not know if the principal was contemplating suicide. Therefore, the booklet was not illegal, as the third requirement could not be proved in any particular case.

An offence may be committed under s 2 even if no attempt to commit suicide is made by the other person. In *R v McShane* (1977), a wealthy old lady who lived in a nursing home was given drugs by her daughter in an attempt to persuade the mother to kill herself, so that the daughter could inherit. The daughter was found guilty.

In *R (on the Application of Pretty) v DPP* (2002), Diane Pretty suffered from motor neuron disease, which was a degenerative condition, and she did not have long to live. Although she was paralysed from the neck down she was mentally competent. She wanted to decide when and how she died but she needed her husband to help her to die. Under s 2(4) of the Suicide Act, a prosecution can only take place with the consent of the Director of Public Prosecutions (DPP). She wanted an undertaking from the DPP that if her husband helped her to die, he would not be prosecuted under s 2(1) of the Suicide Act 1961 for assisting her suicide. The DPP refused to give such an undertaking and Diane Pretty applied for judicial review. She claimed that the refusal breached her rights under the Convention or, alternatively, that s 2(1) of the Suicide Act 1961 was incompatible with the Convention as it imposed a blanket ban on assisted suicide. She relied on Arts 2 (right to life), 3 (right not to be subjected to degrading treatment), 8 (private and family life) and 14 (rights in Convention without discrimination). The case reached the House of Lords where, as regards Art 2, Diane Pretty claimed that the right to life included the right of self-determination, which covered the right to commit suicide with help. The court said that Art 2 was based on the principle of sanctity of life and it provided a guarantee that no individual should be deprived of their life. 'The purpose of Art 2(1) is clear. It enunciates the principle of the sanctity of life and provides a guarantee that no individual "shall be deprived of life" by means of intentional human intervention' (Lord Steyn). The court said that a state did not have to make assisted suicide legal to comply with the Convention. Lord Steyn added:

> It does not require the state to repeal a provision such as s 2(1) of the 1961 Act. On the other hand, it is open to a democratic legislature to introduce such a measure. Our Parliament, if so minded, may therefore repeal s 2(1) and put in its place a regulated system for assisted suicide (presumably doctor assisted) with appropriate safeguards.

In *Pretty v UK* (2002), the European Court of Human Rights confirmed that the right to life did not include a right to assisted suicide. By refusing to give an undertaking that Mr Pretty would not be prosecuted, the DPP was not in breach of Art 2.

There is a growing practice of taking people abroad and helping them to die in countries where it is legal to do so. The question arises whether helping someone in such a way could lead to prosecution under s 2(1). This issue was highlighted in *Re Z (An Adult: Capacity)* (2004). Mrs Z suffered from a progressive and incurable brain disease and was looked after by her husband. Mrs Z's condition had deteriorated and she wished to end her life but did not have the physical capability to do so. Her husband agreed to take her to Switzerland where it is lawful to help someone to die. The local authority found out and brought the case to court. The court held that Mrs Z had the mental capacity to make the decision about dying and understood the consequences. The local authority had fulfilled its duties to her. Although her husband was free to take her abroad, the court pointed out that by doing so he could be committing an offence under s 2(1).

Is there a right to obtain help from a doctor to commit suicide? (This is called physician-assisted suicide, as mentioned by Lord Steyn above.) If a patient asked a doctor for a fatal dose of pills and the doctor handed over the pills, would that be an offence under s 2? It would seem to fall within s 2(1). It has been argued that patients should have the right to ask their doctor for help to commit suicide, as this would give the patient control over when they die. The House of Lords Select Committee was against a change in the law. Paragraph 262 stated: 'As far as assisted suicide is concerned, we see no reason to recommend any change in the law. We identify no circumstances in which assisted suicide should be permitted, nor do we see any reason to distinguish between the act of a doctor or of any other person in this connection' (*Report of the Select Committee on Medical Ethics* (HL Paper 21, Session 1993–94)).

In the US, in *Vacco v Quill* (1997), a court had ruled that a State law, which made assisted suicide for the terminally ill a criminal offence, was unconstitutional under the Fourteenth Amendment, which provides for equal protection. It was argued that patients can ask for removal of life sustaining treatment, but those not on life sustaining treatment cannot obtain help to die and are therefore treated unequally, so physician-assisted suicide should be made legal. The Supreme Court overruled this decision in *Vacco v Quill* (1997), and said that there was a fundamental distinction between refusing treatment and actively ending life. This decision maintains the distinction between leaving a fatal dose of pills for a patient and giving the patient a lethal injection. The Oregon Death With Dignity Act 1994 provides for an adult patient, who is suffering from a terminal illness and who has expressed a wish to die, to make a written request to a doctor for medication to end their life. There must be two witnesses who sign the written request to confirm that the patient is acting voluntarily. The patient's condition must be confirmed by a second doctor. There must be a period of 48 hours between the written request and the prescription for medication.

The issue of physician-assisted suicide raises both legal and ethical issues. In particular, the fact that if introduced in the UK, it would transform the role of the doctor from being seen as a healer, to someone who could effectively kill patients.

EUTHANASIA

The word 'euthanasia' means bringing about a gentle and easy death. It is usually used in the context of killing someone with a terminal illness, who is in great pain. The idea of euthanasia has provoked a debate on whether it should be allowed by law. Those against euthanasia argue that the principle of the sanctity of life should be followed, which is based on the Christian principle that it is wrong to take a human life. However, the principle of the sanctity of life is not an absolute one and, in exceptional circumstances, it is permissible to kill, for example, in self-defence or war. Those in favour of euthanasia argue on the basis of the principle of respect for autonomy: that people have a right to decide when they die and how they die. This is exemplified in the demand for a 'right to die' and was highlighted in the recent case concerning Diane Pretty.

There are a number of ways in which euthanasia may be categorised:

(a) voluntary, involuntary and non-voluntary:

- voluntary – the patient asks for their life to be ended;
- involuntary – ending the patient's life without a request or against the patient's wishes;
- non-voluntary – ending the life of an incompetent patient who is unable to express their views;

(b) active and passive:

- active – a positive act to end the patient's life;
- passive – an omission which leads to the patient's death.

There is a long history of attempts to pass legislation that would make euthanasia lawful. In 1936, a Euthanasia Bill provided for someone over 21, who was suffering from an incurable illness, to sign a form requesting euthanasia. This had to be witnessed by two people. A euthanasia referee would then interview the patient and, eventually, the case would go to court, which could authorise euthanasia. The Voluntary Euthanasia Bill 1969 allowed a patient over 21 years, who was certified by two doctors as suffering from an incurable disease, to request euthanasia in writing. Since that time, a number of other Bills have been introduced, but without success.

In January 2004, the Assisted Dying for the Terminally Ill Bill was introduced in the House of Lords by Lord Joffe. This Private Members' Bill has been prompted by developments since the House of Lords Select Committee on Medical Ethics reported in 1994. These include legalisation of euthanasia in the Netherlands and in Oregon, which have provided some evidence of how a system of euthanasia operates. A number of terminally ill people have travelled to Switzerland to be helped to die, such as Reginald Crew, who suffered from motor neuron disease. Some doctors have admitted that they have helped terminally ill patients to die at the patients' request. The Bill would allow a competent adult with a terminal illness who was suffering unbearably to receive medical assistance to die. Clause 1(1) provides: 'Subject to the provisions of this Act, it shall be lawful for a physician to assist a patient who is a qualifying patient, and who has made a declaration in accordance with this Act that is for the time being in force, to die.' A doctor would be able to provide the patient with the means to end their life or, if the patient was physically unable to do so, the doctor could end their life. Certain qualifying conditions must be met under cl 2. The doctor must: be told by the patient that the patient wishes to be assisted to die; examine the patient to see that the patient is not incompetent; determine that the patient is suffering unbearably because of a terminal illness; tell the patient of his diagnosis, prognosis, the process of being assisted to die and the alternatives; if the patient persists, satisfy himself that the request is voluntary; and refer the patient to a consultant to confirm the diagnosis. Clause 3 provides that the doctor must ensure that a specialist in palliative care sees the patient to discuss the option of palliative care. Under cl 4, the patient must sign a written declaration, as set out in the Schedule. This must be witnessed by two individuals, one of whom is a practising solicitor. The solicitor must be satisfied that the patient is known to the solicitor or has proved his identity; it appears the patient is of sound mind and has made the declaration voluntarily; and the solicitor is satisfied that the patient understands the declaration. The other witness must also know the patient or have had his identity proved, and it must appear to the witness that the patient is of sound mind and has made the declaration voluntarily. The patient and witnesses must sign and witness the declaration respectively at the same time and in the presence of the others. The consultant or any member of the care team, a relative or partner of the patient cannot witness the declaration. Under cl 6, a patient may revoke his declaration orally or in any other way and without regard to his physical or mental condition. Clause 7 provides that no person shall be under a duty to participate in diagnosis or treatment under the Act to which he has a conscientious objection. Clause 10 provides that a doctor acting in good faith who assists a patient to die, or attempts to do so, in accordance with the requirements of this Act shall not be guilty of an offence. The Bill draws in part on the Dutch legislation but it is unlikely to become law.

Active euthanasia

Active euthanasia, which is a deliberate act to end the life of the patient, is prohibited in English law and would lead to a charge of murder or manslaughter. In *R v Cox* (1992), an old lady who suffered from rheumatoid arthritis was in great pain and wanted to die. She asked Dr Cox to end her life. The doctor gave her an injection of potassium chloride, which is a poison and has no painkilling effects. She died a few minutes later. Dr Cox was convicted of attempted murder. The judge said: '... if he injected her with potassium chloride for the primary purpose of killing her, of hastening her death, he is guilty of the offence charged ...' The doctor's motive of helping to put the patient out of her misery was immaterial. It was unclear, on the evidence, whether the patient was so close to death that she would have died anyway. Dr Cox was given a sentence of one year's imprisonment, suspended for 12 months. In fact, Dr Cox was only charged with attempted murder because the body had been cremated and it would have been difficult to prove he had caused her death.

There is an exception to the above rule that a doctor cannot do an act that ends the life of a patient. This involves the ethical principle of 'double effect'. This principle says that a person can do an act that has a good objective if the *intention* is to produce the good objective but *in fact* it has a bad effect. There must be a sufficient reason to risk the bad effect. An example of how this might work is if a doctor gave a terminally ill patient, who was in great pain, an injection of painkilling drugs, but these had the side effect of shortening the patient's life. In *R v Adams* (1957), Dr Adams gave large doses of morphine to an elderly patient who had suffered a stroke and, as a result of these injections, she died. Devlin J said:

> ... a doctor who was aiding the sick and dying need not calculate in minutes, or even hours, and perhaps not in days or weeks, the effect upon a patient's life of the medicines which he administers or else be in peril of a charge of murder. If the first purpose of medicine, the restoration of health, can no longer be achieved, there is still much for a doctor to do, and he is entitled to do all that is proper and necessary to relieve pain and suffering, even if the measures he takes may incidentally shorten life.

Dr Adams argued that he had given these doses to relieve pain and that shortening the patient's life was merely incidental to this purpose. He did not give the morphine with the intent to kill his patient. He was found not guilty. In 1999, Dr David Moor injected a patient with a lethal amount of diamorphine but was found not guilty of murder. He argued that he gave the drug to ease pain:

The family of the victim did not want Dr Moor to be prosecuted. In fact, Dr Moor had admitted to killing over 300 patients in this way and such practice is not uncommon amongst general practitioners. If doctors were allowed to kill patients, this would have a profound effect, not only on the role of the doctor, but also on the view taken of doctors by patients. Doctors would not then be viewed as healers.

The case of the conjoined twins, *Re A (Children)* (2001), seems to be a step towards active euthanasia because it involved the ending of Mary's life for the benefit of her twin sister Jodie.

Outline of euthanasia in The Netherlands

Until recently, active euthanasia was a criminal offence in The Netherlands. Article 293(1) of the Dutch Criminal Code provides: 'A person who terminates the life of another person at that person's express and earnest request is liable to a term of imprisonment ...' In addition, Art 294(1) provides that 'A person who intentionally incites another to commit suicide, is liable to a term of imprisonment ...'; and Art 294(2) provides that 'A person who intentionally assists in the suicide of another or procures for that other person the means to commit suicide, is liable to a term of imprisonment ...'.

However, a doctor could claim the defence of necessity (or *force majeure*) under Art 40 if they acted in the face of conflicting duties. In 1984, the Royal Dutch Medical Association set out guidelines which had to be followed before euthanasia was carried out, and these were subsequently confirmed by the courts. The guidelines provided as follows:

• the patient must make a voluntary request;

• the request must be well considered and persistent;

• the patient must be in intolerable suffering (not necessarily physical);

• euthanasia must be a last resort;

• euthanasia must be performed by a doctor;

• the doctor must have consulted with an independent doctor.

In addition, the doctor had to follow the procedure that had been agreed by the Royal Dutch Medical Association and the Ministry of Justice in 1990. The doctor carrying out euthanasia had to tell the local medical examiner that he was doing so; the examiner reported to the district attorney; and the attorney decided whether or not to prosecute. Doctors who followed the above guidelines and procedure were unlikely to be prosecuted. In the *Alkmaar* case (1985), a doctor was prosecuted under Art 293 after giving lethal injections to a 95 year old patient who was seriously ill and had no prospects of recovery. The patient had said she wanted to die. The Supreme Court held that the defence of necessity or *force majeure* under Art 40 could apply where there were conflicting duties, which were, in this case, to uphold the law against taking life and to act in the patient's best interests. It was considered that the doctor had acted in accordance with medical standards and he was acquitted. This case was widely seen as confirming the acceptability of active voluntary euthanasia if the guidelines were followed. In the later case of *Chabot* (1992) (see Otlowski, M, *Voluntary Euthanasia and the Common Law*, 1997, Oxford: OUP, p 405), a depressed patient who had unsuccessfully attempted suicide (but who was not suffering from any other illnesses) consulted Dr Chabot for therapy. After one month, the patient still wanted to die and Dr Chabot provided her with a lethal dose, which she took in his presence. He was prosecuted under Art 294. The Supreme Court accepted that euthanasia was available to a patient with a psychiatric illness and that the defence of necessity was available to a doctor in such cases. But Dr Chabot was found guilty because, although he had consulted seven other doctors, none of them had examined the patient, so there was no other evidence the doctor had acted in an emergency. However, no punishment was given because of the circumstances and the evidence that it was likely that the patient would have committed suicide anyway. This decision was seen as widening the availability of euthanasia and a step down a slippery slope.

A study of the practice of euthanasia in The Netherlands, the *Remmelink Report* (1991), reported that, in 1990, there were 2,300 cases of active voluntary euthanasia and 400 cases of assisted suicide (about 2% of all deaths). Although this could be seen as dispelling fears that thousands of patients were being killed, the number of cases not reported is unknown. A more recent study of euthanasia in The Netherlands concluded: 'the reality is that a clear majority of cases of euthanasia, both with and without request, go unreported and unchecked. Dutch claims of effective regulation ring hollow' (Jochemsen, H and Keown, J, 'Voluntary euthanasia under control? The latest empirical evidence on euthanasia in The Netherlands', *Journal of Medical Ethics*, 1999, vol 25(1), pp 16–21). In 1999, legislation was proposed to legalise euthanasia.

In 2001, the Dutch Parliament passed legislation giving doctors immunity from prosecution for mercy killing and assisted suicide if they follow certain conditions ('Dutch become first to legalise euthanasia' (2000) *The Times*, 29 November). This article states that Dutch doctors already perform euthanasia on 3,200 patients each year. The new law, the Termination of Life on Request and Assisted Suicide (Review Procedures) Act 2001, amends the Dutch Criminal Code to allow euthanasia. Article 293(1) still makes euthanasia a criminal offence. However, Art 293(2) provides: 'The offence referred to in the first paragraph shall not be punishable if it has been committed by a physician who has met the requirements of due care as referred to in Article 2 of the Termination of Life on Request and Assisted Suicide (Review Procedures) Act and who informs the municipal autopsist ...'

The requirements of due care are set out in Art 2 of the Act. The physician must: (a) be satisfied that the request by the patient was voluntary and well considered; (b) be satisfied that the suffering is lasting and unbearable; (c) tell the patient about the disease and his prospects; (d) check that the patient is convinced that there is no other reasonable solution; (e) consult at least one other independent physician who has seen the patient; and (f) terminate the life or assist the suicide with due care. All six requirements must be complied with. The physician has to report all cases to the regional review committee and must establish all the six requirements to the satisfaction of the committee. If this is done, there is no need for the Public Prosecution Service to be informed. These requirements are very similar to the previous guidelines although the second doctor must now see the patient, which was not previously required. As regards children, Art 2(3) and 2(4) of the 2001 Act provide that children between 16 and 18 years, who have a 'reasonable understanding' of their interests, may make a written statement requesting termination of life if their parents have been involved in the process, although the parents do not have to consent. For children between 12 and 16 years, the consent of the parents is required. Under Art 2(2), if a patient over 16 years is incompetent but has previously made a written statement requesting termination of his life, the physician can follow that request. The requirements of due care still apply. This changes the previous law under which living wills were not binding.

The new law is not vastly different from previous practice but nonetheless it does mark the State allowing euthanasia and assisted suicide:

> The Dutch Government simply now formally and unambiguously recognises what has been going on for a decade, which is that euthanasia is practised on a large scale in the Netherlands, that physicians have generally adopted certain rules of 'careful practice' and that they have often been open and frank about this. [De Haan, J, 'The new Dutch law on euthanasia', *Med LR*, 10, 2002]

Passive euthanasia

This is the ending of life by an omission to act. In fact, it covers situations of non-treatment, withdrawal of treatment and refusal of treatment. The legal position can be summed up in the words of the writer Arthur Clough: 'Thou shalt not kill but needs't not strive officiously to keep alive.' The law recognises a distinction between an act and an omission. However, in the context of medical care, health staff owe a duty to the patient and an omission to act to help the patient would be a breach of that duty. A layperson may also be under a duty to act to help another close relative. In *R v Stone and Dobinson* (1977), the defendants were a man aged 67 years, of low intelligence, and his mistress, who was mentally inadequate. They took Stone's sister into their home. The sister, who was in her 50s, developed anorexia nervosa and became bedridden. The defendants did not call a doctor to see her or obtain any other outside help. A month after taking to her bed, she was found dead as a result of blood poisoning from infected bedsores. It was held by the Court of Appeal that the defendants had taken on the duty of caring for the sister and were grossly negligent in failing to carry out that duty. They had omitted to summon help and were convicted of manslaughter.

But is this distinction between acts and omissions always clear? If a doctor switches off the ventilator of a patient who has no chance of recovery, is this an act? In *Airedale NHS Trust v Bland* (1993), Lord Goff gave the example of a doctor switching off a machine as compared to an interloper who maliciously switches it off and stated that, 'the doctor, in discontinuing life support, is simply allowing his patient to die of his pre-existing condition; the interloper is actively intervening to stop the doctor from prolonging the patient's life, and such conduct cannot possibly be categorised as an omission'. Mason, McCall-Smith and Laurie point out that categorising switching off a machine as an omission is 'untenable' (*Law and Medical Ethics*, 6th edn, 2002, London: Butterworths).

Even if a distinction can be made legally between killing and letting die, can the distinction be justified from an ethical standpoint? It may be argued that both the intention and the consequences of an act and an omission are the same and, therefore, there is no moral difference between them. In *Bland*, Lord Browne-Wilkinson commented:

> How can it be lawful to allow a patient to die slowly, though painlessly, over a period of weeks from lack of food but unlawful to produce his immediate death by a lethal injection, thereby saving his family from yet another ordeal to add to the tragedy that has already struck them? I find it difficult to find a moral answer to that question. But it is undoubtedly the law ...

NON-TREATMENT

In some medical situations, medical staff follow a policy of non-treatment. Examples include certain newborn babies and incompetent adults. The issue of non-treatment involves considering the question of the extent of the duty to act to save someone's life. The Catholic doctrine of ordinary and extraordinary means is relevant here. This doctrine was set out in a directive issued by Pope Pius XII in 1957:

> Man has a right and a duty in case of severe illness to take the necessary steps to preserve life and health ... But he is obliged at all times to employ only ordinary means ... that is to say those means which do not impose an extraordinary burden on himself or others.

The Pope added that 'ordinary' means depended on the 'circumstances of persons, places, times and cultures'. In applying this doctrine, it is not simply a question of deciding whether a proposed treatment is ordinary or extraordinary and, if it is ordinary, it must be given. It must also be considered whether the burden of the treatment would be too much or out of proportion to the benefit.

Another difficulty is if a patient refuses to co-operate, so that treatment cannot be given. In *Re D (Medical Treatment: Mentally Disabled Patient)* (1998), the patient was a 49 year old man who had spent most of his life in psychiatric hospitals and lacked the capacity to consent. He needed kidney dialysis but, because he would not co-operate, the hospital gave him an anaesthetic each time he needed dialysis. The hospital sought a declaration that it was lawful not to give him treatment if he would not co-operate in the future. The court held that if, in the opinion of the doctors, it was not practicable to give him treatment, then it was lawful not to give treatment. This case can be contrasted with *Re JT (Adult: Refusal of Medical Treatment)* (1998), in which the patient, a 25 year old woman who lived in a mental hospital, suffered liver failure. She refused dialysis and said that she wanted to die. The court found that the patient did have mental capacity and, therefore, she could refuse treatment, so her refusal was binding on the hospital.

Neonaticide

The difficulties posed by non-treatment are highlighted in the case of newborn babies (neonates) who are born with severe disabilities, in particular with brain damage. Originally, such babies simply died, but as medical technology progressed it became possible to keep some of them alive. The question arises on what basis should this decision be made? Should such babies be kept alive even if their life will be short and painful? The common thread in all cases of non-treatment is that treatment is futile or is not in the patient's 'best interests'. In *R v Arthur* (1981), a baby was born with Down's syndrome but was otherwise healthy. The parents rejected the baby and Dr Arthur wrote in the notes: 'Parents do not wish it to survive, nursing care only.' Dr Arthur gave the baby an injection of a painkilling drug dihydrocodeine, which also had the effect of suppressing its appetite. The baby died three days later. Dr Arthur was initially charged with murder but this was reduced to attempted murder. The judge asked the jury to consider whether Dr Arthur was merely carrying out a holding operation or whether he had done a positive act to kill the baby. Dr Arthur was found not guilty of attempted murder by the jury. Farquharson J said:

> If a child is born with a serious handicap – for example, where a mongol has an ill-formed intestine whereby that child will die of the ailment if he is not operated on – a surgeon may say: 'as this child is a mongol I do not propose to operate; I shall allow nature to take its course.' No one could say that the surgeon was committing an act of murder by declining to take a course that would save the child.

> Equally, if a child not otherwise going to die, who is severely handicapped, is given a drug in such an excessive amount by the doctor that the drug itself will cause his death and the doctor does that intentionally, it would be open to the jury to say: 'Yes, he was killing: he was murdering that child.' It is very easy to draw the line between those two examples. They are opposite ends of the spectrum. It is very much more difficult to say where the line should be drawn in relation to this case.

The judge has been criticised for making a distinction between acts and omissions in the case of a doctor, who is under a duty to the patient (Kennedy and Grubb, *Medical Law*, 3rd edn, 2000, London: Butterworths).

Before the above case, the courts had considered a similar situation in *Re B (A Minor) (Wardship: Medical Treatment)* (1981), where a baby was born with

Down's syndrome and had a blockage of the intestine which could be treated. The parents refused to consent to treatment, even though, without it, the baby would die within a few days. The baby was made a ward of court. The Court of Appeal said that the baby should be given the chance to live and authorised the operation. The court had to consider the wishes of the parents and the doctors but, ultimately, it had to make a decision that was in the best interests of the child. The court took into account that if the operation was successful, the child would survive for between 20 and 30 years but would not have a normal existence. Although the wishes of the parents were taken into account it was in the interests of the child that the operation be performed. Templeman LJ said:

> There may be cases, I know not, of severe proved damage where the future is so certain and where the life of the child is so bound to be full of pain and suffering that the court might be driven to a different conclusion, but in the present case the choice which lies before the court is this: whether to allow an operation to take place which may result in the child living for 20 or 30 years as a mongoloid or whether (and I think this must be brutally the result) to terminate the life of a mongoloid child because she also has an intestinal complaint. Faced with that choice I have no doubt that it is the duty of this court to decide that the child must live.

These two cases seem to contradict each other, as in *Re B* the operation was authorised, but Dr Arthur was not guilty for not carrying out an operation. It is likely that *Re B* will be followed and that doctors are under a duty to treat babies with Down's syndrome.

In the following case, the baby was dying and there was little that could be done for it. *Re C (A Minor) (Wardship: Medical Treatment)* (1989) concerned a baby who was born with fluid on the brain and who was severely mentally handicapped. The baby had a short life expectancy. The Court of Appeal said that the baby was both mentally and physically handicapped. Lord Donaldson MR quoted the judge from first instance:

> In so far as I can assess the quality of life, which as a test in itself raises as many questions as it can answer, I adjudge that any quality to life has already been denied to this child because it cannot flow from a brain incapable of even limited intellectual function. Inasmuch as one judges, as I do, intellectual function to be a hallmark of our humanity, her functioning on that level is negligible if it exists at all. Coupled with her total physical handicap, the quality of her life will be demonstrably awful and intolerable.

The Court of Appeal ordered that the hospital be allowed to treat the baby to relieve pain and suffering rather than to prolong its life.

The court examined what was relevant to 'best interests' in *Re J (A Minor) (Wardship: Medical Treatment)* (1990). J was born prematurely, suffered brain damage and often needed ventilation. The likelihood was that he would be blind and deaf and unable to speak. Although J was not dying, the question for the court was what should be done if future ventilation was needed. The Court of Appeal, in exercising its wardship jurisdiction, took account of the fact that the child would have a poor quality of life; further ventilation may cause the child's condition to worsen; and ventilation was an invasive procedure for a baby, along with the accompanying use of a nasogastric tube, drips and taking of blood samples. Both the doctors and the parents believed that it would not be in the child's best interests to ventilate him if he stopped breathing and the court agreed with this. Taylor LJ said that the three important principles which the courts follow are: (a) that they act in the best interests of the child; (b) respect for the sanctity of life imposes a strong presumption in favour of preserving it; and (c) the courts never sanction steps to terminate life. They try to look at the position from the point of view of the patient. Lord Donaldson MR said that the sanctity of human life was important. It was also important to look at the position from the assumed point of view of the patient and very severely handicapped people find a quality of life rewarding which others would find intolerable. However, in some cases it will not be in the interests of the child that it have treatment which will cause suffering and no benefit. Account had to be taken of the poor quality of life enjoyed by the child, the fact that he had been ventilated for long periods already and the poor prognosis. However, it is difficult to know what a baby's view would be.

A further case, also called *Re J (A Minor) (Medical Treatment)* (1992), concerned a child of 16 months who suffered brain damage after a fall when he was one month old. As a result, the child was mentally and physically handicapped, being blind and suffering from epilepsy. He needed feeding by nasogastric tube and constant attention. The consultant stated that 'it would not be medically appropriate to intervene with intensive therapeutic measures such as artificial ventilation if J were to suffer a life threatening event'. The local authority applied to the High Court under the Children Act 1989 for the court to determine if treatment should be given in those circumstances. At first instance, Waite J made an order that treatment should be given, including ventilation, if J were to suffer a life-threatening event. J's mother was in favour of this order but the local authority appealed. The Court of Appeal had to consider whether a court should require a doctor to provide treatment, which the doctor considered was not in the best interests of the patient. Lord Donaldson MR stated: 'The order of Waite J was wholly inconsistent with the law as so stated and cannot be justified upon the basis of any authority known to me.' He went on to explain that such an order lacked certainty as to exactly what treatment was required, that health authorities lacked resources and that it was for them to make the choices about the use of resources. The court said that it would be wrong for a court to order treatment against the doctor's clinical judgment.

Recently, in *Re Wyatt (A Child) (Medical Treatment: Parents' Consent)* (2004), the High Court considered the position of Charlotte Wyatt, who was born prematurely in October 2003 weighing 458 grams. She suffered from brain damage, had breathing difficulties and kidney problems. She could feel pain. Medical opinion was that she would never be able to leave hospital and the doctors were unanimous that it was not in her best interests to resuscitate her if the need arose. Her parents wanted treatment to be continued to maintain Charlotte's life. It was held that the decision had to be made on the basis of best interests, which included welfare interests. It was not in her best interests to give her aggressive treatment. It was up to the doctors to give treatment, which they believed was right, or to withhold treatment.

In these types of cases, the courts will not take on the role of telling doctors to give treatment against the medical judgment of the doctors; they tend to follow the wishes of the doctors. In *Re C (A Minor)* (1998), a 16 month old baby suffered from an incurable spinal disease, spinal muscular atrophy, and was likely to die within a relatively short time. She was in the intensive care unit and on ventilation. She weighed only five and a half kilograms. The doctors proposed stopping ventilation and, if there was a relapse, not re-ventilating. The doctors believed that such treatment was futile and would simply cause further suffering without providing any benefit. The parents were Jews and, although they agreed to stop ventilation, they wanted ventilation to be given in the future, if the baby needed it. The doctors now wanted the approval of the court for what they proposed. The court allowed the hospital not to give treatment in the future. It considered that this would be in the best interests of the child, taking into account guidelines from the Royal College of Paediatrics and Child Health. The court would not make the hospital give treatment against the medical decision of the doctors.

In *Re A (Children)* (2000), the case of the conjoined twins, the parents disagreed with the doctors and did not want the twins to be separated. The Court of Appeal allowed the operation to go ahead on the basis that it was the lesser of two evils and by killing Mary this would allow Jodie the chance to lead a relatively normal life. This case can be distinguished by the fact that it concerned a positive act rather than not treating.

A more unusual situation is where the parents are in conflict with the wishes of the doctors but are against giving their child further treatment. In *Re T (A Minor) (Wardship: Medical Treatment)* (1997), a child was born with a liver defect and would die within two years without a transplant. The doctors believed that a transplant was in the best interests of the child and that it was likely to be successful. Both parents were health professionals and were used to looking after sick children. They refused to consent to the transplant because of the pain and suffering that it would inflict on the baby and considered that it would be better for the baby not to have intrusive surgery. The mother took the baby abroad to live. The local authority brought the case for the court to determine the position. At first instance, the judge considered that the parents' opposition was unreasonable and granted the application by the doctors for the operation to be carried out. On appeal, the Court of Appeal said that the welfare of the child was the paramount consideration but the wishes of the parents were also important. The main task of the court was not to decide if the wishes of the mother were reasonable. 'This mother and this child are one for the purpose of this unusual case and the decision of the court to consent to the operation jointly affects the mother and son and it also affects the father' (Butler-Sloss LJ). A number of factors had to be taken into account, including the wishes of the mother, who was against the operation; the fact that the baby had already had an unsuccessful operation to correct the liver problem; and the fact that the mother had gone to live abroad and would have to bring the baby back to the UK for the operation. Forcing the mother to agree would not be in the best interests of the child, as the mother would then have to look after the child. The court said that the best interests of the child required that treatment should be left up to his 'devoted parents'. The court refused to sanction the operation and set aside the order of the judge at first instance. This decision has been criticised by Fox and McHale, in 'In whose best interests?' ((1997) 60 MLR 700), who point out that 'construing the mother and child as one permitted the Court of Appeal to minimise the potential conflict between the interests of the woman and child'. They point out that courts frequently decide against the wishes of the parents in Jehovah's Witness cases. Was the decision in *Re T* really in the child's best interests?

MERCY KILLING

Mercy killing is active euthanasia, and is the deliberate killing of someone. It will usually consist of killing a person who is terminally ill and in great pain in order to relieve their suffering. In English law, this is murder. The fact that the defendant is acting from good motives is irrelevant. In *Airedale NHS Trust v Bland* (1993), Lord Mustill stated:

> That 'mercy killing' by active means is murder ... has never, so far as I know, been doubted. The fact that the doctor's motives are kindly will for some, although not for all, transform the moral quality of his act, but this makes no difference in law. It is the intent to kill or cause grievous bodily harm which constitutes the *mens rea* of murder, and the reason why the intent was formed makes no difference at all.

In *R v Cox* (1992), Dr Cox injected his patient with a lethal substance in order to relieve her pain and Dr Cox was given a suspended sentence. The courts usually take a sympathetic view where someone kills a relative to put them out of their pain and such defendants are often convicted only of manslaughter: a person who carries out the mercy killing of a member of their family has the defence of diminished responsibility available, which has the effect of reducing the charge to manslaughter. However, it would be extremely unlikely for a doctor to be able to raise this defence. The suggestion of creating a separate offence of mercy killing, which would carry a maximum sentence of two years' imprisonment, was examined by the Criminal Law Revision Committee in its *14th Report* in 1980. The Committee rejected creating a new offence. More recently, in 1994, the House of Lords rejected creating a new offence of mercy killing. 'To distinguish between murder and "mercy killing" would be to cross the line which prohibits any intentional killing, a line which we think essential to preserve' (House of Lords Select Committee on Medical Ethics).

PERMANENT VEGETATIVE STATE

The 'permanent vegetative state', also known as the 'persistent vegetative state' (or PVS), is a condition in which the cortex of the brain (the part responsible for thinking and the senses) is destroyed but the brain stem (which controls reflexive functions, such as the heartbeat, breathing and digestion) continues to function. The patient can breathe unaided but such a patient cannot communicate with the world and feels no pain. However, the patient in PVS is not dead.

In *Airedale NHS Trust v Bland* (1993), Tony Bland was crushed in the Hillsborough tragedy in 1989 and was diagnosed as being in PVS. He could still breathe but was fed liquefied food through a nasogastric tube. He had been in this state for nearly three years and it was accepted by medical staff that he would never become aware again. The hospital applied to the court for a declaration that they could withdraw life sustaining treatment, including feeding. The parents and doctors were agreed on this action. It was argued against withdrawing feeding that this was a breach of the doctors' duty to treat. The House of Lords said that feeding could be regarded as 'medical treatment' because it required the fitting and use of a nasogastric tube and was quite different to normal methods of feeding. 'The insertion of the tube is a procedure calling for skill and knowledge, and the tube is invasive of the patient's body to an extent which feeding by spoon or cup is not' (Sir Thomas Bingham MR). The court had to answer this question: in what circumstances, if any, could a hospital withdraw life-sustaining treatment, with the result that the patient would die? The court said that there was a distinction between acts and omissions in law. If an act done with the intent to kill led to death, that was murder, but an omission with the same result was not an offence. There is an exception if a person is under a duty to act. Stopping artificial feeding was an omission, not an act and could be seen as part of the doctors' duty of care to the patient in this case. But a doctor is not under a duty to continue treatment, including artificial feeding, if the position of the patient is hopeless.

The next question was whether the doctors were under a duty to continue to treat Tony Bland. Because he was not able to consent to treatment, he could only be treated, in accordance with *Re F* (1990), if the treatment was in his best interests. This had to be assessed by the '*Bolam* test' of whether such treatment was in accordance with 'a responsible body of medical opinion'. The patient was unconscious and there was no hope of any improvement in his condition. It was therefore in the patient's best interests that the treatment should be stopped and the court allowed this. The judges recognised that a point could be reached where there was no duty to continue to treat. Lord Browne-Wilkinson went so far as to say that there could be a duty not to treat if:

> ... there comes a stage where the responsible doctor comes to the reasonable conclusion (which accords with the views of a responsible body of medical opinion) that further continuance of an intrusive life support system is not in

the best interests of the patient, he can no longer lawfully continue that life support system: to do so would constitute the crime of battery and the tort of trespass to the person. Therefore, he cannot be in breach of any duty to maintain the patient's life.

In *Bland*, the court stepped beyond the existing boundaries in allowing passive euthanasia of patients in PVS.

The House of Lords also considered the procedure to be followed in situations where doctors wished to withdraw treatment from a patient in PVS. Sir Stephen Brown had said that a declaration should be obtained from the court in all cases of PVS. In the Court of Appeal, Sir Thomas Bingham MR said:

> This was in my view a wise ruling, directed to the protection of patients, the protection of doctors, the reassurance of patients' families and the reassurance of the public. The practice proposed seems to me desirable. It may very well be that, with the passage of time, a body of experience and practice will build up which will obviate the need for application in every case.

The House of Lords confirmed that this guidance should be followed. The Official Solicitor issued *Practice Note (Official Solicitor: Vegetative State)* (1996), which sets out the procedure for applying to the court in such cases. This is now part of the *Practice Note (Official Solicitor: Declaratory Proceedings: Medical and Welfare Decisions for Adults Who Lack Capacity)* (2001). In 'Appendix 2: Permanent Vegetative State Cases', it is provided that the purpose of the proceedings is to determine whether the patient is in PVS. The concern of the court is whether the patient has any awareness or whether there is likely to be any change. The approach of the courts is compatible with the Convention following *NHS Trust A v M; NHS Trust B v H* (2001). Applications should be made to the Principal Registry and will normally be heard by the President of the Family Division.

What is the position if the family objects to withdrawing treatment? In *Re G (Persistent Vegetative State)* (1995), a motorcyclist, aged 24, was badly injured in an accident in 1991 and was diagnosed as being in PVS. In 1994, his wife and his doctors wished to withdraw artificial feeding but his mother wished feeding to continue. The hospital applied to the court for a declaration to allow withdrawal of feeding. The court accepted that doctors should consult relatives about their views and that relatives may be able to give guidance on what the patient would want to do in the particular circumstances, but the views of relatives could not determine treatment. The court took into account guidance from the British Medical Association (BMA) on the views of those close to the patient, which said that their wishes cannot determine the treatment. The declaration was granted and feeding was withdrawn.

Since *Bland*, there have been a number of cases dealing with similar situations but some of them have clearly been outside the boundary of PVS. In *Frenchay Healthcare NHS Trust v S* (1994), after taking an overdose of drugs, the patient was diagnosed as being in PVS. The patient's condition remained unchanged for two and a half years. The patient was fed through a tube inserted through the stomach wall, but this tube became dislodged. Doctors believed that it would be against the patient's interests to insert another tube. The hospital obtained a declaration that it did not need to replace the tube. The Court of Appeal rejected the appeal, which was made on the ground that there should have been more time for an independent medical report to have been made. The court said that the patient had no prospect of recovery and it was not in his best interests to re-insert the tube. As regards best interests, Sir Thomas Bingham MR said: 'It is, I think, important that there should not be a belief that what the doctor says is the patient's best interest is the patient's best interest. For my part I would certainly reserve to the court the ultimate power and duty to review the doctors' decision in the light of all the facts.' The decision in *Frenchay* had to be made quickly because of the emergency that arose when the feeding tube became dislodged. In *Re D* (1997), a 28 year old woman suffered brain damage after a car accident. She did not meet the criteria for PVS as laid down by the Royal College of Physicians, although she had no awareness. She remained in this condition for six years. When her feeding tube became dislodged, a declaration was sought that it did not need to be replaced. The court granted this declaration. In *NHS Trust A v Mrs M, NHS Trust B v Mrs H* (2001), the two patients had been in PVS for three years and nine months respectively. Declarations were sought on withdrawing feeding and this was supported by the families. The High Court granted the declarations. It also considered the effect of Arts 2, 3 and 8 of the Convention (see below, 'Human Rights Act 1998').

After the *Bland* case, a Select Committee of the House of Lords considered the issue of euthanasia (*Report of the Select Committee on Medical Ethics*, HL No 21, Vol I, 1994, London: HMSO). The Committee considered the arguments for euthanasia but was firmly against changing the law on intentional killing:

> That prohibition is the cornerstone of law and social relationships. It protects each of us impartially, embodying the belief that all are equal. We do not wish that protection to be diminished and we therefore recommend that there be no change in the law to permit euthanasia.

The Committee also pointed out that legalising voluntary euthanasia would put pressure on the old and the sick to request death.

One potential problem is whether a woman in PVS who is pregnant should be given treatment and feeding so that the foetus could reach full term and be born. The guidance from the BMA makes provision for such cases.

Pregnant PVS patients

The BMA recommends that no decision to withdraw treatment should be made within the first 12 months, thus the question of whether it is morally appropriate to keep a pregnant woman alive for the sake of the foetus alone does not arise.

Bland has been criticised by a number of academics, including John Keown, who has said that the decision has left the law 'prohibiting active, intentional killing but permitting (if not requiring) intentional killing by omission, even by those under a duty to care for the patient' ('Restoring moral and intellectual shape to the law after *Bland*' (1997) 113 LQR 481).

REFUSAL OF CONSENT TO TREATMENT

Competent patients

Can a competent patient refuse life saving treatment even if they know that doing so will lead to their death? In *Re T (Adult: Refusal of Medical Treatment)* (1992), the Court of Appeal said that a competent adult had the choice to accept or refuse such treatment. The courts are trying to maintain a balance between the interests of the patient and the interests of society in maintaining life. In *Bouvia v Superior Court of California* (1986), Bouvia was a mentally competent 28 year old but was completely paralysed, had arthritis and was in constant pain. She was totally dependent on others. She had to lie flat in bed all the time. She had a further life expectancy of 20 years. She wanted to die and refused food but doctors inserted a nasogastric tube against her will in order to feed her. The court authorised removal of the tube, saying that Bouvia had the right to refuse life sustaining treatment. 'It certainly is not illegal or immoral to prefer a natural, albeit sooner, death than a drugged life attached to a mechanical device' (Beach JA). But does the patient in such a situation intend to die, or are they simply intending to avoid the pain?

In *Ms B v An NHS Hospital Trust* (2002), the High Court was faced with a similar decision. Ms B was 43 years old. She had suffered a haemorrhage in her spinal column in 1999. Following this, she made a living will stating when she wanted treatment to be withdrawn. Her condition worsened and she became tetraplegic and was paralysed from the neck down. She was dependent on a ventilator for breathing. She confirmed that she wanted to be taken off the ventilator despite the alternative of rehabilitation, although her condition could never improve. A psychiatric assessment said that she was not capable of making a decision. Some time later, it was decided that she did have capacity to make the decision. She made a second living will in August 2001, setting out that she wanted treatment to be withdrawn. The hospital continued to treat her. Ms B started proceedings to resolve the matter. The court said that in assessing capacity it was not for the assessor to substitute his own values for those of the patient, unless the illness had affected the patient's capacity. Although there was a presumption that the patient had capacity, it was important to look at the effect of treatment or refusal of treatment. A high level of capacity was needed where a refusal of treatment would lead to death, as in Ms B's case. The court refused to accept the defendant's argument that as Ms B had not tried rehabilitation she could not have capacity. It was not possible to experience something before choosing in many medical situations. The court said that Ms B did have capacity from August 2001 and was entitled to damages for being given treatment after that time. She was entitled to refuse treatment even though this would inevitably lead to her death.

If a patient refuses a particular type of treatment, can they demand another treatment? In *R (on the Application of L) v Newcastle Primary Care Trust* (2004), L, who was a haemophiliac, refused treatment with plasma derived Factor VIII and requested treatment with another type of Factor VIII. The hospital refused to give him that particular treatment. It was held that a person of full age and capacity could refuse treatment, even if this meant that they would die. The hospital was not under a duty to provide a particular treatment.

Patients who are no longer competent

If a patient decides, when competent, not to be treated if they develop certain conditions, do medical staff have to follow their wishes? The ethical principle of respect for autonomy requires the wishes of such a patient to be followed, but is this the law? In North America, the concept of the 'advance directive' (or living will) has been established for some time. An advance directive is a statement, made when the patient is competent, setting out what treatment they want or do not want if they become incapacitated. If the patient specifies in the advance directive the treatment they would want, this is qualified to the extent that medical staff would decide whether such treatment was appropriate, as no one can demand a particular treatment. The Canadian case of *Malette v Shulman* (1990) is a clear example of how an advance directive works. A patient was taken to hospital, unconscious, after a road accident. She was carrying a card which stated that she was a Jehovah's Witness and did not want a blood transfusion under 'any circumstances'. Dr S gave her a blood transfusion that saved her life. The court said: 'A doctor is not free to disregard a patient's advance instructions any more than he would be free to disregard instructions given at the time of the emergency.' The court added that a patient could reject treatment, even if to do so had harmful consequences. This was a battery and the doctor was liable to pay damages.

In English law, the legal status of an advance directive is beginning to be clarified by the courts. The courts accepted the idea of such advance directives in *Re T* (1992), where Lord Donaldson MR commented that, 'if clearly established and applicable in the circumstances', they would bind the doctor. A *Practice Note* (1994) states:

> The High Court exercising its inherent jurisdiction may determine the effect of
> a purported advance directive as to future medical treatment ... In summary,

the patient's expressed views, if any, will always be a very important component in the decisions of the doctors and the court.

In *Re AK (Adult Patient) (Medical Treatment: Consent)* (2001), the patient was 19 years old and suffered from motor neuron disease. He lived at home but was on a ventilator and needed 24 hour nursing care. He was not able to speak and was fed through a tube. His only communication was through the movement of one eyelid, which would soon stop but he was still able to think and understand. In July 2000, when he was told that he would lose movement in his eyelid, he communicated to the medical staff that he wanted his ventilator turned off. This was confirmed on a number of later occasions. Two weeks after he lost the ability to communicate, the health authority applied to the court for a declaration. The court said that an adult patient of sound mind and full capacity can refuse treatment. An advance indication of the patient's wishes is valid but care must be taken to make sure that it still represents the patient's wishes. It was particularly important in situations like the present that the patient had freely given consent. The declaration was granted. The courts also considered an advance directive in *HE v A Hospital NHS Trust* (2003). D was being brought up as a Muslim but her parents separated and she went to live with her mother. Both D and her mother became Jehovah's Witnesses. Some years later, when D was an adult, she needed surgery for a heart condition. In February 2001, she signed an advance directive refusing blood but it also provided that the advance directive could only be revoked in writing. In April 2003, she became ill and before being taken to hospital in an ambulance she told her family, 'I don't want to die'. On admission, it was found she needed a partial amputation and a blood transfusion. Her mother told the hospital about the advance directive. She was likely to die within 36 hours without a transfusion and her father, HE, applied to the court to allow a transfusion. HE argued that D was engaged to a Muslim and was changing back to the Muslim faith. She had stopped attending Jehovah's Witness services. The court confirmed that a competent adult had an absolute right to refuse medical treatment. A competent adult could make an advance directive that remains binding if they become incompetent. There were no formal requirements to create an advance directive. It could be oral or in writing and could be revoked orally or in writing. Even if made under seal, it could be revoked orally. Any condition in an advance directive to make it irrevocable or to impose formal conditions for revocation was contrary to public policy and void. Whether an advance directive existed and whether it was still valid was a question of fact. On the facts of the case, saying 'I don't want to die' was not of particular significance but the fact that D had given up her faith on which the advance directive was based was significant. It was up to those seeking to show the advance directive was still valid to prove it, in this case, the mother. The declaration was granted. The courts also considered issues of competence and advance directives in *NHS Trust v T (Adult Patient: Refusal of Medical Treatment)* (2004). T had a long history of psychiatric problems and suffered from a borderline personality disorder. She harmed herself by cutting herself and on several occasions needed emergency blood transfusions. In January 2004 she signed an advance directive stating that she did not want any more blood. Her main reason for refusing was because she believed that her own blood was evil and would contaminate any new blood she was given. The claimant trust sought a declaration to authorise treatment for T. The court heard evidence from the psychiatrist responsible for T, who stated that when T made the advance directive she was in a state of 'disordered thinking brought about by her mental disorder'. The court said that T's belief that her blood was evil showed a disorder of the mind and that she was incompetent. If T was not given a blood transfusion she would die. The treatment was in her best interests and a declaration was granted.

In *St George's NHS Trust v S* (1998), the court set out guidelines for medical staff to follow in dealing with patients who require invasive treatment. Part of these guidelines provide:

(iii) Where the patient has given an advance directive, before becoming incapable, treatment and care should normally be subject to the advance directive. However, if there is reason to doubt the reliability of the advance directive (for example, it may sensibly be thought not to apply to the circumstances that have arisen), then an application for a declaration may be made.

The difficulties with advance directives include the following:

- Does the statement cover the situation which arises? If it does not, then medical staff could ignore it.
- Would the patient change their mind when in the actual situation which has arisen, if they could communicate? This leaves medical staff with the flexibility to ignore the advance directive.
- The actual wording of the directive may be unclear and open to different interpretations as to exactly what the patient wanted.

The Law Commission, in Report No 231, *Mental Incapacity* (1995), proposed that legislation should be passed to give advance directives legal effect. The Commission did not want basic care, pain relief or feeding to be included. The government did not include advance directives in their proposals for reform (see *Making Decisions*, referred to in Chapter 2). But the Mental Capacity Bill 2004 incorporates advance directives, which it refers to as 'advance decisions'.

The BMA's guidance, *Withholding and Withdrawing Life-Prolonging Medical Treatment* (1999), provides as follows:

10.1 Where a patient has lost the capacity to make a decision but has a valid advance directive refusing life-prolonging treatment, this must be respected.

The guidance explains that if an advance directive names an individual whom the patient wishes the healthcare team to consult, this may be useful in making treatment decisions, although the wishes of that individual are not legally binding:

10.3 A valid advance refusal of treatment has the same legal authority as a contemporaneous refusal and legal action could be taken against a doctor who provides treatment in the face of a valid refusal.

The legal action contemplated would be a claim for battery.

The guidelines produced in August 2002 by the General Medical Council (GMC) emphasise that a valid advance directive is legally binding (*Withholding and Withdrawing Life-Prolonging Treatments: Good Practice in Decision-making*):

Adult patients who cannot decide for themselves

14 Any valid advance refusal of treatment – one made when the patient was competent and on the basis of adequate information about the implications of his/her choice – is legally binding and must be respected where it is clearly applicable to the patient's present circumstances and where there is no reason to believe that the patient had changed his/her mind.

If it is known that the patient would refuse treatment, but he has not explicitly said this, what is the position of medical staff? In the US, in such circumstances, the concept of 'substituted judgment' may be used. This means that a person (proxy) puts themselves in the position of the incapacitated person and makes a decision on the basis of what that person would have wanted, taking into account their knowledge of that person. In *Airedale NHS Trust v Bland* (1993), the House of Lords rejected the use of the substituted judgment test. Lord Goff said '... I do not consider that any such test forms part of English law in relation to incompetent adults, on whose behalf nobody has power to give consent to medical treatment'. One important limitation of such a test is that it can only be used if the patient has been competent at some time; they cannot make any choice for the permanently incompetent. However, Mason, McCall-Smith and Laurie (*Law and Medical Ethics*, 6th edn, 2002, London: Butterworths, p 519) have argued that the substituted judgment test is better than the best interests test with incompetent patients, because it is based on the patient's autonomy rather than the paternalistic approach of best interests.

In *Regina (Burke) v GMC* (2004), the court said that in decisions about withholding or withdrawing life-prolonging treatment, if the patient has expressed their wishes or made an advance directive, doctors must follow their wishes.

'DO NOT RESUSCITATE' ORDERS

A do not resuscitate (DNR) order (or do not attempt to resuscitate, DNAR) is a direction which is put in the patient's notes, stating that the patient should not be resuscitated if their heart or lungs stop working. When this happens, it may be possible to restart the heart and breathing with treatment known as cardiopulmonary resuscitation (CPR).

In February 2001, a statement was issued by the BMA, the Resuscitation Council and the Royal College of Nursing, entitled *Decisions Relating to Cardiopulmonary Resuscitation*, which replaces earlier guidelines. They include the following provisions (in summary):

2 Presumption in favour of attempting resuscitation

If no advance decision has been made about attempting resuscitation and the wishes of the patient are unknown, there should be a presumption that resuscitation will be carried out.

5 Competent adults

The key question in deciding whether to attempt resuscitation is whether it is able to provide any benefit to the patient. If patients ask that no DNAR order is made, this should be respected.

6 Incapacitated adults

No one can give consent to medical treatment for an adult who lacks capacity. People close to the patient should be kept informed and be involved in decision making to reflect the patient's views, but it should be made clear that their role is not to take decisions for the patient.

9 Refusal of treatment

Resuscitation must not be attempted if it is contrary to the sustained wishes of a mentally competent adult. A refusal does not have to be in writing to be valid.

11 Responsibility for decision making

The overall responsibility for DNAR orders rests with the consultant or GP in charge of the patient's care. He or she should be prepared to discuss the decision with other health professionals involved in the patient's care. Blanket policies that deny resuscitation to groups of patients, for example, all those in a nursing home or over a certain age, are unethical and probably unlawful under the Human Rights Act 1998 as being discriminatory.

The courts examined DNR orders in *Re R (Adult: Medical Treatment)* (1996), in which a 23 year old patient had cerebral palsy, malfunction of the brain, epilepsy and other ailments. He had a very low state of awareness and could not eat, but responded to pain and pleasure. He lived in a residential home and was taken to hospital, suffering from chest infections and fits. The consultant issued a DNR order, to which the patient's mother agreed. Staff at the day centre that the patient attended objected to this DNR order. The court considered the evidence that resuscitation might cause further brain damage, and the chances of resuscitation being successful in a residential home were low. The court declared that withholding resuscitation and antibiotics was lawful. Sir Stephen Brown P said: 'In this case there is no question of the court being asked to approve a course aimed at terminating life or accelerating death. The court is concerned with circumstances in which steps should not be taken to prolong life.'

In practice, the use of such orders has caused problems, with patients often being unaware that a DNR order has been made for them. There are still question marks over the involvement of patients and over decisions about the quality of life decisions for those patients. However, the above guidelines should help to make the position of individual patients clearer.

The BMA's *Withholding and Withdrawing Life-Prolonging Medical Treatment* (1999) sets out detailed rules for healthcare staff in making decisions on treatment. The rules cover adults with capacity, advance directives, adults lacking capacity, children and young persons under 18.

THE HUMAN RIGHTS ACT 1998

A number of Articles from the Convention have been used in this area of medical law to try and establish rights for the patient. They include Art 2, the right to life, Art 3, the right not to be subject to inhuman or degrading treatment, Art 8, the right to respect for private and family life, Art 9, the right to freedom of thought and religion, and Art 14, the right to enjoy Convention rights without discrimination.

In 'Do not resuscitate orders and the Human Rights Act 1998' ((2000) 150 NLJ 640), Maclean considers the use of DNR orders made for old people without asking them. Maclean argues that Arts 2, 8 and 14 of the European Convention on Human Rights may be relied on. Article 8 was considered in *Gaskin v UK* (1989), where the European Court of Human Rights said that a child who was brought up in a local authority care home was entitled to see personal files about himself, because these contained information about his childhood and development. A failure to give individuals access to information about themselves was a breach of Art 8. Using this right would entitle a person to information about their treatment, for example, a decision not to resuscitate them. This would not, however, give the patient the right to demand treatment, because of Art 8(2), which provides for exceptions which are in accordance with the law and for the protection of health or morals. Under Art 2, the state has a duty to protect NHS patients in its care by doing what is reasonable (*Osman v UK* (2000)). Article 14 could operate if there was a blanket ban on treatment for older patients.

Article 3 may also be used by the families of patients kept on life support machines who wish the machines to be switched off. However, in *A NHS Trust v D* (2000), it was held that allowing doctors to withhold medical treatment, even involving a specific decision, was not a breach of Art 2 or 3, provided that the decision was made in the best interests of the patient.

Both the House of Lords in *R (on the Application of Pretty)* and the European Court of Human Rights in *Pretty v UK* (2002) considered the application of Convention rights in the appeals by Diane Pretty. She claimed that the DPP's failure to agree not to prosecute her husband if he helped her to commit suicide was a breach of her Convention rights. It was argued that Art 2 gave a right to life, including a right to choose whether to carry on living. Allowing help to commit suicide would not be in conflict with Art 2, otherwise countries which allowed assisted suicide would be in breach of it. The House of Lords said that Mrs Pretty's interpretation, the right to end her life, was the exact opposite of the right to life. This was confirmed by the European Court of Human Rights: 'Article 2 cannot, without a distortion of language, be interpreted as conferring the diametrically opposite right, namely a right to die; nor can it create a right to self-determination in the sense of conferring on an individual the entitlement to choose death rather than life.' As regards Art 3, it was argued that the state had an obligation not to inflict degrading treatment and a positive duty to prevent it happening, and by not allowing her help to die this was in effect imposing degrading treatment on her. The House of Lords said that suffering from a natural illness could be within Art 3 if it was made worse by treatment or lack of treatment, but here the government had not caused any ill treatment. It would be stretching the meaning of the word treatment to cover allowing her help to commit suicide. The European Court of Human Rights said that the request here would require the State to allow action to end life, which could not be derived from Art 3. Articles 2 and 3 could be read together as protecting life and were based on the principle of sanctity of life. It was claimed that Art 8, the right to private and family life, included a right of self-determination, which itself covered a right to choose when to die. The House of Lords said that Art 8 prevented interference with how a person lived their life but not how they died and did not include a right to die. Even if it did apply, the restriction under s 2(1) of the Suicide Act 1961 could be justified under Art 8(2) in protecting the rights of others, that is, those at risk of being coerced into suicide. The European Court of Human Rights disagreed with the House of Lords and said that Art 8 did confer a right of self-determination on a competent adult. In the case of medical treatment, a competent adult patient could refuse treatment which might lead to their death, and imposing such treatment would interfere with their physical integrity, which is protected by Art 8. The European Court endorsed the statement of Lord Hope in the House of Lords, that how she chooses to pass the closing moments of her life is part of living, and stated:

> The very essence of the Convention is respect for human dignity and human freedom. Without in any way negating the principle of sanctity of life protected under the Convention, the court considers that it is under Art 8 that notions of the quality of life take on significance. In an era of growing medical sophistication combined with longer life expectancies, many people are concerned that they should not be forced to linger on in old age or in states of advanced physical or mental decrepitude which conflict with strongly held ideas of self and personal identity.

Mrs Pretty was prevented by law from choosing to avoid a distressing end to her life that was a breach of her private life under Art 8(1). However, the European Court added that, under Art 8(2), the ban on assisted suicide was justified as necessary to protect life and therefore protect the rights of others, particularly the vulnerable. The argument under Art 9 was that the right to freedom of thought and belief gave a right to act in accordance with those beliefs. Mrs Pretty believed in the right to have help to commit suicide and wanted that belief carried out. The House of Lords said that Art 9 did not give a right to do acts in pursuance of any particular beliefs they held. The European Court of Human Rights said that all opinions did not constitute beliefs in the sense covered by Art 9. There was no violation of that Article. The argument under Art 14 was that she was discriminated against because she was treated less favourably than able-bodied people. The House of Lords said that as they had determined that there was no breach of the Convention, Art 14 did not apply, as it was dependent on another Convention right. The European Court of Human Rights said that Art 14 had to be considered because Art 8(1) applied. But to introduce a distinction between those able and unable to commit suicide would undermine the protection given by the Suicide Act 1961 because it would increase the risk of abuse. There was no breach of Art 14.

The position of patients in PVS was considered in *NHS Trust A v Mrs M; NHS Trust B v Mrs H* (2001). The court dealt with a number of questions concerning Convention rights. Was a patient in PVS alive and entitled to the protection of Art 2? The court said that the patient's brain stem was still functioning and the patient was therefore alive and covered by Art 2. The wording of Art 2 provides that 'No one shall be deprived of his life intentionally…'. Did withdrawing artificial feeding amount to an intentional deprivation of life? The court said that deprivation of life meant a deliberate act rather than an omission. Withdrawing treatment based on clinical judgment is an omission. Does Art 2 impose a positive obligation to provide treatment? The court said that if a decision to withdraw treatment was made in the patient's best interests and in accordance with a responsible body of medical opinion, the duty under Art 2 was fulfilled. It did not impose an absolute obligation to provide treatment. Did Art 8, respect for family life, give relatives the right to respect for their wishes about the treatment of the patient? The court said that it was unlikely that families have rights under Art 8 that are separate from the patient's rights. Did continuing treatment which was futile amount to inhuman and degrading treatment under Art 3? The court said that the patient needed to be aware of the treatment and a patient in PVS was not aware. This latter point is open to question, as a person could be mentally incompetent and unable to appreciate the fact that they were subject to degrading treatment. Would this mean that they were not then covered by Art 3?

The European Court of Human Rights applied Art 8 in *David and Carol Glass v UK* (2004). David had severe mental and physical disabilities. When he was 11 years old, he needed an operation for a breathing problem. His mother, Carol, did not want him to be given diamorphine as she believed that it would affect his breathing. The hospital gave him diamorphine. Carol eventually took the case to the European Court of Human Rights. The court said that the treatment of David against his mother's wishes was a breach of his right to physical and moral integrity under Art 8. It was a breach of both David's rights and his mother's.

The High Court has recently reconsidered the legal position, both at common law and under the Human Rights Act 1998, in *Regina (Burke) v General Medical Council* (2004). This was a challenge to the GMC guidance, *Withholding and Withdrawing Life-Prolonging Treatments: Good Practice in Decision-making* (2002). Mr Burke suffered from a degenerative brain disease and was concerned about his position in the future when he would need artificial feeding. The court said that the guidance could be criticised in four ways; first, the guidance put emphasis on the right to refuse treatment rather than to require treatment; secondly, it failed to emphasise that a doctor who was unable or unwilling to carry out the patient's wishes had a duty to provide treatment until he could find another doctor to do so; thirdly, it did not sufficiently acknowledge the presumption in favour of life-prolonging treatment, which should be given unless this made the patient's life intolerable from the patient's viewpoint; and fourthly, it failed to emphasise the legal requirement to obtain court approval for withdrawing feeding in certain circumstances. The court also said that the guidance was incompatible with Art 2, not to deprive someone of their life, Art 3, not to subject someone to degrading treatment, and Art 8, not to interfere with private life, which included personal autonomy and dignity. Withdrawing artificial feeding before the patient went into a coma would in principle be a breach of Arts 3 and 8 as the patient would be subject to suffering. The GMC are appealing against parts of the judgment.

SUMMARY – DEATH

1 *Definition of death*
   - Brain stem death accepted by courts: *R v Malcherek & Steel* (1981) – switched off ventilator.
   - Questions: time of death; organs for transplant; anencephalic babies.

2 *Suicide*
   - Suicide not a crime since Suicide Act 1961, but s 2(1) of the Suicide Act makes it an offence to aid, abet, counsel or procure suicide: *Attorney General v Able* (1984); *R (on Application of Pretty) v DPP* (2002) – Pretty wanted agreement of DPP that her husband would not be prosecuted under s 2(1).
   - Physician-assisted suicide: would be within s 2(1); but contrast US Oregon Death With Dignity Act 1994.

3 *Euthanasia*
   - Sanctity of life/principle of respect for autonomy.
   - Assisted Dying for the Terminally Ill Bill 2004 – provides medical assistance to die.

- Active euthanasia: deliberate act to end life – legally murder or manslaughter: *R v Cox* (1992); *R v Adams* (1957).

- The Netherlands: Termination of Life on Request and Assisted Suicide (Review Procedures) Act 2001: requirements – request voluntary; suffering unbearable; patient told of prospects; patient accepts no other reasonable solution; two doctors see patient – can end life.

- Passive euthanasia: end life by omission, for example, by non-treatment and withdrawal; medical staff under duty to treat; is distinction between killing and letting die valid?

4 *Non-treatment*
- Distinction between ordinary and extraordinary means.

- Patient refuses to co-operate: no need to treat: *Re D* (1998).

- Neonaticide: newborns with brain damage are given nursing care only: *R v Arthur* (1981); but *Re B (A Minor) (Wardship: Medical Treatment)* (1981) – blockage of intestine – duty to treat.

- Courts act in best interests of child: presumption in favour of preserving life; courts do not order termination of life; courts follow medical judgment; note decision in *Re T (A Minor) (Wardship: Medical Treatment)* (1997) – child with liver defect.

5 *Mercy killing*
- Killing someone who is terminally ill and in pain – murder.

6 *Permanent vegetative state*
- PVS patient is not brain dead: but no need to feed and treat: *Airedale NHS Trust v Bland* (1993).

- Cases seem to have expanded situations where treatment can be stopped.

- Criticisms of *Bland*.

7 *Refusal of consent to treatment*
- Competent patients: can refuse life saving treatment: *Ms B v An NHS Hospital Trust* (2002) – paralysed from neck down and had capacity to refuse.

- Patients no longer competent: advance directives (or living wills); Canadian case *Malette v Shulman* (1990); courts must follow patient's wishes: *R (Burke) v GMC* (2004).

- Do not resuscitate orders: these are lawful; but some problems over decisions.

8 *Human Rights Act 1998*
- Main Articles are Art 2, right to life; Art 3, right not to be subject to degrading treatment; Art 8, right to respect for private and family life.

- *Pretty v UK* (2002), *David and Carol Glass v UK* (2004).

CHAPTER 10

PROPERTY IN THE BODY AND TRANSPLANTS

INTRODUCTION

This chapter will examine issues surrounding ownership of the human body and parts of the body. The widespread practice of taking parts of children's bodies after their death for research purposes has highlighted some of the problems that the law faces, such as who has the legal right to bodies or body parts after death. The inquiries at Bristol Royal Infirmary and Alder Hey Children's Hospital in Liverpool followed allegations that body parts of dead children had been removed without consent. The subsequent reports by Professor Ian Kennedy and Michael Redfern have made numerous suggestions for reform of the law. Many of these have been incorporated in the Human Tissue Act 2004. The substantive provisions of the Act are not in force at the time of writing and are not expected to be brought into force until April 2006. This chapter will also explain the law relevant to the transplant of organs from dead bodies and from live donors. It will also briefly consider transplants from animals to human subjects (xenotransplants). The first organ transplants took place in the 1950s, using kidneys, and a wide range of organs and tissue may now be transplanted, including corneas, livers, hearts and lungs. The transplant of organs and body tissues raises many ethical and legal issues and the law has lagged behind medical developments in this field. The demand for organs greatly exceeds the supply and there are approximately 6,000 patients waiting for an organ (UK Transplant). A growing number of commentators now believe that people should be allowed to sell their organs, most notable amongst these is John Harris. From a Kantian perspective, others should not be used merely as a means to an end, and this would rule out transplants from live donors. The utilitarian approach would consider the overall benefits of transplants and would not rule them out in principle. On this basis, a kidney transplant would be preferred to dialysis, which costs £25,000 for one patient for a year.

PROPERTY IN THE BODY

The question of whether someone can own their body raises difficult ethical and legal issues. As John Harris has pointed out, just because no one else owns my body, this does not mean that I do ('Who owns my body?' (1996) 16 OJLS 55). The concept of owning oneself is difficult to understand. The ideas of ownership and property are legal inventions, which set out the relationship between people and things and enable people to own things.

This facilitates trade, which underpins the working of society. Applying the concept of ownership to oneself seems alien. There is also the question of ownership of parts of the body. Many would frown on the idea of someone selling a part of their body, as this would not be treating their body with respect in accordance with the principle of autonomy. The idea of buying and selling bodily organs can be seen as treating parts of the body just like other goods. This is sometimes referred to as 'commodifying' the body.

The law has accepted that some regenerative parts of the human body may be classed as property. In *R v Welsh* (1974), the defendant was convicted of the theft of a urine sample he had given and, in *R v Rothery* (1976), the defendant was convicted of stealing a sample of blood he had given, which was to be tested for alcohol.

The Human Organ Transplant Act 1989 regulates live transplants and makes it a criminal offence to buy or sell organs (s 1). However, the Act does not deal with ownership of organs. The difficulties faced by courts dealing with the problem of ownership of body parts can be illustrated by the US case of *Moore v Regents of the University of California* (1990). Moore had hairy-cell leukaemia and his spleen was removed to slow down the progress of the disease. The doctor, Dr Golde, used some of the cells from his spleen to conduct research and develop new cells, which were patented and then sold to a drug company. Moore did not know about this at the time. Later, he found out and sued the doctor and the hospital, the Medical Center of the University of California at Los Angeles. He claimed conversion for using his property; breach of fiduciary duty, as the doctor had not acted in good faith by not disclosing his personal interest from developing new cells; and lack of informed consent because Moore did not know what they were going to do with his cells and had not consented to using his spleen for research purposes. The majority of the court held that it was inappropriate to recognise property in the body for two reasons: (a) there were no precedents; and (b) it would hamper medical research, because the owner could then prevent others from using their tissue. As regards the claim in conversion, Panelli J said: 'To impose such a duty, which would affect medical research of importance to all society, implicates policy concerns far removed from the traditional two-party ownership disputes in which the law of conversion arose.' To establish conversion, Moore would have had to prove interference with his right of ownership or possession. Once his spleen had been removed, he did not have possession of it and the court could find no authority showing patient ownership of body parts that had been cut out. Moore did not own the patent of the new cells because they had been developed by someone else. His claim for conversion therefore failed, but the university hospital was found liable for breach of fiduciary duty and trespass. The court's decision was based on public policy that research on human tissue should not be hampered. Even though Moore had no right to the cells developed, the university hospital obtained a patent for them and made millions of dollars from them. This seems unjust on the patient and illustrates that existing laws are not able to effectively solve such problems.

The Nuffield Report

The question of tissue ownership was considered by the Nuffield Council on Bioethics in Chapter 9 of *Human Tissue: Ethical and Legal Issues* (1995).

Someone from whom tissue is removed has no claim by statute: the Human Tissue Act 1961, the Human Organ Transplant Act 1989 and the Anatomy Act 1984 imply that tissue is given freely. At common law, the matter has not been decided, probably because tissue removed in the course of treatment is not wanted and tissue removed to give to others is a gift.

If tissue is removed in the course of an operation, the patient may be seen as abandoning it, and it is then in the possession of the hospital.

It could be argued that, when tissue is removed, it becomes the property of the patient. The patient may waive this right to it. In *Venner v State of Maryland* (1976), the court said that when a person does nothing and says nothing about rights of ownership, the inference is that he intends to abandon the material. Thus, there is a presumption in favour of abandonment. However, if the circumstances were such that abandonment could not be presumed, then, if no consent was given, property rights would not necessarily pass.

Another approach is to argue that, once tissue is removed, it becomes property but it is not owned by anyone until it is brought under dominion (that is, control), as with a wild animal.

The Nuffield Report then said that the approach of English law was unclear and suggested the following approach:

(a) any consent to treatment would imply that any tissue removed would be regarded as abandoned;

(b) any tissue removed for donation would be regarded as a gift. If it was used for another purpose, however, this could lead to a claim;

(c) if tissue is removed with the intention of keeping it for the future use of the donor (for example, blood), the donor could claim that tissue. Note that embryos have their own statutory framework of consent;

(d) if tissue is removed without the explicit knowledge and consent of the patient, any claim over use will depend on the general consent given.

The Nuffield Report has been criticised by a number of writers, such as Mason, McCall-Smith and Laurie, who say that it is based on the premise that people see no value in parts removed from their bodies. They point out that it is no longer true that parts cannot be valuable, for example, due to developments in biotechnology. The *Moore* case is the classic example. The Nuffield Report fails to deal with the right to own the parts of one's body.

What is the legal position as regards dead bodies and parts of dead bodies?

The original common law rule, as set down in *Dr Handyside's Case* (1749), was that there was 'no property in a corpse'. This rule was qualified in *R v*

Kelly (1998), where the defendant and an accomplice stole various body parts from the Royal College of Surgeons. The defendant was an artist and wanted to use the parts in sculptures. They were both charged with theft and claimed that no one could own a dead body or the parts of a body, so the parts could not be stolen. They were convicted and appealed. The Court of Appeal said that the common law rule that there was no property in a corpse only applies to the corpse or parts of it which remain in their natural state. If parts of a corpse 'had acquired different attributes by virtue of the application of skill, such as dissection and preservation techniques, for exhibition and teaching purposes', then they were capable of being property. The parts taken had been used as specimens and could be regarded as property. The Royal College of Surgeons was in possession of the body parts. The defendants were found guilty of theft. The court added that the common law might recognise property in human body parts, even when those parts had not acquired different attributes, if they had attracted a 'use or significance beyond their mere existence', for example, as an organ transplant or for the extraction of DNA. As regards a corpse, the general rule was that the law recognises no property in a corpse. A corpse, or part of it, cannot be stolen. It is up to Parliament to change that principle.

If a right to body parts was recognised, who would have such a right? In *Dobson v North Tyneside HA* (1997), the claimant's daughter had died from a brain tumour and the claimant argued that the hospital had been negligent in not diagnosing the condition on time. The hospital had preserved the brain in paraffin and later disposed of it. It was also claimed that the hospital was liable in conversion for destroying the brain. The Court of Appeal held that there was no property in a corpse unless it had undergone a process of human skill, such as embalming. The preservation of the brain in paraffin was not on a par with embalming and the claimant had no right to possession of, or property in, the deceased's brain. Therefore, the claim in conversion failed. Neither did the claimant have the evidence to prove negligence. The court added that the executors have a limited right of possession of a corpse for the purposes of burial. The court approved the Australian case of *Doodeward v Spence* (1908), which concerned a two-headed foetus that had been preserved in a jar. The High Court of Australia said:

> ... a human body, or a portion of a human body, is capable by law of becoming the subject of property. ... when a person has by the lawful exercise of work or skill so dealt with a human body or part of a human body in his lawful possession that it has acquired some attributes differentiating it from a mere corpse awaiting burial, he acquires a right to retain possession of it, at least as against any person not entitled to have it delivered to him for the purpose of burial ... [Griffith CJ]

These decisions still leave questions unanswered. Do the executors have the right to return of the body and all the parts? Exactly what work needs to be done for a corpse or body part to become property? Kelly says that preserving something is sufficient.

TRANSPLANTS

Transplants from dead bodies

At common law, the relatives of a deceased person have a right to the body for the purposes of disposal, but it is questionable whether this includes the right to donate organs from that body. In the early part of the 19th century, Burke and Hare dug up bodies and sold them to the Edinburgh Medical School, and then went on to murder people for the same purpose. It was only after their conviction for murder that the Anatomy Act 1832 was passed to regulate the use of dead bodies. This Act allowed people to give their body for medical purposes after their death. The law is now largely contained in the Human Tissue Act 1961, as amended by the Corneal Tissue Act 1986.

Section 1(1) of the Human Tissue Act 1961 provides that:

> If any person, either in writing at any time or orally in the presence of two or more witnesses during his last illness, has expressed a request that his body or any specified part of his body be used after his death for therapeutic purposes or for purposes of medical education or research, the person lawfully in possession of his body after his death may ... authorise the removal from the body of any part ... for use in accordance with the request.

Section 1(2) provides that the person in lawful possession of the body may authorise removal of parts if, after making 'such reasonable inquiry as may be practicable', they have no reason to believe that:

(a) the deceased expressed an objection to his body being used; or

(b) a surviving spouse or any surviving relative of the deceased objects to the use.

The above means that the deceased can allow removal of organs (s 1(1)) or, if enquiry shows no objections from relatives, the hospital (or nursing home, etc) in lawful possession of the body may authorise removal (s 1(2)). The provision about making enquiries gives hospitals some degree of flexibility: where, for example, relatives cannot be contacted reasonably quickly, the hospital could allow removal. However, the wording of the section may also be viewed as too vague and open to different interpretations. For example, what relatives must be consulted? Is it just close relatives or more distant ones? The Code of Practice gives some guidance on this point. But what if relatives cannot be contacted; is this situation covered by such reasonable inquiry as may be practicable? If not, can the hospital rely on s 1(7), below?

The Department of Health's Code of Practice on *Diagnosis of Brain Stem Death – Including Guidelines for the Identification and Management of Potential Organ and Tissue Donors* (1998) provides that the person responsible for making enquiries has to 'make such reasonable enquiries as may be practicable'. In most situations, it is sufficient for doctors to discuss the matter of a transplant with a relative who had close ties with the deceased.

The relative will be able to provide information on whether the family would object to a transplant. 'There is no need to establish a lack of objection from all relatives before authorising the removal of organs.' The guidelines also state that if the patient has a donor card or is on the Organ Donor Register, there is no need to ask the relatives if they object, although it is good practice to take their views into account.

Can children donate organs after their death? A *Gillick* competent child may be able to do so, although the point has not been decided.

Section 1(4) of the Human Tissue Act provides that the removal of parts must be carried out by a doctor, who must be satisfied 'by personal examination of the body that life is extinct'. An exception is made for eyes, which may be removed by other sufficiently qualified staff acting on the instructions of a doctor.

Section 1(5) provides that a coroner may stop an organ from being removed for transplant if the organ is needed as evidence at an inquest.

Section 1(6) of the Act provides that no authority to remove parts may be given by someone who only has possession of the body for the purpose of burial or cremation. This makes it clear that an undertaker who has possession of the body cannot give permission to remove organs.

Section 1(7) gives authority to those having the 'control and management' of hospitals or other institutions where a body is lying to give permission for body parts to be removed for transplant. This allows those in control of the institution to allow removal of body parts even though the dead person has not consented to removal. It may also be argued that this could be used if the relatives cannot be traced.

The Human Tissue Act 1961 does not provide any sanctions for its breach. Some arguments have been proposed that there could be liability in criminal law or the law of tort:

- Criminal law: in *R v Lennox Wright* (1973), the defendant, using forged qualifications, obtained a job as a doctor in a hospital. He removed eyes from a dead body and was charged with doing an act contrary to s 1(4) of the Human Tissue Act 1961 (before amendment of the Act, removal had to be carried out by a doctor). The court held that it was a common law offence to disobey a statute and the defendant was convicted. However, in the later case of *R v Horseferry JJ ex p IBA* (1987), the court said that if there was no express provision in the Act for an offence, then it must be taken that Parliament did not intend to create one.

- Tort: a claim for nervous shock is a possibility if the requirements of *Alcock v Chief Constable of South Yorkshire Police* (1991) and *Page v Smith* (1995) are met. Claiming as a secondary victim could cause a difficulty with the requirement of the claimant seeing the event or its aftermath. The organ would not be removed in the presence of relatives, so they would have to see the body shortly afterwards.

Criticisms of the Human Tissue Act 1961

There are a number of problems with the meaning and effect of the Act. The phrase 'lawfully in possession of his body' has been taken to mean that, if the person dies in hospital, the hospital managers are in possession until the body is given to the executors, but there is an argument that the executors have the legal right to possession. The requirement for the hospital to make 'such reasonable inquiry as may be practicable' to see if the 'surviving spouse or any surviving relative' objects before removing organs has also caused difficulties. What is reasonable action here? If the spouse or relative objects, then the hospital has the right to remove the organ under s 1(1), but would be unlikely to do so. This effectively gives relatives a veto. But the Act does not take an unmarried partner into account. What is the position if the person has no relatives? Another difficulty is the fact that it is unclear whether there is any sanction for breach of the Act.

Beating heart donors

With transplants from dead bodies, the organ needs to be removed quickly before they degenerate through lack of oxygen. Some hospitals followed a practice of 'elective ventilation', whereby patients in a coma who suffered respiratory arrest were put on an artificial ventilator. This allowed the organs to be kept in good condition until the hospital was ready to transplant them. In 1994, the Department of Health issued guidelines stating that such practice was a battery, because it was not done in the best interests of the patient. Although these patients are 'brain stem dead', Mason, McCall-Smith and Laurie, in *Law and Medical Ethics* (6th edn, 2002, London: Butterworths), say that there is opposition to such transplants because they appear to be taking organs from a living patient. They say that such fears are 'irrational' and suggest that issuing a death certificate before removing the organ would set the minds of relatives at rest.

Removal and retention of organs

The practice of removing organs after death was highlighted by the inquiries into procedures at Bristol Royal Infirmary and Alder Hey Children's Hospital in Liverpool. The evidence showed that organs of dead children were taken without consent. It was found that these practices were widespread throughout the NHS and it caused suffering to those families involved, particularly where a number of body parts had been taken. Many of the families said that had they been asked they would have consented to organs being taken. Following the Redfern Report, in January 2001, into practices at Alder Hey Children's Hospital, the government set up the Retained Organs Commission in April 2001 under the chairmanship of Professor Margaret Brazier. The main aims of the Commission were to oversee the return of organs and tissue to relatives in accordance with their wishes and in a single process to avoid multiple funerals; to determine how to deal with the disposal of organs and tissue which did not need to be returned; and to improve public understanding of the need for retention of organs and tissue. It also advised the government on a new framework for the collection and retention of human tissue and organs and advised that commercial dealings in body parts should be illegal. The Commission was finally closed on 31 March 2004. The Department of Health in conjunction with the NHS Department of the Welsh Assembly also produced a consultation report in 2002, *Human Bodies, Human Choices: the Law on Human Organs and Tissue in England and Wales*. The report emphasises that organs and tissue should only be removed and retained for purposes for which patients have given consent. If a patient has died without expressing their wishes about organ removal, then it should be up to those closest to that patient to make the decision. The Human Tissue Act 2004 makes it an offence to take parts or relevant material from a dead body without an 'appropriate consent' from the patient or a nominated representative (see ss 1, 2 and 3).

Transplants from live donors

(a) The common law

The rules dealing with transplants from living donors come from both the common law and statute. At common law, a person cannot consent to being killed or seriously injured. In *R v Brown* (1993), the court said that people could not give a valid consent to being harmed. In the case of donating an organ, the donor must consent. Distinctions must be made between:

- donating one of two kidneys, where the remaining kidney will keep the donor alive, and donating a single organ, such as the heart. Clearly, in the latter case, this would kill the donor and would not be legally allowed; and

- donating regenerative tissue (which can reproduce), such as bone marrow, and non-regenerative tissue, such as a lung (which cannot reproduce). With regenerative tissue, donation will not normally harm the donor overall. It is now possible to transplant part of a liver, which can then reproduce.

In 'The law relating to organ transplantation in England' ((1970) 33 MLR 353), Gerald Dworkin set out three conditions for donation of an organ:

(a) the patient must give a free and informed consent – it is important to see that a patient is not donating under pressure from relatives;

(b) the operation must be therapeutic and for the patient's benefit – removing an organ from the patient can hardly be seen as for their benefit but it may be, psychologically, if they are donating it to their child;

(c) there must be a lawful justification – donating organs is seen as a benefit to society and can be justified.

A competent adult may therefore legally consent to donating certain organs and tissues. It is important to ensure that any such donation is not made under pressure.

Incompetent adults

An incompetent patient is not able to consent to donating an organ. Medical treatment may be given to an incompetent patient if it is in their 'best interests' (*F v West Berkshire AHA* (1989)). The difficulty is that donating an organ cannot easily be seen as being in the donor's best interests. The Law Commission, in its report, *Mental Incapacity* (No 231, 1995), suggested that the donation of non-regenerative tissue by a mentally incapacitated person should automatically be referred to the court. They said that 'organ donation will only rarely, if ever, be in the best interests of a person without capacity, since the procedures and their aftermath often carry considerable risk to the donor'.

There have been some examples where donations have been allowed. In the US case of *Strunk v Strunk* (1969), the court allowed a kidney transplant from a mentally handicapped man of 27 years of age, with a mental age of 6, to his brother. The evidence was that the donor was very attached to his brother. The donor lived in an institution and relied greatly on visits from his brother. If his brother died, this would have a great impact on the donor. However, the US courts have not always followed such an approach. In *Curren v Bosze* (1990), the Illinois Supreme Court considered a case involving three year old twins who lived with their mother, Ms Curren. The father, Mr Bosze, was not married to the mother and did not live with them. Mr Bosze had other children by other women and one of these children was Jean Pierre, who suffered from leukaemia and needed a bone marrow transplant. Jean Pierre would die within a short time if he did not have a transplant, and other family members were not compatible. Mr Bosze wanted the court to order that the twins should be tested and, if found compatible, that they should be ordered to donate bone marrow. The twins had only met Jean Pierre twice and had not been told that he was a half brother. Ms Curren argued that it was not in the twins' best interests that they should go through the pain and risks of such a procedure. The court agreed that in the circumstances it was not in the twins' best interests and refused to sanction the tests.

In *Re Y (Adult Patient) (Transplant: Bone Marrow)* (1996), Y was a physically and mentally handicapped 26 year old. She lived in a residential home. Her sister had a bone marrow disorder and wanted Y to be tested, with a view to donation of bone marrow. Y was incapable of consenting to the procedure and the question was whether it was in Y's best interests to undergo such a procedure. The court took into account the close relationship between Y and her mother and sister, who visited Y at the home, and the adverse effect that the death of the sister would have on Y. If the sister was not helped by Y, she would have a much lesser chance from another donor. If Y's sister died, the mother would be left with a grandchild to look after and would have less time to visit Y. There was also evidence that the family was very close. It was held to be in Y's best interests that the procedure should go ahead because it would maintain and improve her relations with her mother and sister and the continuing visits would keep contact with the outside world. The court saw Y's best interests as being the social and emotional gains. The court added that in those cases involving an incompetent adult donor, it was desirable that an application be made to the court. Note that this case involved regenerative bone marrow and it remains to be seen if the English courts will follow *Strunk v Strunk*.

Children

Can a minor donate an organ? Such a procedure would not be treatment for the minor but would be for the benefit of someone else. If a child is young and is not *Gillick* competent, then it would require the consent of the parents to allow the child to donate an organ. Strictly, the parents can only give this consent if it is in the 'best interests' of the child. The US courts have agreed to such donations in a number of cases. *Hart v Brown* (1972), involved two identical seven year old twin sisters, one of whom needed a kidney transplant. The parents sought a declaration from the court that the parents had the right to consent to a transplant from the healthy twin. The court heard evidence that a successful transplant would be a benefit to the donor, who would then have a happy family. The court considered it unjust to stop the parents in circumstances where their motives could be reviewed by a court, and it granted the declaration. The US case of *Strunk v Strunk* (1969) and the UK case *Re Y* (1996) both involved incompetent adult donors, but by analogy it may be argued that donation by a child to a sibling or parent could be viewed as being in the child's best interests. Donating an organ would mean that the sibling, for example, survives and this is a benefit to the donor. However, although bone marrow transplants have been sanctioned by the UK courts, it is unlikely that they would agree to a kidney transplant.

As regards children over 16, in *Re W* (1992), which concerned giving medical treatment to a 16 year old without her consent, Lord Donaldson, speaking about s 8 of the Family Law Reform Act 1969, said that the Act only covered treatment and diagnosis and did not cover donating blood or organs:

> The doctor has a duty to act in the best interests of the patient. It is inconceivable [that] he should act in reliance solely on the consent of an under age patient, however *Gillick* competent, in the absence of supporting parental consent. He may be advised to apply to the court for guidance, as recommended by Lord Templeman in *Re B* (1987).

A particular difficulty with donations by children is to ensure that they are voluntary and not made under family pressure. Should children be allowed to donate organs to people other than close family members? As a general rule, this would be unlikely to be in the best interests of the minor and may allow exploitation of children.

Similar issues arise with minors receiving transplants. A *Gillick* competent child could consent but, in practice, a doctor would be unlikely to carry out a transplant without the consent of parents. Parents may refuse consent, as happened in *Re T* (1996), where the parents refused a liver transplant for a young baby as they did not want the baby to go through further pain and suffering. Can a minor refuse to have a transplant of an organ to them? In *Re M (Child: Refusal of Medical Treatment)* (1999), a 15 year old girl suffered heart failure and was likely to die without a transplant. She said that she did not want to die but she did not want someone else's heart. The High Court had to balance the risks of the operation and the fact that M did not want it, against the fact that without it she would die. The court held that it was in her best interests to have the transplant. This decision raises the question of how far a court should go in authorising treatment against the wishes of a minor. One consideration is that only 'reasonable force' may be used, but the provision against inhuman or degrading treatment in Art 3 of the Convention must also be considered.

The law on transplants and minors needs a set of clear rules, which will be of benefit to all those involved in such procedures. The British Medical Association (BMA) has said that 'only competent adults should be considered as live organ donors' (*Organ Donation in the 21st Century* – see below).

Patients in a permanent vegetative state (PVS)

A patient in PVS exists using their own heart and lungs and they are not brain stem dead. It would be unlawful to use their organs for transplant. It has been argued by Hoffenberg, Lock, Tilney *et al* that waiting for them to die naturally after withdrawing feeding means that the organs will be useless for transplant. However, it is illegal to kill them. Nevertheless, either changing the definition of death to include them or exempting PVS patients from the legal prohibition on killing, so that a lethal injection could be given, would have benefits. It would save the futile use of resources and would provide suitable organs for transplant. They estimate that there are around 1–2,000 patients in PVS in the UK and these patients could be a source of organs ('Should organs from patients in permanent vegetative state be used for transplantation?' (1997) *The Lancet* 1320).

(b) Statute

The law is contained in the Human Organ Transplants Act 1989. The Act was passed after Turkish nationals sold kidneys in the late 1980s and the transplants were carried out by surgeons in London. The Act defines 'organ' as 'any part of a human body consisting of a structured arrangement of tissues which, if wholly removed, cannot be replicated by the body' (s 7(2)). This distinguishes between parts of the body that can regenerate, such as blood, skin and bone marrow, and parts that cannot, such as kidneys, heart, liver and lungs. Only dealings in the latter are prohibited.

The main aim of the legislation is to prevent all commercial dealings in organs. Section 2(1) provides that it is an offence: (a) to remove an organ from a living person intended to be transplanted to another; or (b) to transplant an organ removed from a living person to another, unless the donor and donee are genetically related within the terms of s 2(2).

Under s 2(2):

... a person is genetically related to –

(a) his natural parents and children;

(b) his brothers and sisters of the whole or half blood;

(c) the brothers and sisters of the whole or half blood of either of his natural parents; and

(d) the natural children of his brothers and sisters of the whole or half blood or of the brothers and sisters of the whole or half blood of either of his natural parents ...

The relationship has to be proved by a genetic test under the Human Organ Transplants (Establishment of Relationship) Regulations 1989.

If a relationship cannot be established within the above requirements, for example, a transplant between spouses, then the transplant is treated as being between unrelated donors and various restrictions apply. Under the Regulations, the doctor responsible for the donor must refer the matter to the Unrelated Live Transplants Authority (ULTRA). Under s 2(3) of the Human Organ Transplants Act 1989, the Secretary of State may, by regulations, provide that the prohibition under s 2(1) does not apply in cases where no payment is made and the conditions in the Regulations are met. The Human Organ Transplants (Unrelated Persons) Regulations 1989 provide, under reg 3:

(a) no payment has been made;

(b) the doctor who referred the matter to ULTRA has clinical responsibility for the donor;

and the following conditions are satisfied, except where the removal of the organ is for the medical treatment of that donor:

• the doctor has explained the nature of the procedure and the risks;

• the donor understands the nature of the operation and the risks;

• the donor's consent was not obtained by coercion or offer of payment;

• the donor understands that he can withdraw the consent;

• the donor and recipient have both been interviewed by a suitable independent person who confirms to the Authority that the conditions have been met.

Section 1(1) of the 1989 Act makes it an offence to make or receive payment for an organ which is to be transplanted in Great Britain or elsewhere; or to agree to find someone willing to supply an organ for payment; or to initiate any arrangement for payment for an organ; or to take part in the management of any body involved in such arrangements. Section 1(2) makes it an offence to advertise for the supply of organs for payment and s 1(3) provides that 'payment' does not include costs and expenses of the donor in connection with the supply, including loss of earnings.

One of the aims of the Human Organ Transplants Act 1989 was to prevent commercial dealings in live organs, which it achieves. The Act also distinguishes between related and unrelated donors and, with unrelated donors, rules have been put in place to ensure that such donors make the decision freely and without pressure. However, although the Act prevents payment to a related donor, it overlooks the fact that a related donor may be under various other pressures, for example, psychological pressure from their family to agree to donate an organ. It has been argued that all live donors should be protected. The BMA has said that 'all live donations should be subject to the same rigorous assessment, either by ULTRA or by some other mechanism, to ensure that the potential donation is truly voluntary and free from pressure' (*Organ Donation in the 21st Century: Time for a Consolidated Approach*, June 2000).

Liability for defective organs

If a transplanted organ is defective or carries a virus, the donee may be able to take legal action against the donor or the hospital. The possible claims would be in negligence or under the Consumer Protection Act 1987. A claim in negligence would most likely be taken against the hospital, as the donee would be unlikely to be at fault. The Consumer Protection Act 1987 imposes strict liability for damage caused by a defective product. There are a number of particular stumbling blocks in bringing such a claim. First, is an organ a 'product'? Although 'product' is defined in the Act as 'any goods', which has been held to include blood (*A and Others v National Blood Authority* (2001)), it has not been decided whether it includes organs. Secondly, the goods must be 'defective', which occurs if the safety is not such as persons generally are entitled to expect. The standard to which donees are entitled will depend on the organ being transplanted, the expertise available, etc. Thirdly, the Act makes the 'producer' liable and defines 'producer' as including the manufacturer, producer of raw materials, the processor, the importer into the European Union and the supplier. Can the donor, or the doctor who carried out the operation, or the hospital which acquired the organ, or UK Transplant fall within this definition? The 'supplier' is only liable if they do not identify who they obtained the product from. The doctor, hospital and UK Transplant could all be within the meaning of 'supplier'. The identity of the donor would be kept confidential so they would not become liable. Fourthly, under s 4(1)(e), there is a defence if a producer of such products could not have discovered the defect, given the state of scientific knowledge at the time. A hospital would have a possible defence if it could show that the defect could not have been discovered.

XENOTRANSPLANTATION

Xenotransplantation (or xenografting) is transplanting an organ from an animal to a human being. This practice is a potential solution to the organ shortage. Research and experimentation on such transplants have been carried on for many years. Valves from pigs' hearts have been used successfully for humans since the 1960s and a number of transplants of animal organs have been attempted, but with no great success. In 1984, in the US, a baby was given a baboon's heart ('The Baby Fae case' (1987) 6 Medical Law 385) and survived for three weeks; since then, a range of organs from various animals have been transplanted.

There are two main areas of concern about this practice. First, there are scientific worries that humans would reject such organs and that animal diseases could spread to humans. The development of immunosuppressant drugs and transgenic animals (which have human genetic material) results in less rejection. There are concerns that humans will contract animal diseases as a result of transplants. A man who was given a baboon's liver in Pittsburgh in 1992 contracted a virus from the baboon ((1999) *The Independent*, 1 October, p 13).

Secondly, there are ethical concerns about the use of animals for transplants. Is it morally acceptable to use animal organs for transplant into humans? From a utilitarian viewpoint, it is acceptable to use animals for such purposes if their suffering is outweighed by the benefit to people. Against this, many have argued that using animals for transplants causes them suffering, which outweighs any benefits to humans. Others say that we kill animals to eat, so using their organs is no worse than that. Downie ('Xenotransplantation' (1997) 23 J Medical Ethics 205) argues that there is a moral difference between eating animals, which is 'natural', because many animal species do it, and transplanting animal organs, which is 'unnatural', because only humans do it. Downie urges developing mechanical organs and improving the donation of human organs instead. Mason, McCall-Smith and Laurie (*Law and Medical Ethics*, 6th edn, 2002, London: Butterworths) highlight the difficulties ahead if humans were to use animal brains, and the cost of such procedures.

Two reports have been carried out on xenotransplants. The Nuffield Council of Bioethics issued a report entitled *Animal to Human Transplants: The Ethics of Xenotransplantation* in 1996. This report raised concerns about the use of primates for transplants because of their closeness in evolutionary terms to humans, and suggests the use of non-primates, such as pigs, instead. The Report also draws attention to the fact that using primates on a large scale would have implications for endangered species like chimpanzees and there is the risk of transmission of diseases to the recipient of the organ and thence to the human population. In 1997, a Government Advisory Group on Xenotransplantation, under the chairmanship of Professor Ian Kennedy, said that the benefits to humans would outweigh the suffering to animals, which could be minimised. However, they recommended that no trials should take place for the present, because of the risk of diseases being transmitted to humans. There have not been any animal to human transplants in the UK. Following the Kennedy Report, the government set up the Xenotransplantation Interim Regulatory Authority (UKXIRA) in 1997 to oversee developments in this area, including assessing safety. Approval for carrying out a xenotransplant must be given by the Secretary of State and this is done through UKXIRA, which deals with applications on a case by case basis. To date no such approval has been given.

HOW CAN THE SUPPLY OF ORGANS BE INCREASED?

Three possible methods of achieving this are suggested below.

(a) Allow the sale of organs

Under s 1 of the Human Organ Transplant Act 1989, buying or selling organs for transplant from live donors or from dead bodies is a criminal offence. It is argued that if people were allowed to sell their organs, this would increase the supply available for transplant. Under the principle of autonomy, a person should be allowed to do what they want with their own body, including selling their organs. The sale of organs would help people who were dying. Some have argued in favour of allowing organ sales. One of the foremost proponents of a market in donor organs is John Harris:

> There is a lot of hypocrisy about the ethics of buying and selling organs and indeed other body products and services – for example, surrogacy and gametes. What it usually means is that everyone is paid but the donor. The surgeons and medical team are paid, the transplant co-ordinator does not go unremunerated, and the recipient receives an important benefit in kind. Only the unfortunate and heroic donor is supposed to put up with the insult of no reward, to add to the injury of the operation. [Erin, C and Harris, J, 'An ethical market in human organs' (2003) 29 J Medical Ethics, p 137]

The writers propose a scheme with one purchaser like the NHS and where no direct sales are allowed and organs are distributed on the basis of medical priority. Others in favour of allowing sales include Radcliffe-Richards, Daar *et al*, who, in 'The case for allowing kidney sales' ((1998) *The Lancet* 351), claim that the arguments against the sale of kidneys are weak. They point out that the commonest objection is that it will exploit the poor, but argue that preventing such vendors selling causes them more harm because it takes away another option for them. They also argue that the claim that it is risky to the vendor must be set against people doing risky jobs for high pay or taking part in dangerous sports for pleasure. A poor vendor takes a lesser risk for a potentially greater reward, like saving a relative's life or getting themselves out of debt. The authors say that a ban on sales is not justified: 'feelings of repugnance among the rich and healthy, no matter how strongly felt, cannot justify removing the only hope of the destitute and dying.' They are in favour of a controlled market of some sort.

Many arguments have been put forward by those against allowing organ sales. Professor Alastair Campbell is a leading opponent of organ sales. He points out the important difference between donating a kidney because you care for someone and selling a kidney, which is treating it as a commodity. He has also highlighted the fact that a study of the market for organs in India shows that 87% of vendors had worse health and greater debts than the population at large, thus negating the argument that allowing them to sell would be a benefit to them. Campbell also says that there is no evidence that allowing sales of organs would increase the supply:

- it would exploit the poor, who would be the ones likely to sell;
- it would expose vendors to the risks and pain of the operation;
- allowing sales would make body parts and, therefore, human beings seem like mere commodities;
- no one could give a truly voluntary consent to such a risky procedure; and
- it would undermine the existing system of altruistic donation of organs as donors would want to be paid.

The sale of organs from dead bodies would encourage relatives to agree to transplants, but raises fundamental concerns over our respect for the dead and how we treat dead bodies.

(b) A system of opting out

The current system under the Human Tissue Act 1961 is an 'opting in' one, under which people may carry a donor card, allowing their organs to be used on death, or they may register on the National Register in Bristol. This has not proved wholly successful as, although around 70% of the adult population say that they would donate their organs on death, only 30% are registered as organ donors, approximately 11 million in May 2004.

A number of attempts have been made to change the present 'opt in' system, to a system under which individuals have to 'opt out' of donating their organs. This system is also known as 'presumed consent'. It is used in a number of European countries, including Italy, Spain and Belgium. There are some ethical concerns with this system, as the onus is on the individual to object and it seems like inertia selling. If individuals did not bother to register their objection, organs could be removed against their actual wishes. However, there is now wide support for such a change. The BMA supports a system of opting out. It believes that as a majority of the population are in favour of donation, that is a good reason for presuming consent. A system of keeping a register of those who object would be cheaper and such a system would save relatives from having to make a decision at the time of death. It should be noted that there is some difficulty in ascertaining the number of people in favour of donating and different figures have been produced by UK Transplant and the Retained Organs Commission.

In February 2004, the Organ Donation (Presumed Consent and Safeguards) Bill was introduced in the House of Commons. In introducing the Bill, Siobhain McDonagh MP stated: 'It is estimated that for the average patient, compared with dialysis, a kidney transplant saves £191,000 over nine years, which is the median graft survival time.' Clause 1 of the Bill proposes that, where a person has not registered an objection during his lifetime, organs may be removed after death in anyone over 16 years except where information is provided by a person's spouse or partner (or if none by a parent or child of the deceased) that the donor had expressed an objection, or that donation would cause distress to the person's spouse or partner (or if none, parent or child of the deceased). Clause 3 provides that no organ may be removed unless two doctors, independent of the transplant doctor, are satisfied that the person is dead.

(c) A system of required request

Under this system, medical staff would be under a legal duty to ask the relatives of the deceased patient for permission to remove organs. This system is used in the US under the Uniform Anatomical Gift Act 1987. The evidence shows that such schemes are not very successful, partly because of the difficult position that medical staff face, in that they have to ask the relatives, who are already facing a traumatic situation, about removal of organs. A report by the Kings Fund Institute (New, B, Solomon, M, Dingwall, R and McHale, J, *A Question of Give and Take*, 1994, London: Kings Fund Institute, p 59) says that this approach has not had a major impact because it is not enough to simply pass legislation: this must be backed up by training and commitment.

THE HUMAN RIGHTS ACT 1998

Could a patient needing a transplant rely on Art 2, the right to life, to demand treatment? The European Court of Human Rights has accepted that resources are not unlimited and the State only has to do what is reasonable. Therefore, it is unlikely that Art 2 would be of great help to patients needing transplants. Another possible argument is based on Art 3, the right not to be subjected to inhuman or degrading treatment. It could be argued that failure to provide a transplant meant that the patient was subject to such treatment in having to undergo alternative treatment. Article 14, freedom from discrimination, could also be useful, for example, in the situation in 1999 where the Great Northern Hospital in Sheffield accepted a donation of organs from a dead person on the condition that they would be used only for a white donee. The Human Tissue Act 1961 does not prohibit attaching conditions to the donation of organs, but Art 14 could be used to say that this was discrimination against black patients.

REFORM

In June 2000, the BMA set out its suggestions for reform of the transplant system in *Organ Donation in the 21st Century: Time for a Consolidated Approach*. It identified problems with the existing system, including difficulties with the interpretation of current legislation; the fact that the NHS Organ Donor Register had not been successful, in that less than 14% of the population had registered, it was not effective in keeping track of donors and it was not routinely checked when an organ was available; and the concern that organs would be removed before the patient was dead, which arose from confusion caused by the use of the term 'brain stem death'. They suggested that the term 'death confirmed by brain stem tests' would be clearer.

The BMA proposed a system of presumed consent (opt out) and identified the Belgian system as a model. In Belgium, a register of non-donors is operated and people may register their objection at their local town hall. Additionally, an organ will not be taken if there is an objection from a close relative or spouse, unless that objection is contrary to the stated wishes of the deceased. The BMA wants a public debate and public support for the change to presumed consent.

It was also considered that elective ventilation was not realistic at present, because of practical and ethical difficulties. Some suggestions were rejected, including payment of live donors, that bodies should automatically be used for donation regardless of the wishes of the individual, required request and conditional donations.

The recommendations include:

- a single, comprehensive piece of legislation dealing with organ donation;
- up to date guidelines to determine death by brain stem tests before organs are removed;
- the removal of the distinction between related and unrelated live donors, with all live donations subject to the same assessment by ULTRA or other appropriate body;
- legal authorisation of invasive procedures after death to preserve organs;
- introduction of a system of presumed consent for adults.

The BMA has also formed the Transplant Partnership with 17 other organisations to campaign for a radical review of the system of organ donation.

Parliament has passed the Human Tissue Act 2004 to provide a legal framework for the donation, storage and use of bodies, organs and tissue. The Explanatory Notes to the Act, para 4, state: 'It is intended to achieve a balance between the rights and expectations of individuals and families, and broader considerations, such as the importance of research, education, training, pathology and public health surveillance to the population as a whole.' When the substantive provisions of the Human Tissue Act 2004 are in force, they will repeal the Human Tissue Act 1961, the Anatomy Act 1984 and the Human Organ Transplants Act 1989 insofar as they apply to England and Wales.

The Act is divided into three parts. Part 1 deals with the removal, storage and use of human organs and tissue for purposes set out in Sched 1, including anatomical examination; determining the cause of death; education or training relating to human health or research; establishing after death the effectiveness of drugs; obtaining scientific or medical information about a living or deceased person; public display; and research into disorders and transplantation.

Part 1 of the Human Tissue Act 2004 covers the following:

- Authorisation for scheduled purposes (as mentioned above) with 'appropriate consent' (s 1).

- Section 2(1) provides what 'appropriate consent' means; (2) appropriate consent of child means his consent where the child is alive; (3) or where the child is alive and has neither consented nor refused consent, and either is not competent to give consent or fails to do so, a person with parental responsibility may give consent; (4) where the child has died and the activity is one within sub-s (5), 'appropriate consent' means his consent in writing; (5) this sub-section applies to an activity involving storage for use for public display or, if it is not excepted material, anatomical examination; (6) consent in writing under sub-s (4) is only valid if (a) it is signed by the child in the presence of at least one witness who attests the signature, or (b) it is signed at the direction of the child and in his presence and the presence of one witness who attests the signature; (7) where the child has died and the activity is not one to which sub-s (5) applies, 'appropriate consent' means (a) if a decision to consent or a decision not to consent was in force immediately before he died, his consent or (b) if (a) does not apply, the consent of someone with parental responsibility for him immediately before he died, or if no one had parental responsibility, the consent of someone in a qualifying relationship at that time.

Note that 'children' covers anyone under 18 years old.

- Section 3 appropriate consent of an adult; (2) where the person is alive, this means his consent; (3) where the person has died, and the activity is one to which sub-s (4) applies, 'appropriate consent' means his consent in writing; (4) this sub-s applies to an activity involving storage for use or use for public display or, if it is not excepted material, anatomical examination; (5) consent in writing under sub-s (3) is only valid if (a) it is signed by the person in the presence of at least one witness who attests the signature or (b) it is signed at the direction of the person concerned, in his presence and the presence of at least one witness who attests the signature, or (c) it is contained in a valid will of the person; (6) where the person concerned has died and the activity is not within sub-s (4), 'appropriate consent' means (a) if a decision to consent or not to consent was in force immediately before he died, his consent or (b) if (a) does not apply and he has appointed someone under s 4 to deal with consent after his death, consent under that appointment or (c) if neither of these apply then the consent of someone in a qualifying relationship to him immediately before he died; (7) where the person concerned has appointed someone under s 4 to deal with consent after his death, the appointment shall be disregarded for the purposes of sub-s (6) if no one is able to give consent under it; (8) if it is not reasonably practicable to communicate with a person appointed under s 4 within the time available, he shall be treated for the purposes of sub-s (7) as not able to give consent.

- Section 4: nominated representatives. An adult may appoint one or more persons to represent him after his death in relation to consent for the purposes of s 1; (2) an appointment may be general or limited to consent in relation to one or more activities specified; (3) the appointment may be oral or in writing; (4) an oral appointment must be made in the presence of two witnesses present at the same time; (5) a written appointment is only valid if it is signed by the person making it in the presence of one witness who attests the signature, or is signed at the direction of the person making it in the presence of one witness who attests the signature, or is contained in a valid will; (6) where two or more persons are appointed, they shall be treated as able to act jointly and severally unless it is provided that they act jointly; (7) an appointment may be revoked at any time; (10) a person may not act under an appointment unless he is an adult.

- Section 5: prohibition of activities without consent. This section makes it an offence for a person if he does something within s 1(1), (2) or (3) without appropriate consent, for example, retaining organs; it is a defence to prove that he reasonably believes that he does have consent, or the activity is not covered by the Act.

- Section 6: activities involving adults who lack capacity to consent. Where an activity involves storage for use for a purpose in Pt 1 of Sched 1 or use for such a purpose, and the material is from the body of an adult and lacks capacity to consent, and no decision of his to consent or not to consent is in force, there shall be deemed to be consent of his to the activity if it is done in circumstances of a kind specified by regulations.

- Section 7: powers to dispense with need for consent. If the Human Tissue Authority is satisfied that material is from a living person and it is not reasonably possible to trace that person and it is desirable to use the material in the interests of another person to obtain scientific or medical information about the donor, then the authority may deem consent to be in place.

- Section 8: restriction of activities with donated material. This section makes it an offence to use or store donated material for something which is not a qualifying purpose. A qualifying purpose includes purposes in Sched 1, medical diagnosis or treatment, decent disposal or a purpose specified in regulations. Donated material includes the body of a deceased person or material from a body which has been donated.

- Section 9: existing holdings. This covers the body of a deceased person or relevant material from a body. Use or storage for use for a scheduled purpose does not need a consent under s 1(1) if the material is held immediately before the day s 1(1) comes into force.

- Section 10: existing anatomical specimens. This section makes provision for a person dying in the three years immediately before s 1 comes into force; if authority has been given under the Anatomy Act 1984 and s 1 comes into force before the anatomical examination has been concluded. The authority is treated as appropriate consent under s 1 for the storage of the body or parts or use for anatomical examination. If the examination was not concluded, the authority is regarded as appropriate consent to storage for educational and research purposes.

- Section 11: coroners. This section provides that nothing under Pt 1 applies to anything done for the purposes of a coroner.

Part 2 deals with the creation of a Human Tissue Authority and the regulation of activities involving human tissue:

- Section 13: creates a body corporate, the Human Tissue Authority (HTA).

- Section 14: remit. Sets out activities within the remit of the HTA, including: removal of material from a human body; use of the body or relevant material from a human body for scheduled purposes; storage of anatomical specimens or former anatomical specimens; disposal of bodies or relevant material. It excludes certain activities from the remit of the Authority relating to the body of a person who died before the day this section comes into force or material from such a body, and at least 100 years have elapsed since that person's death. Under sub-s (5) in this section, relevant material does not include blood or anything derived from blood.

- Section 15: general functions. The HTA will maintain a statement of general principles which should be followed in carrying out the activities; providing guidance, ensuring compliance, providing information and advice, monitoring developments and advising the Secretary of State.

- Section 16: licence requirements. This section makes provision that no activity to which the section applies can be carried out without a licence from the HTA. The activities include: anatomical examination; postmortems; removal from the body (other than for anatomical or postmortem) of relevant material for a purpose other than transplant; storage of anatomical specimens; storage of the body of a deceased person or relevant material (not being within anatomical specimen); use for public display. Sub-section (3) allows the Secretary of State to make regulations making exceptions from the requirement for a licence, for example, an individual using human tissue for research.

- Sections 17–25. Provisions concerning who is permitted to act under a licence; reconsideration of licensing decisions; appeals; conduct of activities under the licence; and breach of licences (s 25 makes it an offence to breach the licence requirements of s 16 unless he reasonably believes either that the activity is not covered by s 16 or that he acts under the authority of a licence).

- Sections 26–29: codes of practice. Provision for the HTA to prepare codes of practice for those carrying on activities within its remit; sets out qualifying relationships for the purposes of consent under ss 2 and 3 (spouse or partner, parent or child, brother or sister, grandparent or grandchild, etc); provisions for failure to observe codes; approval of codes by the Secretary of State.

- Section 30: anatomical specimens. This section makes provision for an offence to be committed if a person has an anatomical specimen on premises for which there is no licence in force; certain exceptions are made, for example, if the person has possession for the purpose of transporting it.

- Section 32: trafficking. This section makes it an offence to give or receive a reward for the supply of, or the offer to supply, any controlled material; to seek to find someone willing to supply, or offer to supply; or initiate or negotiate any arrangement involving the giving of a reward for supply; or take part in the management of a body of persons whose activities include such arrangements. The section allows payment in money or money's worth for reimbursing expenses (the section extends the prohibition on buying and seeing organs from the Human Organs Transplants Act 1989 to all human material intended for transplants).

- Section 33: restriction on transplants involving a live donor. Sub-section (1) makes it an offence if person removes any transplantable material from a living person intending it to be used for transplantation, and knows or might reasonably be expected to know that the person is alive; and (2) makes it an offence if he uses for the purposes of transplantation any transplantable material which has come from a living person, knows or might reasonably be expected to know that the material has come from a living person. The Secretary of State may make regulations to provide that sub-ss (1) and (2) do not apply if the HTA is satisfied that no reward has been or is to be given in contravention of s 32, and such other conditions as specified in the regulations are satisfied.

- Sections 39–40: exceptions. These sections make an exception from the activities covered by the Act and the requirement for a licence, of anything done to prevent or detect crime or to bring a prosecution (s 39); and makes an exception for a body or material from a body used as a religious relic (s 40).

Part 3 deals with a number of miscellaneous matters:

- Section 43: preservation for transplantation. Where a body of a deceased person lying in a hospital, nursing home or other institution may be suitable for transplantation, it shall be lawful for the person having control of the management of the institution to preserve part for transplantation and to retain the body for that purpose; this authority ceases to apply when it is established that consent has not been and will not be given.

- Section 44: surplus tissue. Provision that material consisting of or including human cells which has been taken from a person's body in the course of medical treatment, diagnostic testing or research, which ceases to be used or stored for a purpose under Sched 1, may be disposed of as waste.

- Section 45 makes it an offence to have any bodily material intending that any human DNA in it should be analysed without consent.

- Section 46 provides that the Secretary of State may amend the Act by regulations to comply with Community obligations.

There has been widespread support for the Human Tissue Act 2004 from organisations such as the BMA. However, there are also concerns that it is too complex and may stop some doctors carrying out research.

SUMMARY – PROPERTY IN THE BODY

1 *Property in the body*
   - Can someone own their body? Problems shown in US case: *Moore v Regents of the University of California* (1990) – used cells to develop new cells.
   - Nuffield Report 1995: treat tissue as abandoned, or a gift.
   - Legal position: common law – no property in a corpse: *R v Kelly* (1998) – application of skill.

2 *Transplants*
   - Dead bodies; s 1(1) of the Human Tissue Act 1961: person in lawful possession can authorise removal of parts; meaning of reasonable inquiry; no authority to remove parts if only have possession for purposes of burial; problems: no sanction for breach of Human Tissue Act; matters of interpretation.
   - Beating heart donors: patients on ventilator do not appear dead.
   - Live donors – common law: cannot consent to being killed; a competent adult can donate certain organs; incompetent adults cannot consent, but could it be done under best interests? US case: *Strunk v Strunk* (1969) – gave kidney to brother; English courts allow bone marrow transplants; children, if not *Gillick* competent, need consent of parents – but not in best interests, children over 16 years not covered by Family Law Reform Act 1969, so apply to court.
   - Live donors – statute: under s 2(1) of the Human Organ Transplants Act 1989 it is an offence to remove an organ or transplant an organ from a living person unless genetically related; if not related, must have permission from ULTRA and

certain conditions must be met – no payment, risks explained, etc; also offence to make or receive payment for an organ.

3 *Liability for defective organs*
  - Claim in negligence.
  - Possible claim under Consumer Protection Act 1987, but certain hurdles.

4 *Xenotransplantation*
  - Concerns about spread of disease from animals to humans.
  - Ethical concerns about such use of animals.

5 *Increasing the supply of organs*
  - Sale of organs; opt out system; required request.

6 *Human Rights Act 1998*
  - Possible argument for Art 2, the right to life.

7 *Reforms*
  - Human Tissue Act 2004 sets out requirements for consent; creation of Human Tissue Authority and need for a licence to remove tissue (substantive provisions of the Act not due to come into force until 2006).

APPENDIX A

MODEL CONSENT FORM

This has been issued as a model consent form by the Department of Health and is available at www.dh.gov.uk.

**[NHS organisation name]
consent form 1**

**Patient agreement to investigation
or treatment**

Patient details (or pre-printed label)
Patient's surname/family name...............................
Patient's first names ....
Date of birth ....
Responsible health professional...............................
Job title ....
NHS number (or other identifier)................................
Male   Female
Special requirements .... (eg other language/other communication method)

To be retained in patient's notes

Patient identifier/label

Name of proposed procedure or course of treatment (include brief explanation if medical term not clear) ....
....
....

Statement of health professional (to be filled in by health professional with appropriate knowledge of proposed procedure, as specified in consent policy)

I have explained the procedure to the patient. In particular, I have explained:

The intended benefits ....
....
....
Serious or frequently occurring risks ....
....
....
Any extra procedures which may become necessary during the procedure

    blood transfusion...

    other procedure (please specify) ....
....

I have also discussed what the procedure is likely to involve, the benefits and risks of any available alternative treatments (including no treatment) and any particular concerns of this patient.

    The following leaflet/tape has been provided ....

This procedure will involve:

    general and/or regional anaesthesia   local anaesthesia   sedation

Signed:..   Date .. ..
Name (PRINT) ....   Job title ....

Contact details (if patient wishes to discuss options later) ....

Statement of interpreter (where appropriate)

I have interpreted the information above to the patient to the best of my ability and in a way in which I believe s/he can understand.

Signed ....   Date ....
Name (PRINT) ....

Top copy accepted by patient: yes/no (please ring)

Statement of patient

Patient identifier/label

Please read this form carefully. If your treatment has been planned in advance, you should already have your own copy of page 2 which describes the benefits and risks of the proposed treatment. If not, you will be offered a copy now. If you have any further questions, do ask – we are here to help you. You have the right to change your mind at any time, including after you have signed this form.

I agree to the procedure or course of treatment described on this form.

I understand that you cannot give me a guarantee that a particular person will perform the procedure. The person will, however, have appropriate experience.

I understand that I will have the opportunity to discuss the details of anaesthesia with an anaesthetist before the procedure, unless the urgency of my situation prevents this. (This only applies to patients having general or regional anaesthesia.)

I understand that any procedure in addition to those described on this form will only be carried out if it is necessary to save my life or to prevent serious harm to my health.

I have been told about additional procedures which may become necessary during my treatment. I have listed below any procedures **which I do not wish to be carried out** without further discussion. ....
....
....
....

Patient's signature .... Date...............................
Name (PRINT) ....

A witness should sign below if the patient is unable to sign but has indicated his or her consent. Young people/children may also like a parent to sign here (see notes).

Signature .... Date ....
Name (PRINT) ....

Confirmation of consent (to be completed by a health professional when the patient is admitted for the procedure, if the patient has signed the form in advance)

On behalf of the team treating the patient, I have confirmed with the patient that s/he has no further questions and wishes the procedure to go ahead.

Signed:... Date .. ..
Name (PRINT) .... Job title ....

Important notes: (tick if applicable)

See also advance directive/living will (eg Jehovah's Witness form)

Patient has withdrawn consent (ask patient to sign /date here) ....

Guidance to health professionals (to be read in conjunction with consent policy)

What a consent form is for

This form documents the patient's agreement to go ahead with the investigation or treatment you have proposed. It is not a legal waiver – if patients, for example, do not receive enough information on which to base their decision, then the consent may not be valid, even though the form has been signed. Patients are also entitled to change their mind after signing the form, if they retain capacity to do so. The form should act as an *aide-memoire* to health professionals and patients, by providing a check-list of the kind of information patients should be offered, and by enabling the patient to have a written record of the main points discussed. In no way, however, should the written information provided for the patient be regarded as a substitute for face-to-face discussions with the patient.

The law on consent

See the Department of Health's *Reference guide to consent for examination or treatment* for a comprehensive summary of the law on consent (also available at www.doh.gov.uk/consent).

Who can give consent

Everyone aged 16 or more is presumed to be competent to give consent for themselves, unless the opposite is demonstrated. If a child under the age of 16 has "sufficient understanding and intelligence to enable him or her to understand fully what is proposed", then he or she will be competent to give consent for himself or herself. Young people aged 16 and 17, and legally 'competent' younger children, may therefore sign this form for themselves, but may like a parent to countersign as well. If the child is not able to give consent for himself or herself, some-one with parental responsibility may do so on their behalf and a separate form is available for this purpose. Even where a child is able to give consent for himself or herself, you should always involve those with parental responsibility in the child's care, unless the child specifically asks you not to do so. If a patient is mentally competent to give consent but is physically unable to sign a form, you should complete this form as usual, and ask an independent witness to confirm that the patient has given consent orally or non-verbally.

When NOT to use this form

If the patient is 18 or over and is not legally competent to give consent, you should use form 4 (form for adults who are unable to consent to investigation or treatment) instead of this form. A patient will not be legally competent to give consent if:
- they are unable to comprehend and retain information material to the decision and/or
- they are unable to weigh and use this information in coming to a decision.

You should always take all reasonable steps (for example involving more specialist colleagues) to support a patient in making their own decision, before concluding that they are unable to do so. Relatives **cannot** be asked to sign this form on behalf of an adult who is not legally competent to consent for himself or herself.

Information

Information about what the treatment will involve, its benefits and risks (including side-effects and complications) and the alternatives to the particular procedure proposed, is crucial for patients when making up their minds. The courts have stated that patients should be told about 'significant risks which would affect the judgement of a reasonable patient'. 'Significant' has not been legally defined, but the GMC requires doctors to tell patients about 'serious or frequently occurring' risks. In addition if patients make clear they have particular concerns about certain kinds of risk, you should make sure they are informed about these risks, even if they are very small or rare. You should always answer questions honestly. Sometimes, patients may make it clear that they do not want to have any information about the options, but want you to decide on their behalf. In such circumstances, you should do your best to ensure that the patient receives at least very basic information about what is proposed. Where information is refused, you should document this on page 2 of the form or in the patient's notes.

APPENDIX B

USEFUL WEBSITES

www.bma.org.uk	British Medical Association
www.dh.gov.uk	Department of Health
www.ethox.org.uk	The Ethox Centre (Oxford) (ethics research)
www.gdc-uk.org	General Dental Council
www.gmc-uk.org	General Medical Council
www.hmso.gov.uk	Her Majesty's Stationery Office (Acts of Parliament)
www.hfea.gov.uk	Human Fertilisation & Embryology Authority
www.kcl.ac.uk/depsta/law/ research/cmle/index.html	King's College London Centre of Medical Law and Ethics
www.kingsfund.org.uk	The Kings Fund (London)
www.linacre.org	The Linacre Centre for Healthcare Ethics
www.the-mdu.com/gp/index.asp	Medical Defence Union
www.medico-legalsociety.org.uk	Medico-Legal Society
www.medicalprotection.org	Medical Protection Society
www.nmc-uk.org	Nursing & Midwifery Council
http://nmap.ac.uk	Nursing, Midwifery and Allied Health Professions
www.omni.ac.uk	OMNI (Organising Medical Networked Information)
http://rdn.ac.uk	RDN (Resource Discovery Network)
www.ethics-network.org.uk	UK Clinical Ethics Network
www.uktransplant.org.uk	UK Transplant

INDEX